The Fashion Game

GORDON KENDALL

PEARSON

Boston   Columbus   Indianapolis   New York   San Francisco   Hoboken
Amsterdam   Cape Town   Dubai   London   Madrid   Milan   Munich   Paris   Montréal   Toronto
Delhi   Mexico City   São Paulo   Sydney   Hong Kong   Seoul   Singapore   Taipei   Tokyo

Senior Acquisitions Editor: Lindsey Gill
Editorial Assistant: Nancy Kesterson
Director of Marketing: David Gesell
Marketing Manager: Stacey Martinez
Senior Marketing Coordinator: Alicia Wozniak
Marketing Assistant: Les Roberts
Program Manager: Maren L. Beckman
Project Manager: Janet Portisch
Procurement Specialist: Deidra M. Skahill
Art Director: Jayne Conte
Cover Designer: Karen Noferi
Manager, Rights and Permissions: Mike Lackey
Cover Art: © Image Source Plus/Alamy
Media Director: Leslie Brado
Lead Media Project Manager: April Cleland
Full-Service Project Management: Susan McIntyre, Cenveo© Publisher Services
Composition: Cenveo© Publisher Services
Printer/Binder: Courier/Kendallville
Cover Printer: Lehigh-Phoenix Color/Hagerstown
Text Font: 45 Helvetica Light

Credits and acknowledgments borrowed from other sources and reproduced, with permission, in this textbook appear on the appropriate page within text.

Library of Congress Cataloging-in-Publication Data

Kendall, Gordon T.
  The fashion game / Gordon Kendall. —First edition.
    pages cm
  ISBN 978-0-13-511789-7 a0135117895
1. Fashion—Textbooks. 2. Clothing trade—Textbooks. I. Title.
  TT518.K46 2014
  746.9′2—dc23
                          2014004962

10 9 8 7 6 5 4 3 2 1

www.pearsonhighered.com

ISBN 13: 978-0-13-511789-7
ISBN 10: 0-13-511789-5

brief contents

contents

acknowledgments

Publishing, like fashion, is a game. It has been my pleasure to team with Pearson Education, and its "players." I wish to thank Vern Anthony, Doug Greive, Sara Eilert, Janet Portisch, Alicia ("Woz") Wozniak, Amanda Cerreto, and, of course, Laura Weaver, publishing's most patient editor, for their support of this project as it took various developmental turns. As well, I would like to thank Susan McIntyre and Cindy Miller of Cenveo© Publisher Services for assistance with this text's final manuscript. They were always available and helpful in bringing about what has become *The Fashion Game*.

Thanks, too, is due other players. These include the previously unknown to me, but certainly influential, reviewers. Their insights— gleaned from years of education, research, and teaching— ultimately helped determine the content of *The Fashion Game*. The efforts of these contributors are greatly appreciated. They include:

Debra Powell, The Art Institutes
Elena Karpova, Iowa State University
Patricia Cunningham, The Ohio State University
Robert Battle, Nassau Community College
Kathleen Colussy, The Art Institutes
Dhona Spacinsky, Academy of Couture Art
Della Reams, Virginia Commonwealth University in Qatar
Doris Treptow, Savannah College of Art and Design
Jim McLaughlin, Florida State University
Laurabeth Allyn, Cazenovia College
Cherie Bodenstab, Fashion Institute of Design and Merchandising

Other fashion education professionals I would like to acknowledge include Marilyn Sullivan, Fashion Marketing Coordinator of Dallas's El Centro College, professional mentor and friend. I value the insights and suggestions she, her students, and colleagues offered about this project during my association with the college. Over the last year of this project, the faculty, staff, and students of L.I.M. College, New York, offered informative feedback and encouragement, all beneficial toward completion of this project. Especially, I would like to thank fellow textbook author and L.I.M. Dean of Academic Affairs, Michael P. Londrigan, for his interest and encouragement. How did this all begin? I would be remiss if I did not mention Dr. Beth Wuest, Associate Vice President for Institutional Effectiveness at Texas State University, who, not really so long ago, offered positive, realistic suggestions about my career change into fashion merchandising.

My personal team includes those who experienced this project along with me, always asking, hopefully, how "the book" was progressing. I acknowledge with thanks the talented, concerned, and insightful friends who kept me on track:

Dr. Wayne R. Kirkham, MD, and Sally L. Kirkham, PhD, of Dallas, Texas: gracious, encouraging, always "A little bit crazy, Man!" and ever the more lovable.

Throughout, Harlen Fleming and Eric Bown of Chicago remained interested in and supportive of *The Fashion Game*. Bill Taylor, family friend for two generations, Gene W. Voskuhl, MD, David J. Rodriguez, and Anita (Ani) and Pedro Nosnik, MD, made up my Dallas team of well wishers, too. Thanks, guys! The longtime "Austin Gang," Carla Cox, Michael Helferich and Gene Brenek, Laura Martin and Brian Watkins, Lucius and Lynn Bunton, and Susan Adler, MD, and Marvin Zellner, MD, always encourage my writing endeavors. Thanks to them as well!

Virginia Regier, accomplished writer and newspaper editor in her own right, remains an attentive listening ear and source of insights about the writing and publishing processes. I appreciate and thank her for her interest in and support of all my writing endeavors.

Michael Regier, to whom I dedicate this text—may *The Fashion Game* serve as testament to your belief in me and my abilities.

author biography

Gordon T. Kendall, JD, MBA, is a freelance author based in New York and New Jersey. He has served on the adjunct fashion merchandising faculty at Southwest Texas State University (now Texas State University) in San Marcos, Texas. He has also served as a lecturer and member of the fashion advisory committee at El Centro College in Dallas, Texas. He is an executive member of the New York (Manhattan) Chapter of Fashion Group International and a Professional Member, International Textile and Apparel Association (Pending). As well, he is an adjunct faculty member at L.I.M. College, New York. His previous titles include: *Designing Your Business: Strategies for Interior Design Professionals* (2003) and *Fashion Brand Merchandising* (2009) as well as articles about fashion history, design, retail, and brand management.

instructor resources

DOWNLOAD INSTRUCTOR RESOURCES FROM THE INSTRUCTOR RESOURCE CENTER
To access supplementary materials online, instructors need to request an instructor access code. Go to www.pearsonhighered.com/irc to register for an instructor access code. Within 48 hours of registering, you will receive a confirming email including an instructor access code. Once you have received your code, locate your text in the online catalog and click on the 'Instructor Resources' button on the left side of the catalog product page. Select a supplement, and a login page will appear. Once you have logged in, you can access the instructor material for all Pearson textbooks. If you have any difficulties accessing the site or downloading a supplement, please contact Customer Service at http://247pearsoned.custhelp.com.

overview of *The Fashion Game*

With *The Fashion Game*, whether you are a student, a young fashion or fashion retail professional, or simply an interested consumer, you will discover why and how exciting things happen in fashion.

The Fashion Game offers new, fresh perspectives on the timeless, ever-evolving subject of fashion. It does so by putting you as closely as possible in the middle of what really happens in fashion . . . participating at a runway fashion show . . . working with a fashion designer as a new season's collection is born . . . being a retail store buyer . . . texting about what you see worn by others on the street, blogging about your impressions of fashion's newest directions, or showing your research related to its earliest beginnings. In short, this text makes real the very jobs you may have thought about for yourself, and provides insights as to what really goes on in fashion and fashion retail. Mostly, it makes clear how you, too, can and will be part of the fashion game!

Many fashion merchandising texts follow a sequential approach, one that traces a fashion "idea" from its initial development through to a final, finished product, ending eventually with consumers. However clear such an approach may be for explaining the production of fashion products, it does not address the interconnectedness, the interdependence of the people responsible for making fashion happen. They do not and, indeed, cannot work in isolation from each other. Their relationships with each other are the core of the fashion game concept. What follows is designed to help you find your way in the complex, interconnected, always fascinating realm that "is" fashion: the stores, designers, and brands—all the things you love! As with any profession, no matter your passion, you must have factual knowledge. From there, it's up to you how you use that information. This text seeks to be your "go to" for such basics, a resource to keep as you establish your fashion career.

The Fashion Game frames textbook-necessary information and places it into a concise, highly readable format. It includes clear topical explanations meshed with interesting projects, the very kind of work you will carry out in your career. These activities really are there for a reason! They serve as practical previews of what occurs in the "real-life" fashion game arena. Along with chic images and graphics, this text also seeks to impart a sense of humor as well as a clear understanding about fashion. Here you will find many of the things you will need

to know about fashion, fashion retail, and those businesses related to them, but more than that, in ways you will enjoy pursuing.

But let's be honest: If you find the following information "boring," not what you expected, then, okay. Are fashion and its many related careers really for you? For example, many aspire to positions as retail store buyers. Great! But to get there? Most established buyers started as assistant buyers, a tough, low-paying job. On top of that, all of them had to be "numbers" people—that is, they had to have above-average quantitative skills. How to read that: "They had to be 'good at' math!"

This text explores everything the world of fashion designers, fun stores, "red carpet" outfits, and brands are about. To be part of it, you need to know how multimillion, even billion-dollar industries and individual businesses work, and who makes the hard decisions about how they will operate. Also, as you study these pages, ask yourself this: Are you willing to devote personal hard work, to give your own heartfelt drive and determination toward becoming what this text terms a fashion game "player"? Knowledge, hard work, savviness about how to use these tools—these are just a few of the things that fashion, in all its many forms, is about. Anything else?

Personal skills. A career in fashion includes networking, connecting with people you may not have met previously, and may not even personally like when you do! As well, you will find it necessary to always keep your "fashion eyes" on—to become better able to gauge what consumers feel, what they are willing to purchase, those things that people feel represent who they "are," —and to always be on the lookout for opportunities to sell to meet those needs. Don't forget, by the way, that all your knowledge, impressions, and ideas must ultimately and positively affect your own, or your company's profitable "bottom line." Fashion is a business, after all. Are you ready? To get started, get comfortable with idea of a text attuned to you and your goals, one with the purpose of introducing you to the concepts you will need to know to become the fashion game "player" you want to be! So, for now, what does this mean for you?

The Fashion Game will teach you how to read and understand, instantly and intently, information reported in "the trades." These are the print publications, blog postings, and Internet sites communicating to fashion and retail professionals what is happening. Often, these sources are days, weeks, sometimes even months ahead of those intended for consumers. Thanks to *The Fashion Game,* you should be able to keep up with the more detailed and more technical information found in professional sources. Using the paradigm of "game," "players," and "rules" (about which you will soon know more) will make it possible for you to establish your own highly important fashion legacy.

With these goals in mind, then, as well as all the other tasks demanding your time, what is the quickest, best way to get to know *The Fashion Game,* to gain maximum benefit from your time with it and, ultimately, to enjoy it? As you follow the responses to the kinds of questions you might ask, you will find out.

Is *The Fashion Game* Right for You?

Anyone interested in fashion should find *The Fashion Game* useful and enjoyable!

With so many fields of study and careers related to everything fashion, it should come as no surprise that there are countless ways this text can and will be helpful. If you just want to know more about fashion, or definitely intend to pursue fashion studies in the following areas, then *The Fashion Game* is for you:

Fashion or costume design
Accessories design
"Technical" fashion design, including garment production and manufacturing
Fashion marketing and merchandising
Retailing
Visual merchandising
Fashion education or consumer sciences
Curatorial (museum) studies

These would be among the obvious disciplines to which this text will introduce you. Whether you are pursuing certificate, two-year associate, or four-year bachelor degree programs, *The Fashion Game* offers information, perspective, and ideas for getting started as you pursue studies in these areas. In other words, this text provides a straightforward way for you to process all the many details about fashion and its related industries you will come across in your studies and work. Are you a student of general business, marketing, or entrepreneurship? This text includes concepts you know from your studies of these disciplines and applies them to the modern fashion and retail industries.

Fashion includes more than clothing and personal accessories. Today, it includes "lifestyle" items as well. These are products enabling stylish, up-to-date living. Think how many fashion designers, such as Ralph Lauren and Vera Wang among others, who offer furniture, housewares, and decorative items. As well, they and others make available home accessories, paint, wallpaper, carpets and rugs, bed and bath linens, even china and crystal. This text, then, should be helpful to you if you are or are studying to be an interior designer, decorator, home products professional, or are simply interested in knowing more about the ways home products are now very much fashion ones as well. The

fashion game concept applies to, and even explains, why so many "designer," branded home products exist.

Have you ever wondered why you see the kinds of fashion items you do in certain stores and not in others? For that matter, have you ever been curious why seemingly similar garments sometimes fit dramatically differently, or carry wildly divergent price tags? Anyone interested in becoming a more informed fashion shopper, looking for answers to questions such as these, should consider what this text has to say as well.

Thanks for taking the time to read this overview and getting to know what's ahead. Now, you understand there is an underlying concept, a central idea to look for. You also know how this text may apply to many different areas of study. As a further preview, when you complete your studies with this text, you will be able to do the following tasks:

1. Identify the four kinds of "players" in the fashion and retail industries and describe their activities and the kinds of items they provide, produce, purvey (sell), or promote;
2. Explain the four "rules" they follow in their professional activities; and
3. Name the one "goal" all fashion game players seek to achieve. (It may surprise you!)

All you will have to do is pick up a trade magazine, or visit an Internet site. You should be able to understand what you find there, because you are able to accomplish these tasks. Do you have further questions about what you will encounter? The following text feature descriptions and content details should help.

How Is *The Fashion Game* Organized?

What's inside? Getting to know how this text has been planned will help you understand even more what it is all about! Twelve sections comprise *The Fashion Game,* each with text, captioned images, learning tools, and projects. You won't be bored! Maybe your semester will be longer, about fifteen weeks, or a quick summer session of twelve weeks. No matter. Refer to your instructor's syllabus for exactly how the text will be presented in class. Whatever the plan: how are the four text parts organized?

Part One: What Is the Fashion Game About?

What is the fashion game? Who participates in it? How does it operate? The first three sections of this text answer these questions, making it easy to identify those known as "fashion game players." As well, it details this simple fact: All the players have one goal. Thus, the second section details the all-important "human" aspect of fashion: consumers. They are the goal of the fashion game. Finally, the third section of this text sets out for you four fun-to-know, easy-to-remember "rules," those guidelines found to inform the actions of the players as they pursue that goal of attracting consumers and operating fashion businesses.

Part Two: Fashion Game Players in Action

Now that you know who they are, what do fashion game players "do"? This part of the text details the activities of those involved in the fashion game. What do they "make," design, sell, or publicize? How do they interact with each other? This part of the text takes a look at the four kinds of fashion game players and their professional activities. You may have an idea about what you want in a fashion career. After this study of the players, what do you think? If you are still undecided about a specific fashion career, what ideas did you glean about how you, fashion, and fashion retail professionals might come together?

Part Three: Fashion Game Issues

Two sections comprise this part of the text. In one, you will explore problems that have arisen as the fashion game has continued, learn to recognize them, and gain insights about how they might be ameliorated. Proliferation of counterfeit merchandise and continuation of sweatshop labor are among the first issues you will study. Perhaps you will find ways to use fashion game rules to achieve lasting solutions to these problems. Social media has become the darling of fashion, a powerful conduit for information about its changes and a platform for many to gain presence. Yet, along with its advances have come concerns about privacy. Fashion involves consumption, use of resources. Is that sustainable? Will fashion be able to continue without some greater concern given to its effects on the environment, on people and the physical conditions in which they live? This part of the text explores these concerns, notes how fashion and retail industries respond, and then uses fashion game rules to suggest outcomes.

Part Four: The Fashion Game in Motion

How is the world changing and how are the fashion and retail industries—and the fashion game—responding to those shifts? Most importantly, what practical steps might you take to be part of these exciting new happenings? The final part contains three sections, one that gives you an overview of the changing "world of fashion" and two that prepare you to enter the fashion game and describe, possible "first moves" in the fashion game, such as internships and entry-level industry jobs.

What Can I Expect?

How do you learn?

Whether you like images as a "visual learner," or like to read written text, there is something for all students in The Fashion Game. The number of photographs you will find are there to help you imprint text concepts through image retention. With them are straightforward, easy-to-understand captions. All four parts contain a **"Part Preview"** with summaries of the individual sections that follow. You will always know what to expect if you begin by reading this feature. **"Fast Forward"** contains an overview of the specific section you are about to study and describes in simple, bullet-style points what you will soon encounter and will need to know. **"Sidelines,"** asides that seek to impart of sense of context for the text discussions that follow, are found scattered throughout each section. A **"Finale"** concluding each section briefly summarizes the major topics just explored.

Fashion information is everywhere. With your iPhone you can go online, use Facebook, Twitter, Pinterest, Instagram, or so many other sources to find information. You may also open this text. How might doing so be as easy as using mobile media? **To make your experience with The Fashion Game text as close to those found with other sources, you will encounter little in the way of referential "interruptions" such as parentheticals references or footnotes.** This text is intended to be easy and pleasant to read.

The **Annotated Bibliography**, found at the conclusion of the text, narrows the near thousand sources used to compile this work down to about 100 books and articles you might be interested in reading. To that end, many of these sources are annotated with brief notes about their importance or special features.

What Features Will Help Me Succeed in Class?

Who doesn't want to do as well as possible?

This, like all texts, contains a great deal of information. Each section contains **"Review Questions: What Did You Discover?"** This feature includes topical review questions and lists of terms and phrases. The concepts and terminology it contains will be important for class, quizzes, or tests, and, as you will later discover, used in any work you undertake in fashion and fashion retail. Additionally, worksheets have been included, so that you may conveniently include answers in each section and have them for later reference. These features should further class success.

How Will This Prepare Me for Working Life?

Will you be ready for the "real" fashion game, working in fashion or fashion retail?

Whichever fashion or retail career you choose, you will need to know a great deal and be able to work with people who possess different skills and come from different professional backgrounds. This text contains a cumulative project intended to bring you, as closely as possible, to the excitement of working with others in fashion-related pursuits. Completing activities at the end of each section will bring you one step closer toward participating in **"Market Day—The Fashion Game Simulation Project"** at the conclusion of your fashion course.

Fashion and retail professionals attend fairs and exhibitions—"markets"—that inform them about and promote new products and services. These include shows featuring new textiles (for now, think fabrics), showcasing innovative manufacturing processes, and, of course, presenting soon-to-be-current fashions. Maybe you are on the way to becoming such a professional, but nothing prevents you from planning and presenting a similar type of "market day" at your school.

What is it about fashion that you like? What fascinates you? What interests you enough to devote time and energy to creatively, thoroughly informing others of your passion? Acting the roles of fashion game "player," or interested consumer, you, or a small group of two to four others, will soon come to see how interdependent everything related to fashion is. Who will be voted "Best of Fair," or receive other commendations for contributions made during the course of this event? Seeking such accolades, you, or your group, will interact with others in challenging, ever-changing ways in this classroom adaptation of the real-world fashion game.

Opening Moves in the Fashion Game

Fashion—it's everywhere, part of every life. It's exciting to study, to pursue professionally, or just to enjoy personally! Does this text contain *everything* that you might need to know about fashion? Of course not. No single source realistically could. This text does, however, highlight much of what you, as a young fashion professional, will need to know. That means you will encounter many terms and concepts to learn, recall, and, better yet, know how to recognize and apply. Once again, when finished with this text, you will know who's who, be able to describe what those professionals do, and understand what's currently being reported about in important trade information sources. You will be better able, in other words, to "talk the talk" of fashion!

Still unsure of what lies ahead?

As you begin your study with *The Fashion Game* all I ask is that you keep an open mind—see what is presented here as a start, as a first, organized source for basic information. As such, it will serve as your entrée to the excitement and opportunity offered by fashion and fashion retail careers. From this starting point, you will then be able to branch out, to explore your own interests, to plan your studies, and to find your career.

I hope that you will agree that you have made your own opening move in the fashion game successfully by considering what this text has to say and then find that its organization and information guides your subsequent "plays" equally well. Good luck!

WHAT IS THE FASHION GAME ABOUT?

Welcome to the game! What can you expect in this very first part of the text?

This part of the text sets out the "basics" of the fashion game, those concepts that go a long way toward explaining how and why fashion is the force that it is, one powerful enough to shape the lives and professions of many. Here is a preview, a first glimpse, of what to expect.

SECTION 1: THE FASHION GAME AND ITS PLAYERS

Who makes fashion what it is?

This first section **introduces the fashion game concept**. It also **identifies "Players," those professionally responsible for fashion goods and services,** showing them at work and describing the activities they carry out in their jobs. It then applies the "game" concept to one contemporary and very big fashion company.

SECTION 2: CONSUMERS AND THE FASHION GAME

Consumers are the goal of the fashion game.

Those who purchase and wear fashion items are consumers. Just like you! Here, you will find out how **consumers shaped fashion's direction** over time. You will also discover how various consumer groups may be described. Further, you will learn factors contributing to consumers' adoption of fashion and its many changes. Simply put, **without consumers, there would be no fashion**. You will explore this idea in more detail as you find out how fashion game players get to know consumers and their needs in order to appeal to them.

SECTION 3: RULES OF THE FASHION GAME

Every game has rules!

The fashion game is no exception to this rule about rules. Here, you will find out about **four guidelines applicable throughout the fashion and retail industries**. It may seem too simple to say that these and only these rules apply. But is it? Over and over, these four seem to apply, motivating the actions of fashion game players. As you explore further, you will encounter these rules and see how fashion businesses big and small follow them.

Still not sure about the "fashion in four" concept? That's understandable. Right now, you are processing all kinds of information from many sources. However, to get you started, think about what you know, what you have learned already. How would you describe "fashion" to someone who did not know anything about it? Where does it come from? Who is responsible for bringing together all the things required to create even one garment? What would you say makes some fashion and retail businesses successful while others fail? The rules of the fashion game, as you will find out, go a long way toward answering those questions. This first section sets the conceptual course for the remainder of *The Fashion Game* text. After completing it, for example, you are prepared to experience "**Fashion Game Players in Action**," the next part. There, you will find out more about the many interactions between and among fashion's "players."

THE FASHION GAME AND ITS PLAYERS

FAST FORWARD

This is where the fashion game starts. After you read this section, you will be able to tell who are its "players," the game's all-important decision makers. This section should interest and inspire you—get you thinking about becoming a player in the fashion game, too.

WHAT YOU SHOULD KNOW ABOUT THIS SECTION:

- It describes the fashion game idea woven throughout this text.
- It introduces you to the players who make fashion such an exciting and dynamic business.
- It describes fashion, retail, merchandising, and other related careers of interest.

(Opposite page) Source: © shock/Fotolia

Fashion Game P.O.V.

What is the fashion game point of view? As you start your study with this text, think for a moment about "What is 'fashion'?" For sure, your answer might include fashion's rich, colorful history and that it now involves many, multibillion-dollar industries devoted to producing fashion goods and other businesses supporting them and fashion retailing and promotion. Fashion is exciting, too. It has something brilliant, something that you want to be part of, happening all the time.

Be honest. What you really think of when you think about fashion are the names associated with it. These are the people, the brands, and the stores that offer the things you want to wear, to have, or to maybe one day be a part of. Just mentioning fashion instantly brings all these impressions to mind!

Sideline:

Often, fashion and retail professionals are quoted in the trade press as saying the "good old days" of just showing creative sketches or one-of-a-kind sample garments to buyers and getting orders are long over. Today, buyers want to see "plans," require you to have a growth "strategy" for your brand, and ask in detail how you are going to "support" the account if they buy from you. What does their use of these kinds of terms suggest to you?

So, how then, might one text bring all these thoughts and ideas together in ways that are meaningful, useful, and even inspiring to you?

Fashion, today, is a game!

So, what, then, is this "fashion game" all about?

Think how much you already know about fashion—the "looks" or styles, the names, the stores, and the people associated with it. Knowing all of this is a great start. But what do you know about the various, varied, and valuable professions and industries responsible for making fashion part of your life? Do you know who these insiders are? What these entities do? Do you have any idea how they interact with each other? Are you ready to learn about these, so that, ultimately, you can participate in the contemporary fashion game?

To begin your discovery, consider this point of view: "fashion" as you know it, is not one, single industry. It is made up of many—from those who provide cloth and buttons to those who sell finished garments and other fashion-related items in the stores you like to visit.

Most of our experiences with fashion start with shopping, and seeing display windows in retail stores. (© CFphotos/Alamy)

The fashion game approach identifies and explores these highly different entities (the "players") and their activities. It also describes why
and how they function as they do (the "rules").

It may surprise you to know that no matter how diverse these players may be—whether
providers of cotton fibers, or purveyors and retailers of the latest, most trend-focused styles—
each follows markedly similar rules. **Each player regardless of how specialized, or unique,
seeks the exact same objective, or "goal."**

Can you think what that might be?

**The overall purpose of this text is not just to describe "rules," "players,"
and the single "goal" that unites them, but to show how all of these
interact with each other.**

Why? Because you will find yourself part of that exciting exchange when pursuing any
career related to fashion. Repeat: *any* career. What will you do as a fashion designer, for
example, when fabrics do not arrive on time? Which other fashion game player will you call to
find out what happened? As a retailer, for another example, how will you work with other players
to make sure you have enough inventory on hand to meet demand? As you build a career, working with other players who are developing professionally themselves, what will your own strategy
be for working successfully with them? What ideas might you gain from this text for doing so?
To answer these questions, consider the following ideas:

First, the fashion game concept believes everything about fashion is related.
Really! No matter how different the aspects of it may seem right now, at the conclusion of
this text, you will come to find out how interconnected each and every player, rule, goal—
everything—is. There is a reason you recognize fashion brands at a glance, for example.
There is a reason garments and accessories are made of the materials they are and why
they are available in particular stores and not others.

**Second, working within the fashion game means balancing the dependency you will
have on other players (and they on you) with the need all of you have for professional
success.** Interconnected and at the same time independent; how will you balance these needs?

Working within these extremes begins with knowledge: gaining the know-how of a fashion
professional. This means knowing and knowing how to use terms and phrases, especially understanding concepts as other professionals do. Here, you will find much necessary, practical
information for a fashion career. Additionally, working within the fashion game context means
gaining an overall sense of how the fashion and retail industries operate. Thus, the fashion game
concept was born. It is a framework, a way of thinking to which you may refer as you seek to
make sense of why, how, and by who makes what you think of as "fashion" work.

Presenting the Fashion Game!

How might you get a better idea of the fashion game? What is an example of it? Who are its
professionals, the players in the fashion game you might encounter? What do they do? Get
ready to find out. You've stood in line for hours, been checked against "the list," and told to
quickly find your seat.

You've just arrived at a fashion show!

Lights go down…music comes up…late arrivals straggle to their seats…and out onto the
runway step the first models.

Fashion shows bring together representatives of almost every occupation involved in fashion and fashion retail. (© Luftbildfotograf/Fotolia)

You've seen them in shopping malls, in stores, through various media. Always, the focus was on the clothes, accessories, and all the exciting things being presented. "What's new for this season?" That's always an interesting question.

At this fashion show, however, consider more than just clothes and accessories. Seasonal fashion shows, especially those of well-known designers or brands, bring together representatives of almost every occupation involved in fashion and fashion retail. Directly or indirectly, as you will come to find out, they are interested in, concerned with, and definitely dependent on what is shown. Consider those in this audience. Who are they and what do they have to do with fashion?

Promoters in the Fashion Game

Among the easiest fashion game players to spot are **promoters**. Front row, dead center, in seats flanking both sides of the runway, they see all and are seen by all. There, for example, several kinds of promoters may be found, especially the **fashion editor**. You will discover others later. Also note that while these players may be easy to spot now, it took years of successful hard work for them to reach front-row status.

Editors scan each ensemble, called a "look," or a "turnout," in the language of fashion, as it is presented. They compare each one to what was shown here before, with what's coming down the runway next, and to what they have seen before elsewhere. Individual details, such as hemlines, are important, but more important are the overall creative themes, ideas, and inspirations espoused by the designer.

Editors look for moods. They gain a sense of how well—or not—the clothes and accessories shown capture, define, and even transcend present-day feelings about fashion, life, and ways of living. Editors convey their thoughts and perspectives to readers of their publications, perhaps even to viewers of television, Internet, and other programs.

Editors communicate through images, text, and other media with the ultimate goal being to stimulate interest in and purchases of fashion items reflecting prevalent fashion moods or trends. You will discover more about the role of editors and other fashion promoters in Section 7,

Fashion editors and stylists use clothes racks to review what is available to present to the public. (Mee Ting/Fotolia)

"Promoters: Supporting the Fashion Game." Today, Anna Wintour currently enjoys front-row, celebrity status as American *Vogue* magazine's editor-in-chief.

The editor may be the one looking for something to say. Next to editors, in prime locations as well, are seated leading editorial fashion directors, or **fashion stylists**. They are thinking about how to present to the public, to those who read magazines, newspapers, and follow fashion, what's being offered. Not just show "outfits," combinations of terrific new items that, together, tell a "story," but how they generate excitement about fashion, its trends, and its new ways of thinking about how to dress. They, like editors, must intrigue consumers, encourage them to adopt—that is, to purchase—fashion products reflecting the new look, the latest trend. Red-haired Grace Coddington of American *Vogue* is one well-known editorial fashion director.

Let's not forget the **models** on the runway. Linda, Naomi, Gisele, and guys, too, like Tyson, Nacho, and David Gandy, are known for their fashion presence. They become the faces, figures, or physiques consumers associate with fashion and with fashion brands and companies. You see them in shows, as you might here, or in internationally published print advertisements, on Internet sites—wherever their presence is needed to further recognition of the fashion companies they represent. Models, as well as editors and stylists, and even the photographers snapping images of the show as it progresses are among **promoters** in the fashion game.

Also in the audience there are **public relations** (PR) professionals, who may have been responsible for producing the show, or hyping it to interest important people in attending. Typically, they, too, are seated where they can best see the action, noting the show's progress and its reception by attendees. Think of the fictional Samantha of *Sex and the City* fame, portrayed by actress Kim Cattrall. Her character was that of a fashion PR guru. If you're a follower of popular culture, it's likely from that example, you're already familiar with how they promote fashion trends, products, designers, models, and events. Promoters connect people to each other, to companies, to brands, to products, and to special events. The presence of celebrities in the audience may be due to the work of promoters like PR professionals, either celebrities' own or those working for the show's designer or sponsor.

"**Sponsors**," another term you may have heard and have certainly seen advertisements for their products in the background of fashion show images, are businesses that underwrite the often considerable financial costs associated with presenting these shows. Venue costs, lighting, special effects, city and other permit fees—it all adds up to multimillion-dollar spectaculars. Mercedes-Benz, Olympus Cameras, L'Oreal Cosmetics, and many hospitality and beverage companies sponsor shows to further the image of their respective brands and companies. In other words, yes, companies do use sponsorship of fashion shows to promote fashion to consumers, but also to build the appeal of their own brands of products—to make cars, cameras, cosmetics, beverages, and a great many other products seem "fashionable" among consumers.

A little farther down the first row is another invited group, busily tapping away on laptop computers. You know these hardcore fashion followers as **bloggers**. They, too, may be thought of as fashion game promoters. They may not intend, specifically, to sell fashion products or services as other promoters might. They are sources of information, "in the moment" perspectives, or personal commentary about what they are seeing, experiencing, even feeling about fashion. Bryan Yambao (a.k.a. "Bryanboy") and Tavi Gevinson ("The New Girl in Town") are two bloggers about whom you may have heard, read, and even, perhaps, followed. Designers and fashion companies actively court influential bloggers to attend and describe what they see in "real time." To participate firsthand via media at a fashion show usually means the blogger has a following. They are "thought" leaders. They are fashion promoters in the larger sense: chronologists of fashion's continued evolution and its ever-changing direction.

Throughout the audience are those texting and "tweeting." These may be fashion industry professionals or just interested observers. They are **microbloggers**, relaying short impressions of what's going on though means such as Twitter. Are they "official" fashion game promoters? You decide. After all, professionals, consumers, everyone lives and works now in a "liquid feedback" world, one that encourages and accommodates all contributions.

Also present in the audience are **fashion forecasters**, another kind of promoter. These are the fashion game players responsible for spotting new style trends and colors to which consumers will respond. David Wolf, of The Doncaster Group, is among the best-known fashion forecasters, responsible for "spot on" fashion, color, and trend projections, for knowing what consumers will want, long before they do! Wolf and others are present to confirm their earlier projections, or to glean new ones from what they see in the show, or in the audience. Their work, too, will be further detailed with that of other promoters.

As you scan the front row further, you notice a group of well-dressed women, and sometimes men, depending on the show. They seem to know everyone and everyone knows them, judging from the number of waves and greetings that others exchange with them, even during the show. Not only that, as the show itself continues, you notice that most of them are already wearing what's shown on the runway. What's remarkable about this is that stores may not stock such garments until months later. Who are these fashion insiders? These are fashion's "uber-consumers," those who buy the most clothes, the most often: **socialites**.

The lifestyles of these highly affluent women and men require their participation in numerous activities where they will be seen, photographed, and talked about. Their front-row presence indicates that they are well known to the "house"—the fashion designer's business—usually because of their many purchases. Socialites function as "ambassadors" in their respective communities, even to the world at large. They interest others in particular fashion designers, brands, styles, products, and stores. Because of their imprimatur, their acceptance, their informal promotion, socialites encourage others' participation in fashion, sometimes as much as any editor or blogger does.

As you scan the front row one more time, you recognize a face you've seen before, maybe on a poster, on television, on film; perhaps on all of the above. You've just spotted a **celebrity**! The fabulously famous have always loved fashion and fashion loves them.

Salma Hayek on the red carpet. Designers get a lot of exposure by dressing celebrities for events. (© MARKA/ Alamy)

Celebrities can become highly influential, maybe even the best known of fashion promoters. For example, it is almost impossible to talk about legendary actress Audrey Hepburn without mentioning French **couturier** (male fashion designer) Hubert de Givenchy. Wearing his designs, she had her famous *Breakfast at Tiffany's* as well as many other memorable moments onscreen and in her personal life. Celebrities in more recent times may not depend on any one designer to quite the same extent as she did. However, actress Renée Zellweger's affinity for clothing by **couturiere** (female fashion designer) Carolina Herrera is one example of the continued draw fashion can have for celebrities.

Some celebrities have fully embraced fashion by becoming fashion game players themselves. Think of Victoria Beckham. The former "Spice Girl" ("Posh") combined her musical celebrity status with acknowledged style sense to form a fashion brand of her own. Her husband, David "Becks" is a sports celebrity who is developing a fashion presence as well. Mary-Kate and Ashley Olsen are other celebrities who turned their personal interests in fashion into thriving businesses. Among their several brands, "The Row," has earned both critical and commercial success.

Whether they remain consumers or become players themselves, celebrities are integral to the fashion game. They become a powerful link between consumers and fashion. They entice consumers, inform their selections, and lead them to purchase as they do. Celebrities become the image associated with particular designers, brands, styles, products, and stores. Tiffany and Company, for example, owes much of its timeless elegance image once again to Audrey Hepburn, who wore that brand's jewelry. Right off the top of your head, you can probably think of contemporary celebrities and the brands with which they are associated: Keira Knightly and, recently, Brad Pitt for Chanel; Natalie Portman for Dior; and Matthew McConaughey for Dolce & Gabbana. The following section explores the relationship of celebrities, fashion, and consumers in more detail.

Editors, stylists, models, PR pros, bloggers, forecasters—these are the fashion game promoters responsible for bridging the gap between fashion that is the idealized image of designers and fashion the item—make that items—you must have when you see them. Because they are often associated with the selling of fashion to consumers, promoters are often thought of as functioning at the "retail level" of the fashion industry.

Celebrities and socialites are highly visible fashion promoters. Each and every one of them becomes important in the fashion game. Through their promotional efforts, they create and further consumers' desire for the latest fashion has to offer. How important is that word "latest"? Very! Why do you think that is?

Promotion is time-sensitive. Its messages and their meanings do not remain interesting forever. For this reason, promoters must be keenly focused on what is "now," the current focus of fashion, how best and who best to convey those impressions. Promoters and, indeed, spokespeople such as celebrities and socialites must move on, change directions when seasons, styles, and other changes occur so as not to be perceived as being out of touch. This is especially true with professional promoters, whose job is to identify and tout fashion's newest developments authoritatively. Socialites and celebrities enjoy the attention they receive wearing the most recent, most exclusive, and, yes, often most expensive clothing and other fashion products. Doing so builds their own fashionable mystique while at the same time promoting the others responsible for the apparel, accessories, jewelry, and other items they sport.

Moving away from promoters, another group of players endeavor to make fashion available to consumers like you when, where, and how you want it!

Fashion Game Purveyors

At different places, up and down both sides on the runway, are groups of men and women who look decidedly "corporate." That's not to say they do not look knowledgeable about fashion; they may even be trendy in appearance. Rather, there is a businesslike air about their appraisal of what's being shown. Something about them suggests that they are concerned about more than just the creativity behind what's being shown. They are looking for what will sell...sell...sell! Because of that focus, these fashion game players work at the "retail level." Who are these new players in the fashion game?

These players in the fashion game are **purveyors**. **They are responsible for actually selling fashion and related items.** Some purveyors may not sell directly to consumers like you, but to other fashion businesses which, in turn, sell to consumers. There are two basic kinds of purveyors when it comes to fashion.

The first kind is known as **wholesalers**. These are "**business-to-business**" **(B2B)** sellers. Wholesalers are in the fashion show audience to see, firsthand, what is being offered for the upcoming season. Then, they will write orders for their selections. When the merchandise is delivered to their businesses, wholesalers will then sell those items to retail stores.

Wholesalers are part of what is referred to as the **channel of distribution**. These are the steps, or "route" fashion goods follow to get from manufacturers into the hands of consumers. As you already know, the world of business is complex and has been made even more so by fast-paced technology and changing commercial practices. Details about the different forms distribution channels take is explored in Section 6, "Purveyors—Bringing Fashion to You."

Other purveyors present at the fashion show include **retailers**. **These are professionals who sell to the end users—consumers.** In other words, they are the **"business-to-consumer" (B2C)** purveyors whom you know, representatives of the stores and boutiques you enjoy shopping in. Retail companies send their fashion directors, lead buyers, and merchandise specialists such as high-ranking allocation planners and managers to shows to see what's being

Retail stores are part of the channel of distribution, making fashion accessible to the marketplace.
(WavebreakmediaMicro/Fotolia)

This shoe display is an example of visual merchandising. (JJAVA/Fotolia)

offered. Retail buyers write orders ("leave paper") for fashion goods after the show. They then sell those items to the general public.

Wholesale and retail purveyors, sellers worthy of first-row status, are the big money! These are the accounts that purchase large amounts of merchandise, or are especially desirable, or both. Their operations may be national or international. Macy's and Kohl's, for example, are retailers that buy large quantities of fashion goods. The Neiman Marcus Group and Saks Fifth Avenue are retailers that purchase large amounts of fashion goods. Yet, as fashion leaders, offering cutting-edge, of-the-moment trends, they are considered highly prestigious as well. In rows farther away from the runway are other purveyors represented by buyers who are working for or who are owners of smaller, regional wholesalers and retailers.

Retailers sell to end users of fashion products—consumers. They do so with the assistance of marketing and merchandising professionals. **Marketers** use principles and techniques of **marketing to identify target segments of the overall consumer population to find the ones most likely to be responsive to new products and services, then plan ways to reach those specific consumers. Merchandisers plan how, how much, when, and where merchandise will be available for those consumers to purchase.** Thus, in the crowd at the fashion show are marketing pros responsible for planning and coordinating all kinds of advertising and promotions to attract the attention of those specific consumers. Others are watching the show with an eye to how to make such goods available in stores, through catalogs, via the Internet, direct mail, television, radio, or all of the above at specific times.

Visual merchandisers are also in the audience. The days of visual professionals being thought of as working in "display," or as "window trimmers" are over. **Visual merchandisers are professionals responsible for planning store environments in distinctive ways and carrying out brand marketing campaigns through merchandise presentations.** Usually working under strict time and budget constraints, they establish a store's image and make holidays memorable for many consumers and profitable for stores.

The audience also includes representatives of other, competing designers or manufacturers. They may be present for any number of reasons. Yet, one of the challenges inherent in the fashion game is how quickly one creative idea disseminates, becoming known and copied at ever faster rates. Not all of those in the audience are looking to illegally copy what they are seeing in this fashion show. Several of them may, in fact, represent fashion companies showing highly similar styles, colors, and details created with ideas obtained through legitimate means. Think about this: Successful professionals in every occupation, including fashion, know their competitors, work with many of the same sources, follow the same trends, and keep abreast of the same issues affecting their industries. This is how they stay current and remain in business. This underscores the connectedness of fashion industries and businesses, of the fashion game itself.

With respect to those "in fashion," these professionals know which other companies, designers, brands, and stores, to name only a few entities, are on the way up, down, or just holding on. They follow designers saying something new, gaining critical interest in the trade press, and notoriety among consumers. It further means that fashion game players use the same color, textile, and trend resources; employ the same forecasters and consumer analysts; read the same trade publications; and, often, know and consult with the same people throughout the industry. They see the same museum exhibits and experience the same cultural and charitable events that spawn fashion ideas as well. No wonder similar design, styling, "moods," and other ideas permeate the fashion industry at the same or nearly same times. As you explore what the fashion game means, later in this part of the text, however, you will find out what— or really, who—determines fashion's course.

Who Made the Fashion Show Possible?

No, it's not the designer who is probably backstage, making sure everything goes according to plan. Designers, as you will see, have their moment at show's end. No, it's those players, there, in perhaps the third and fourth rows back from the runway. There would be no fashion show, no clothes—just piles of sketches—were it not for them.

Many separate sources and makers are required to complete fashion and accessory items. Looking around, you will notice people in the audience who light up at the appearance of a style in an especially attractive fabric, or with distinctive buttons or trims. They are likely representatives of the fabric company that produced the cloth, or maybe makers of the sequins, beads, even zippers appearing on garments in the show. These items are among those producers make available to fashion designers. Maybe these items even inspired the designer as he or she developed the line of garments shown. If you have ever seen or held a beautiful or unique fabric (often referred to as "textile"), you may well understand the power they have to inspire creativity. Who makes such products, which are practical and evocative at the same time, available? These are **providers** in the fashion game. Because they are responsible for the very first "things" that go into or become fashion items, providers are often considered part of the "primary level" of fashion.

Take another look and you will see other fashion game players present at the show. These are the **producers**, those directly responsible for transforming sketches into garments. These audience members are representatives of companies that make what's being shown on the runway. Producers are considered the members of the "secondary level" of fashion. What might you need to know now about the kind of services they perform? Garment production is a complicated, highly controlled, sequential process. Fashion items, such as coats, for example, may be constructed by a single manufacturer or by many different businesses totally apart from designers' companies. In addition to those responsible for constructing all or portions of garments are those who prepare items, such as finishing them and getting them into stores and to consumers.

Because of the many steps involved in fashion production, producers are **supply chain** specialists. They make sure garment or accessory production "flows" with the right raw materials

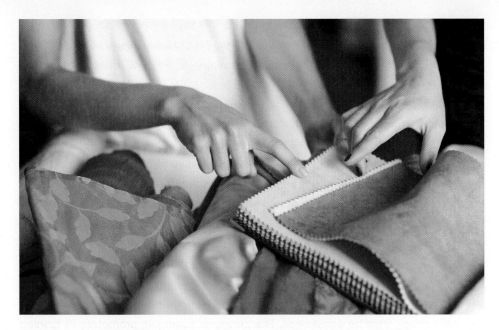

Producers choose appropriate fabrics for the pieces they construct. (Yuri Arcurs/Fotolia)

and progressively finished pieces reaching the correct next manufacturing steps "just in time" on their journey to completion. To that end, they often call on practices such as "Quick Response." Further details about fashion production processes at the secondary level are discussed in later sections. One fashion brand described at the end of this section that has risen to even greater prominence due to its mastery of supply chain processes is Louis Vuitton.

Looking farther back into the audience you may see other kinds of fashion game producers. Well-known designers offer consumers many different products bearing their names. Think of shoes, purses, fashion jewelry, cosmetics, even neckties and underwear. These are among the many different items that often have a "designer" name on them. Where do these things come from and who makes them?

The fashion game players you may see scattered about are representatives of companies that hold **licenses** to use the designer's name. Usually, they are present to see their products being exhibited in the show. These professionals have **paid for the right to use designers' names, logos, or other representative symbols on different products**. Usually, these businesses are better able and more efficient at making these items than the designers or their companies could be. Sunglasses are great examples of licensed products. While almost all major designers offer "name brand" eyewear, in reality only a few specialized companies actually make them.

Finally, the show music thumps to a close. All the models appear on the runway, walking single-file, then clap as the designer appears. Shy designers wave, then duck backstage. The bold ones stride to the end of the runway and give a big salute to the crowd, smiling all the while. Designers are among the most visible fashion game players. Yet, are they the most enigmatic? Using the categories set out here and recalling what you know about fashion already, how might you classify designers: producer, promoter, provider, purveyor, or all of these?

Not sure?

Think about why designers such as Giorgio Armani, Ralph Lauren, and, recently, Michael Kors become so well known. What did they do—besides "just" designing and making clothes—to achieve success? As the lights come up, let's not forget the last few groups remaining. Professionals who study fashion and educate others about its past trends, production processes, and current contributions to culture may be attending this fashion show also. Although their purposes may not be to "sell" fashion to consumers, they, too, are fashion promoters. They further interest in and knowledge about fashion. An overview of several of their activities includes the following examples.

Curators of fashion or costume are responsible for identifying, obtaining, and preserving garments and textiles for observation and study. They may work for museums, academic institutions, even private collectors of fashion. Garments, as well as accessories and other fashion-related items, have become especially sought after as artifacts of the times and circumstances from which they came, as examples of rare degrees of workmanship, as singular works of art in their own right. Curators have mounted museum shows featuring important Hollywood costumes, painstakingly made garments of ancient Chinese royalty, and the work of current designers such as Vivienne Westwood and Jean-Paul Gautier. Past, present, and future museum exhibits present the public with visual, tangible reasons why fashion remains a relevant force in society.

Fashion educators, including professors and workroom instructors attending the show with their classes, **may be considered, like curators, academic promoters of fashion knowledge**. Research, education, and imparting practical, fashion-related skills also keep fashion relevant as new generations of students learn ways to advance fashion's future.

As you leave the fashion show venue, you see a group of people bearing signs and placards, held back by security. Protesters! This, too, is fashion. Shouldn't it be "fun"? Why, then, are some aspects of it so controversial? Maybe the designer whose presentation you just experienced uses fur products, or is thought to employ "sweatshop," or forced labor. These participants are expressing their viewpoints about such issues as **advocates. They seek to raise public awareness.** They are also fashion "promoters" in that they wish to change the ways in which fashion is produced and consumed. Thanks to social media, advocacy groups, comprised of professional organizers and interested consumers, are influential forces. Everyone working in fashion careers must understand who these advocates are and how they can work together to find solutions.

The Fashion Game Dynamic

More than clothes and accessories alone; more than the people who design, make, and sell them; and even more than those who wear them—the exciting interaction of all of these is what we are talking about when we say "the fashion game"! To understand this phenomenon requires, first, acknowledging for whom fashion is, ultimately, intended: consumers. They alone decide whether a style, a color, a brand, or a business will be successful. You will discover more about them and the power they wield in the next section.

Consumers move fashion's direction. They do this through what they pay attention to, certainly what they purchase, and how and when they choose to participate. This has come to mean:

No fashion game player such as a single designer, or any several of them working together, can successfully "dictate" or decree what consumers wear. **Changes in fashion evolve**, occurring gradually, slowly, as consumers become accustomed to and accepting of some developments, while ignoring or forgetting others. While this process, known as **the fashion cycle** has greatly sped up over time and is highly influenced by economic conditions, the fact there are many more fashion trends and style options available now than ever before, does not alter the overall consumer-driven, evolutionary nature of fashion.

Marketing, advertising, promotional activities, "blogs," and "tweets" cannot "put over" any fashion trend, style, product, or brand. **If consumers do not want and fail to accept fashion, no amount of promotion will compel them to do so.**

As never before, consumers have a voice in fashion's direction through avenues such as social media. **Consumers can now offer their insights and comments immediately**, in "real time." How well fashion game players listen to and work with consumers affects their success.

Having such a strong voice as well as self-focused and determined powers, don't consumers expect, somehow, that fashion game players will develop, produce, and offer as quickly as possible exciting clothing, accessories, and other fashion products with "just them" in mind? Certainly, they do not expect fashion game players to offer items to consumers they do not want ("I would *never* wear that!"), to provide them with limited, narrow selections ("Don't you have *anything* else?"), or to fail to consider their feedback ("No one got back to me!").

How, then, are fashion game players able to work, some quite successfully, within the seeming contradictions of consumers' powers and expectations?

Emotional and practical, those fashion game players able to consistently build strong bonds with consumers—and who probably have a degree of luck, too—appear to have found ways to balance consumers' powers with their expectations. By doing so, they thrive in the fashion game!

Think of the challenges entailed in accomplishing those goals. Fashion game players face powerful, demanding consumers on one side as well as numerous competitors on the other. In every market niche, at every "price point" be it couture (high-priced), department store (moderately-priced), or mass-market (low-priced), fashion markets are crowded with products. The players responsible for this all seek consumers. What strategies, then, do fashion game players employ to address the requirements of standing out from crowds of competitors and forming lasting bonds with consumers?

How the Fashion Game Is Played!

The "rules" of the fashion game, as you will discover in subsequent sections, encapsulate these kinds of strategies. Brand marketing and management—"Be a Big Brand"—when carefully thought out and carried out, serve the dual purposes of appealing to consumers and differentiating players from each other. "Branding" is the process by which products and services are given characteristics that add meaning and, ultimately, value that they otherwise would not have. Think of all the different kinds of athletic shoes available: Adidas, ASICS, Nike, Puma, Under Armour, and so many others! Thanks to such practices, each shoe brand carries its own unique images and associations. Right now, you can probably state differences in them, and you can certainly recognize their products, whether you wear, or even like, particular brands.

When focused on specific, targeted consumer groups and their lifestyles (either real or aspired to), brands bring identity, excitement, entertainment, uniqueness, and senses of community and belonging to products and services. Thus, brand building is the way fashion game players form emotional links between their products and consumers.

A shopping mall represents a perfect example of many areas of the fashion game: producers, fashion merchandisers, purveyors, and consumers. (TMAX/Fotolia)

Even so, what good would attractive, desirable, branded products be if they were not available? Practical considerations of producing, distributing, merchandising, and selling their products are other issues fashion game players face. They must address these issues in ways that satisfy consumers' expectations and not incur their powerful wrath.

Making sure "the right products, in the right place, at the right time, in the right quantities," and at the "right price" are available to consumers is one way this challenge has been stated. The remainder of this text explores how this multistep process is carried out by fashion and fashion retail game players in the enterprises they operate. As with all businesses, they must be aware of and integrate legal, ethical, and profitable practices in their professional activities, always with the goals of supporting brands and attracting new consumers.

Fashion Game Focus: Louis Vuitton

Consumers are the fashion game's goal. Recall, however, that the fashion game is a "dynamic interaction." What could be more dynamic than the ever-changing, yet somehow familiar, fashion brand, Louis Vuitton? Previous generations of consumers, fifty and sixty years ago, knew it only as a maker of heavy, hard-sided trunks, suitcases, and bulky travel bags. Think of it now! With widely diverse fashion products, the brand has become one of the most coveted in the world. What happened to make it so? The story of Louis Vuitton is the story of the fashion game and how its players work together.

Vuitton's explosive growth since the late 1970s may be attributed to several factors. Chief among these was increased awareness of how important brands are for all businesses, but especially for fashion ones. Brands, as you will discover later in more detail, define the image, even the substance, of fashion businesses. Whether they use "signature" colors on "iconic" products; evoke luxury, sophistication, or sportiness; no matter their image, fashion brands are the means by which consumers can tell differences among what would otherwise be very similar items. How do fashion game players work with such images to build powerful brands?

With respect to Vuitton, it's emergence as a premier luxury brand resulted from "leveraging the brand," a phrase referring to use of strategies intended to attract as many different purchasing consumers as possible. This, or simply "leverage" are terms employed frequently by fashion and retail professionals. Vuitton's team of sophisticated managers and designers recognized the many impressions the Vuitton name and "L.V." initials evoked: Paris, travel, chicness, as well as the affluence to enjoy such things and the status doing so confers. By working with these beliefs that many consumers already held about the brand, Vuitton developed products and promotions consistent with them. By doing so, they leveraged lingering images of the brand into a full-fledged, high-fashion lifestyle.

Building the Vuitton brand is ongoing. Working with internal and third-party sources as **providers**, the company now offers accessories and garments in an array of textiles and high-quality leathers, besides their recognizable "monogram" canvas. Similarly, they expanded the number of **producers** making their many products to those in Italy and Spain as well as in France. Vuitton works with these sources to ensure consistently high product quality. Doing so maintains brand image and consumer satisfaction. Previous generations of Vuitton customers were known to cut up duffel bags and have the brown-gold fabric made into shoes! There was incredible demand for more products, desires Vuitton identified and used to leverage the brand, to grow it into a vast array of products.

Men's shoes (never offered previously), for example, are now made by Venetian craftspeople "inside" the company as employees, who are skilled in the art of shoemaking but who might not be able to remain in business were it not for Vuitton's ownership. The number of styles now offered far exceeds those possible when consumers had to "make" their own Vuitton shoes. Vuitton's control of product production quality contributes to its appeal. Vuitton better organized its supply chain practices for more efficiency.

Another factor in its success includes the ways in which Vuitton changed its relationship with **purveyors**. Previously, "L.V." goods were haphazardly sold through wholesale, retail, and a few company-run channels. No more! Each Vuitton retail outlet is a company-operated boutique, even if it inhabits spaces leased in other stores. This ensures that only authentic, first-quality Vuitton apparel, accessories, and other items are available. Similarly, the company maintains control over its Internet sales portal to guarantee brand integrity, product and delivery quality, and, of course, consumer satisfaction. Thus, Vuitton streamlined product distribution channels and organized it in ways the company is able to maintain control over at each step.

Vuitton's earlier promotional efforts were largely limited to print advertisements that touted the virtues of its products for luxurious, convenient travel to exotic locales. These may be thought to have formed the brand's descriptive "D.N.A": what it stands for and the message it forms, to which Vuitton returns again and again: not just travel, but adventure made possible, made better, through use of its products. Whether carried by singer, activist Bono and wife, Ali Hewson, in Africa, or beside Angelia Jolie in Cambodia, Vuitton as **promoter** has positioned its products to be the ones sophisticated travelers, or those who wish to be, have and use on their excursions around the world or around town.

Sideline:

Vuitton revives French fashion brand Moynat some thirty-plus years after its successes, reinvigorating Vuitton. Parent company, Groupe Arnault, is reintroducing another French brand, Moynat Malletier (trunk maker). Dating to the 1800s, yet dormant for decades, this brand, known for its "M" logo emblazoned on trunks and traveling bags, is Arnault's latest effort to bring updated production and distribution practices to what might be an otherwise lost fashion company. Currently, the brand is headed by designer Ramesh Nair. A decided "boutique," or small-scale brand, it seems poised for growth in years to come.

Section Finale

With so many things to know about fashion, retail, and subjects such as fashion merchandising related to them, it seems logical to have a framework around which you might organize your newfound knowledge. The fashion game approach allows you to classify professionals ("players") and understand the kinds of work they individually perform. However, its greatest attribute is to facilitate your understanding of how they work together—the dynamics of the fashion game process. How do you think they balance doing both? This section was your introduction to the game and its exciting processes, challenges, and the ways they are addressed by fashion game players as they seek to do just that!

Review Questions: "What Did You Discover?"

1. Identify and describe those identified as fashion game "players." Provide examples of each to help explain who they are and what they do. Using the worksheet "What Is the Fashion Game?" select one you particularly admire and relate their activities to you.

2. As clearly as possible, describe what you believe the fashion game to be. In particular, think about how its players depend on each other, yet must be successful on their own. From your own observations of fashion and what you have learned in this first section, how do "players" appear to strike this balance?

3. What are the "levels" of fashion and what kinds of fashion game players might be found in them?

4. Describe how celebrities further the work of fashion game players.

5. What does it mean to say that consumers "move" the fashion game? What observations are noted here about how they do so?

6. List the "rules" of the fashion game. You will learn more about them in subsequent sections.

7. Describe the (many) activities of different fashion game promoters.

8. What are some of the challenges inherent in the fashion game and what suggestions do you have for how they might be resolved? The answer will be clearer as you complete work with this text. However, based on what you know now, think about these challenges and how you might address them.

9. What is meant by "supply chain" as it relates to fashion products?

10. What processes encompass "channels of distribution"?

11. Why is it important for fashion game players to build "big brands"?

12. Why and how might designers and fashion businesses offer seemingly similar products without having copied from each other?

13. How did Louis Vuitton become symbolic of the fashion game in action?

14. What careers of those listed in this section are of interest to you? Why? Keep your interests in mind as you prepare for the "Market Day Simulation Project" that follows.

Terms to Know

Be sure you know the following terms from this section and can give examples:

Advocates	Channel of distribution	Retailers
B2B and B2C	Supply chain	Consumers
Providers	Visual merchandisers	Curators
Purveyors	Price point	Fashion forecasters
Promoters	Sponsors	Bloggers and microbloggers
The fashion game	Public relations	Celebrities
Fashion editors	Wholesalers	Socialites

Becoming a Fashion Game Player

Project Purpose:	To prepare for the Market Day Simulation Project, this worksheet asks you to select the role you or your group will play and to describe your first ideas of what you might offer.
Step One:	Using the four fashion game player designations: **provider**, **producer**, **promoter**, and **purveyor**, decide which (from the definitions and examples found in this section) appeal to you. Then state why that one correctly defines you. For example: Are you a "people" person? (perhaps promoter roles might be of interest) Are you interested in ways that science affects the development of fashion products such as textiles? (perhaps provider roles might be of interest) Think about your interests in fashion and how they relate to these four designations.
Step Two:	**Describe the job** that fits the category you selected. Refer to section examples for specific job titles/descriptions, if needed. _____ _____ _____ _____
Step Three:	What will you offer at Market Day that reflects your interests in fashion? Is there a product or service you think should be available, but is not? How might you present yourself as an expert fashion stylist or PR pro? SOMETHING got you interested in fashion! What was it? How might you get others excited about you and your idea?

Describe what you are interested in presenting. Do so in terms of fashion game roles and specific job titles. This is an initial idea of yours or your group. You will work out details later!

_____
_____
_____
_____
_____
_____
_____
_____

You may want to give your project idea a "working title," or tentative name. You can change it later, but for now write it here:

_____
_____

Section 1: The Fashion Game and Its Players (Optional Project)

Project Focus:	Based on what you learned from this section, which fashion game player role might be right for you? Here, you will reflect on your personal interests and abilities.

I am most interested in working as the following fashion game player: (Circle only one)

Provider   Producer   Purveyor   Promoter

This/these is/are what functions and activities I know that player performs after reading this section:

_____

_____

_____

_____

This is the education and work experience I now have and how I think it is applicable to the tasks they perform:

My Education:

_____

_____

_____

My Work Experience:

_____

_____

_____

These are the accomplishments I would like to be known for in fashion:

_____

_____

_____

_____

These are the things I think I will need to do in order to reach my goal:

_____

_____

_____

_____

Bringing the Fashion Game to Your Community with Your Help

Purpose: You can learn a great deal about the fashion game just by watching its players in your own community. Observe and record what you find according to the directions below.

Procedure: Locate a department or specialty store in your area that presents fashion shows to the community. This may be any kind of show—one that presents new merchandise and is open to the public, or, if you are able to attend, one supporting a local charity, club, or institution. You may find advertisements for such events in local newspapers, magazines, or through Internet sites and social media postings.

Identify Players of Your Local Fashion Game

Using the chart below and your knowledge of the many kinds of fashion game players, identify those in your community who fulfill game tasks. Be sure to state why you have classified them as one particular type of player. Have fun with your observations and keep this for reference. Why? These may be the very players to whom you will turn for internships and jobs!

Note: To really benefit from this project, be sure to look actively for all four types. Also, gather contact information from those who interest you for possible later follow up when on the hunt for that first big "break" you will make when you enter the fashion game.

Name of Person (Introduce yourself! Ask someone who they are!)	Fashion Game Player (Recall the 4-Ps . . . Provider, Producer, etc.)	Reason for Selecting (What did they do, or say that led you to make that selection?)

CONSUMERS AND THE FASHION GAME

FAST FORWARD

Consumers have shaped fashion's history and, even now, are shaping its future. They are the goal of the contemporary fashion game. Every fashion game player to whom you were introduced previously seeks to attract . . . engage . . . excite . . . and, ultimately, gain new consumers while keeping existing ones. They must in order to be successful. After you read this section, you will know about consumers from the fashion game perspective. These are the people—just like you—who purchase clothing, accessories, and other fashion-related items.

WHAT YOU SHOULD KNOW ABOUT THIS SECTION:

- It describes consumers' roles in shaping the development of modern fashion.
- It outlines recognized fashion consumer groups and their characteristics.
- It explores ways consumers interact with fashion.

2

Get ready to explore the many terms, phrases, concepts, and ways these all-important motivators have continued to shape fashion's development. After you read this section, you will understand why consumers—past, present, and future—influence everything fashion.

Consumers Determine Fashion's Development

The story of fashion has been shaped by consumers and their acceptance—or not—of its many changes. To understand the modern fashion game, recall where the very idea of "fashion" came from. Thinking about that, you may well see not only how consumers have shaped its course, but also how players, then and now, have responded.

Before the sweeping technological advances and resulting social changes of the late eighteenth- and nineteenth-century Industrial Revolution, there were few consumers of what we now would think of as "fashion."

Who do you think those might have been?

Early fashion consumers were royalty and wealthy aristocrats. These elites had the financial ability to acquire finely made clothing and accessories on a regularly changing basis. In marked contrast, farmers, peasants, and others who made up a majority of society owned few, roughly made garments. Often, such items of clothing were handed down from one generation to the next with their only changes being repairs and patches. In these times, centuries long, differences among individuals and their respective social realms could be told by their style of dress.

The distinctive appearance, or "style," of garments and accessories could and did change in accordance with elite whim. The term **"fashion" has come to be defined as the popular manner of dress prevailing at any particular time**. Its use and meaning is further thought to have arisen from these early nobles' adaptation of changing styles.

The more fundamental practice of **"dress," that is, covering the body with some kind of multidimensional garment, or several of them, is tens of thousands of years old**. Remains of its earliest known examples have been dated to about twenty-five thousand years ago.

You will encounter the term "costume" to describe clothing worn by those in the past. Can you distinguish it from "fashion"? Think "representation" for costume and "trend" for fashion. More formally, **"costume" may be thought of as those garments and accessories representative of particular times, places, or persons**. One example shows this distinction: the kilt. When worn by Scottish Highlanders to represent membership in specific families, or clans, and the geographical region where such groups originated, think "costume." When extremely long or short hemmed versions of kilts appear on the runways of Marc Jacobs and Jean-Paul Gaultier? Now, that is "fashion"!

Before advances in production practices, fashion components (particularly fabrics) were handmade and very expensive. Complete garments, too, were produced through painstaking labor, were similarly revered, and were costly. Elites wore embellished clothing, trimmed with furs, gold, silver, and jewels, as outwards signs, visible to all, of their royal or gentrified status.

Such elaborately styled and obviously expensive garments were, indeed, the status symbols of their day; they signified wearers as being rich and powerful. **Sumptuary laws in countries such as England prohibited nonelites from wearing or even owning such finery.** These laws, according to the thinking of the times, prevented "commoners" from fooling others into believing that they were members of the aristocracy, certainly from outwardly appearing above their "true" station in life. It has been argued that such rules were enacted as a means of preserving elite status through the control of dress.

Eighteenth-century "fashion" was accessible to a much smaller group of consumers. Materials were expensive, and most "fashion" garments were handmade. (Mad Pushup/Shutterstock)

Fabrics for clothing were hand-loomed until the late 1800s. (Donald R. Schwartz/Shutterstock)

Practically speaking, nonelites had few apparel options until the 1800s. Some were able to obtain cast-off clothing from elite employers. These were often quite worn out when acquired. Other clothing sources included those obtained from family members, or those obtained through barter, or trade. Purchasing new clothing in shops, as is done today, was rare. Garments were patched and "made over" until nothing useful remained. So precious was cloth and clothing that it was common for elites and nonelites alike to bequeath, or leave to others upon their death, portions of cloth, completed garments, and "accessories" such as leather belts and bags.

Technology Furthers Fashion Development

Industrialization, meaning **technological advances and human reliance on those innovations**, such as better, faster cloth-weaving looms and sewing capabilities brought incredible changes by the mid-1800s. **Cloth became a commodity item: widely available and subject to whatever price markets, not weavers and knit makers, determined.** Over time, market action drove down prices, making cloth, once esteemed and valuable, inexpensive. Garment production, another arduous handcraft like cloth making, advanced to the point where greater volumes of clothing were available at prices affordable by many consumers.

People in developed countries, England, parts of Europe, and the United States especially, became better off financially through advancing technologies. Mills and factories created opportunities previously unavailable. Workers could afford to purchase ready-made clothing. Furthermore, stratified social structures based on birth shifted. In their place came acknowledgment, even respect for personal achievement. One way to demonstrate individual success was through personal appearance. It was no longer "illegal" to wear better clothing. Retailers and advertisements of the times encouraged the purchase of new, better-made clothing as soon as affordable. By the mid-1800s, the ill-clad "commoners" of previous centuries were on their way to becoming today's modern fashion "consumers."

How fashion changed from the early 1800s through 1900.
(sch/Shutterstock)

Modern Fashion Responds to Consumers

Consumers grew in number during the nineteenth and twentieth centuries and they all needed clothing! To meet such demand, **mass production** and **better means of distribution** enabled efficient garment production. Mills that sprang from the Industrial Revolution were able to produce amazing amounts of cloth. Factories of the time were able to make large numbers of garments. These included **ready-to-wear** separates, such as most kinds of men's clothing, women's blouses ("shirtwaists"), and dresses; all of these became widely available and affordable. Fashion magazines and fashion catalogs, such as those of Sears, Roebuck & Co. and Montgomery Ward's, both touted fashion changes and provided convenient means to acquire them. **Mail order**, especially **Rural Free Delivery** (RFD), brought even the most sophisticated goods to rural homesteads. Participation by "regular" consumers in fashion's development was growing.

Greater Consumer Awareness of Fashion

One reason for such involvement was greater awareness of fashion and trends emanating from Paris. By the late 1800s, interested American women could easily follow the fashion innovations of Charles Frederick Worth and other Paris-based designers. Fashion magazines, such as *Harper's Bazaar* (1867) and *Vogue* (1894), were ready sources of such information. Paper dressmaking patterns, based on Worth's and others' designs, appeared as early as the mid-1800s. These further aided consumers' ability to follow French fashion ideas.

More than any one style, or "look," Worth's preeminence in fashion history is based on his establishment of **haute couture, or the design and making by hand of one-of-a-kind clothing**. In contrast to available ready-to-wear, couture clothing is made after it is ordered, sometimes taking months to prepare. Worth is considered the "Father of Haute Couture" for developing this process and establishing standards for it. As well, he introduced, or certainly advanced such then-innovative practices as runway fashion shows of the kind that began your study. Even today, most fashion design businesses continue to employ some elements that originated from Worth, such as seasonal showings of fashion collections with groups of different styles on live models.

Consumers' greater awareness of fashion may have brought about their greater participation, but in times when information traveled slowly, consumers were likely to take as authoritative what retailers offered, magazines portrayed, and style designers themselves proclaimed "should" be worn for particular seasons and on specific occasions. As a result, many local and regional department and specialty stores thrived in their respective areas, as consumers looked to those merchants for fashion guidance. Such deference would change as consumers and their needs and wishes changed in the twentieth century.

Consumers' Changing Lives Affect Fashion

In the early decades of the 1900s, the **growing independence of women** served as a remarkable force for change in society. To begin with, they were actively involved in activities related to World War I. In the United States, they gained the right to vote in 1919. Furthermore, they sought and gained a lasting presence in business and community affairs by the 1920s. These "thoroughly modern" women became discerning, demanding consumers. Among their needs was practicality. The fashion designs of Gabrielle ("Coco") Chanel featured trim, functional suits, her now-famous "little black dress," and, scandalous for then, trousers.

These garments mirrored such needs. Ready-to-wear fashions, much of which was produced in New York City's Garment District, became popular and followed trends emanating from Paris, as they had since Worth's time. Ready-to-wear would continue to grow in importance over the next decades. By the late 1960s, certainly during the 1970s, Parisian designers established and marketed their own ready-to-wear lines to consumers.

Leisure time and recreation became popular consumer pursuits by mid-century. After years of economic troubles brought about by the Depression of the 1930s and the political and social strife of World War II, ending in 1945, such interests were understandable. Consumers sought comfortable, practical clothing. Inventions in fabric and manufacturing technologies during this time, such as the introduction of polyester in 1953, provided fabrics that were cheaper to make than natural fiber ones such as cotton or silk. They were easier to care for and retained their shape and appearance better than handmade garments in high-maintenance natural fiber fabrics. This postwar desire for easy-to-wear clothing, however, did not mean that consumers had turned away from fashion. When it came to fashion, consumers still turned to Paris!

In contemporary culture, the 1950s might be called the "Decade of Paris" thanks in no small part to French fashion designer Christian Dior. He offered attractive, feminine fashions to women. After the "make do" garments of the Depression and the World War II years, his were, indeed, fashion's "New Look" clothes. At first, some consumers and critics thought his use of fabric overly extravagant. Yet, Dior's styles caught on, widely so, and remain among the iconic styles consumers still associate with the 1950s. The "twin set," two color-matched sweaters worn together, for example, was a Dior idea, now a mainstay for such fashion retailers as Banana Republic and J. Crew. Media sources avidly described highlights of Dior's collections—his changing hemline lengths and silhouettes (shapes of garments) were big news—and featured them in newspaper articles, department store advertisements, and television reports. So well known was he and his fashion ideas that even men wondered what Dior would present next season for women to wear. Thanks to his fashion innovations and savvy business management, his name and fashion ideas form the basis of the modern-day Christian Dior fashion brand.

During the post–World War II decades, shopping became for many consumers a favored pastime as there were ever-more exciting and affordable products available. Interest and, indeed, excitement in fashion during this time stemmed as much from where fashion ideas originated as what styles emanated from them. Consumers closely associated Paris with fashion. Yet, there were other venues gaining their own fashion authority.

As Dior rose to preeminence, Italy was beginning its ascent as a fashion source. With foreign assistance, Italian fabric mills and fashion houses began during this same postwar era. By the 1970s, Italy would become a worldwide fashion powerhouse, thanks to these business investments and the creativity of designers such as Cecile Sorrell, Princess Irene Galitzine, and Valentino Garavani.

Fashion Comes to Reflect the Individual

The postwar years saw consumers increase in number as never before, thanks to the baby boom, lasting from 1946 to 1964. You will learn more about this group later in this section. With so many people, demand for more things and for greater choice among them became

Men's clothing became more colorful in the 1960s and 1970s. (iofoto/Shutterstock)

powerful. What consumers came to want more and more was for fashion, for both men and women, to be more reflective of the individual and less about what someone else might think they should wear.

For men, the **Peacock Revolution** of the 1960s brought color and pattern to men's clothing. This shift was in marked contrast to the much more sober clothing men adopted after the war, through the 1950s and into the early 1960s.

For women, the iconic style of the 1960s was the "mini" skirt. Often worn with thigh-high boots, this sometimes radically short dress captured the "youthquake" feel emanating from fashion's new focus: London and its Carnaby Street area. The colorful, body-conscious styles of these times often came from equally colorful and exciting boutiques. These small specialty stores offered selections specifically chosen to appeal to that era's "mod" consumers, those "down" with the new, freer living scene.

Today's All-Powerful Fashion Consumer

How would you like to be told what to wear?

Not likely, right? The late American fashion designer Bill Blass noted that the **"midi" skirt**, a skirt style falling mid-calf, was the last time in his estimation the fashion industry attempted to tell consumers just that. In fall 1970, fashion editors, manufacturers, and retailers attempted to push the style on consumers with little success. The "midi" did, however, spark debate at the time not about what would be fashion's direction, but about who would lead it. In the time since, and as you will discover next, the answer has become clear: consumers. Women, unconcerned about what anyone in fashion thought, did not hesitate to choose more flattering and practical pantsuits. That jacket-and-trouser combination, sometimes paired with a blouse or sweater, became **iconic, or highly representative**, of the 1970s. The "midi," on the other hand, ended up as one of the decade's fashion **"flops," or a style that gained no wide-scale consumer acceptance and quickly passed from the market**.

Current popular culture and fashion styles take inspiration from the 1970s. However, the era itself was economically challenging due to "stagflation," or rapidly increasing prices. Put another way: "Times were tough!" By the 1980s, many people aspired to greater affluence, certainly of appearing prosperous. The 1980s was the era of **"power dressing."** Tailored suits often with exaggerated shoulders became popular examples of this trend among both men and women.

Music and musicians also influenced young 1980s fashion consumers, and they adopted the styles of favored singers or groups. This was the (first) heyday of singer Madonna. Among her lasting style influences were her use of lingerie, "inner wear" as outerwear, for example. Practical, colorful athletic clothing such as tracksuits, too, became common day wear during this time as well.

By the 1990s, consumers demanded value from fashion, its producers, and retailers. This meant lower-priced, "on-sale" goods, available in plentiful quantities. Style trends varied widely as consumers adopted those based on their own interests and needs. "**Hip Hop**" and "Business Casual" styles were reflective of late twentieth-century fashion trends.

As technology became ever-more forceful in the lives of all, the Internet became the go-to source for fashion information and, increasingly, for purchases. By the new century, consumers were only growing in power. That meant players who wished to remain in the game would have to find more innovative ways of engaging and interacting with consumers. Can you think of how they might do so based on your own shopping experiences, even just browsing?

New Consumer Interests Lead Fashion

Technological savvy and price sensitivity are recent consumer interests of note. Technology has enabled those in the fashion and retail industries to know more about consumers. It has also provided consumers with the means to know a great deal more about fashion than they did previously. Information is now readily available, useful, and rewarding to makers, sellers, and users alike.

It is a multichannel, technology-driven environment now! Shoppers expect retailers to allow purchasing through traditional stores, mail and catalog, television and radio, Internet, and mobile devices. Retailers also must support those channels by permitting consumers to mix and match selections and allowing them to buy online and, if they desire, have purchased items delivered directly to them or to the store for pick up. These technological innovations have allowed consumers to influence fashion and those who provide it.

Who does not like a bargain? Consumers of all kinds certainly do. So much so that what is now considered "fashionable" is not based on price alone. Many consumers feel comfortable mixing garments and accessories of often markedly different prices and origins, such as when expensive totes and purses appear with much less expensive athletic clothing. Limited edition jeans, often costing several hundred dollars, teamed with five-dollar rubber flip-flops are another manifestation seen on both men and women. Fashion game players of all kinds are paying attention to consumers' price concerns and finding innovative ways of addressing them.

Star athletes often lend their names to shoe styles to attract customers. (Natalia Glado/Shutterstock)

Price and Quality Interests

The "**masstige**" (mass + prestige) movement underscores efforts on the part of designers to provide fashion and fashionable items at reasonable prices that have the cachet—the status—of more expensive ones. Karl Lagerfeld and Madonna, for example, have leveraged the power of their names and reputations as fashion leaders to attract customers to lower-priced merchandise that they have had a hand in designing. That a movement such as "masstige" could exist, even be recognized, makes clear one thing: **consumers—not designers, stores, or prices— determine what "is" fashion**. As a result, consumers and the related quest for identified, focused (targeted) groups of them are one principle of the fashion game. You will explore that in further detail in the following section.

Consumers' Participation in Fashion Design

What other powers might consumers have? They now want to be part of the fashion process. Technology developed over the past decade has enabled much greater direct participation in the fashion process. Perhaps there is no greater way to have fashion on one's own terms than to design one's own products. **Product customization**, particularly with shoes and accessories, is a theme present and growing in fashions of the first decade of the twentieth century. Companies now offer consumers the ability to be involved in the fashion process. This has been dubbed "crowdsourcing."

> ### *Sideline:*
>
> *Major brands and retailers see crowdsourcing as a way to increase consumer loyalty, while smaller firms build entire businesses from it.*

Social media allows consumers to have fashion on their terms—to shape its products—and share their opinions directly with company decision makers. Facebook, for example, has become a major conduit permitting consumers to have such power, as when fashion brand Burberry broke the three-million fan barrier on Facebook, becoming the most widely followed fashion brand on the social networking site.

Consumers are as interesting and compelling as any style or trend adopted over time. The study and analysis of their many groups offer opportunities for fashion professionals. Those who understand how to reach target markets are uniquely positioned to shape the future course of the fashion game. Considering their importance, how might you identify and better understand consumers?

Getting to Know Fashion Consumers

What do all fashion game players need? From the previous section, recall several of them, their respective roles, and what they seek: magazine editor Anna Wintour needs readers for American *Vogue*; bloggers Bryan Yambao (a.k.a. "Bryanboy") and Tavi Gevinson, The Style Rookie, need followers; PR executives need interesting, interested people to promote and attend their events. They all need fashion-interested consumers who are ready to buy!

Fashion consumers are those who purchase and use information and products related to apparel, accessories, cosmetics, and home and gift items. Every player in the fashion game, no matter how diverse his or her endeavor, needs them. But who "are" consumers?

No two people are alike. That is especially true when it comes to fashion consumers. Their needs, interests, influences—their personal "type"—vary greatly. "Who is the customer?" This is a frequent way fashion and retail professionals ask not about just any, but the one consumer, or **target market** being sought.

Target marketing is the process of identifying specific consumers, those most likely to comprehend, want, and, ultimately, purchase fashion goods and services. To discern any one of these groups, it is important to gain a general understanding of consumers first.

Take a look around the next time you are out among large groups of people. Whom do you see? What are they like? Try to determine what they seem to like or are interested in by what they are doing, saying, even wearing. Whether you are aware of it or not, you are seeing consumer groups and observing but a few of the traits making them distinct. How might these traits be described from the point of view of fashion merchandising and marketing professionals?

Your work in fashion will include learning about consumers as quickly, as cost efficiently, and as thoroughly as possible. What follows is a brief overview of how fashion game players, whether designers, corporate executives, or even small store owners, come to gather and interpret information about consumers. It may seem a long way from fashion, but in reality, this is what fashion is all about: getting to know existing or future consumers and finding ways to satisfy them.

Those involved in fashion and its promotion to consumers may use several approaches to describing consumers. Perhaps the most straightforward way would be to describe groups by gender, specific ages, broader ages, income, location, or some combination of these characteristics. **Fact-based approaches such as these, in which collected data can be measured and mathematically verified, are referred to as demographics.**

A more complicated approach to describing consumers would be that known as psychographics. Think "lifestyle" and you will have a good idea what this approach is about. By using data collected about consumers, their interests, and their motivations, psychographics provide another kind of insight. In very general terms, **psychographics**, such as the commonly used VALS2 system, **consider consumers' personal values and available resources to estimate the kinds of items they purchase and activities in which they engage**.

Psychographics can be used to form a highly accurate understanding about consumers, their motivations and actions, and what they purchase based on those characteristics. At the top of the VALS2 scale, for example, are "innovators." These are consumers with substantial financial resources and desires to obtain the most innovative products when they become available. Others with lesser abilities and interests might, by the same system, shy away from such items, only interested in them, if at all, after many others have already accepted them. At the bottom of the eight-segmented VALS2 system are "survivors," who have little interest in or means to acquire anything other than subsistence products such as food.

Many demographic and psychographic forms of consumer analysis are proprietary. This means that fashion and retail professionals must hire companies specializing in conducting such forms of research and interpreting its results. Both approaches are important tools for identifying target market consumers and are often used together to identify and locate types of consumers sought by fashion game players.

Consumer research is an exciting, exacting application of the social sciences and mathematical statistics. Sociologists, psychologists, demographers, and others advance our understanding of the identity and practices of consumers. Statisticians quantify those findings to give them credibility and relevance. **Analytics** is a term generally used to describe the technological ways consumer information is gathered and scientifically interpreted.

Consumer research may be conducted by or commissioned from specialists by fashion and retail professionals. These may be providers (to understand textile characteristics, such as "easy care," sought by consumers), producers (to find out what styles of garments consumers like or do not like), purveyors (in which stores ascertain what fashion items to stock to meet consumers' expectations), and promoters (to know what to advertise). Information gathered through consumer research is one part of fashion forecasting, a topic discussed in Section 5, "Producers: Designing and Manufacturing Fashion."

Technology has furthered ways of collecting consumer information. Thanks to social media outlets such as MySpace, Facebook, and Internet applications that permit, even entice, consumers to contribute thoughts and suggestions, they are now able to volunteer important information about themselves in collaborations with other consumers and fashion game players.

The field of consumer research is vast, with many sources of information available for exploration. In general, however, those researching consumer information follow several basic steps. The first of these involves defining a question or set of questions to be answered. In other words, stating a problem. For example, fashion designers might be curious about whether consumers would like garments made with a particular kind of fabric, perhaps one about to be or just recently introduced into the market. On the other hand, a fashion retailer might be interested in knowing how well sales for certain items went throughout the entire industry during one particular month. Each question requires information to answer, but what kind and how might it be obtained?

The second step in consumer research involves finding the information necessary to answer the defined question. Some kinds of questions, such as the designer's concerns about fabric preferences, might be addressed by reference to information collected by others. However, it is more probable that such information must be obtained by the designer or his or her company. Information obtained through original research is referred to as **primary data**. Data collected and analyzed by others is known as **secondary data**, such as that found in trade papers such as *Women's Wear Daily*. In this instance, if the fabric in question has not been on the market for long, it is quite likely that secondary data are available and primary data will need to be collected. Primary data may be obtained in the following ways:

Observation: As the name suggests, this method of gathering primary data involves watching how consumers react to products or services. It can be as simple as watching and noting the brands and styles of clothing individuals wear or more intense observations known as counts.

Questionnaires: These are sometimes lengthy sets of inquiries. They may be followed by predetermined sets of responses from which consumers may choose the one best representing their characteristics, opinions, and other information.

Focus groups: Volunteers or groups of people are invited to participate in this form of information gathering. The focus group may meet once or on several occasions over a period of time. The entire process is usually observed and recorded. Market research groups, psychologists, and educational consultants, among others, offer focus group services.

Social media: Another means of gathering consumer data sought to elicit, or "pull," data from consumers is through social media. What is unique about social media sources is that consumers may volunteer, or "push" it out for the benefit of others. Not only that, they do so in their own language and when and where they want. For example, through "tweets" and MySpace and Facebook pages, or even their own blogs and Internet sites, consumers can make others aware of their experiences, impressions, observations, and findings. These, too, are primary sources of information from which those in fashion and retail can learn about consumers and products and how well the two interact.

Social media remains, for now, a fairly new way of gathering data, as application of technology for this purpose has only become available within the past few years. The ability of consumers to post fashion products and service reviews has given them a voice and means to influence others. No matter how exciting it might be for you, as a consumer, to let others know what you think, can you see issues in doing so? What might be some challenges for fashion professionals when interpreting yours and others' inputs?

Quantifying and using information gained from social media may be difficult because one of its strengths is also one of its weaknesses: consumers respond in their own ways. These may not necessarily be in forms statistically easy to interpret. Nevertheless, because consumers often are swayed by others' use of these methods, fashion and retail professionals are interested in finding ways to enable and excite the use of social media. The fashion designer interested in

Sideline:

Through social media, fashion professionals with the fashion brand Coach have learned that female consumers tend to want more frequent interactions with fashion companies; they want such fashion brands as Coach to reach out to them through e-mails and text messages. They further want information about new products and what celebrities and fashion bloggers think of items and how to wear them. Male consumers, on the other hand, value interactions that enhance their knowledge of company products, how they came about, and what their uses are, as also determined by Coach's study of how to improve its social media presence with consumers.

knowing about consumer perceptions of the new fabric might, for example, conduct a focus group, then ask participants to "tweet" those thoughts—whatever they might be—to others. From those who respond, the designer might then have a better idea of how products made up in the fabric might be perceived. Now, truly, is fashion's media age, times in which the means through which consumers obtain information—what app, what tweet, what scan—is as exciting as any actual information they receive.

While engaging in these activities, "publishing" for all to see and read personal images and facts or comments, consumers reveal much about themselves: computer IP numbers can be traced, data given when registering can be sold to others, and information can be disseminated in many ways. Some consumers have no problem with this fact of modern life, feeling that they gain more in access and convenience than they give up, but it gives others pause. What do you think?

Describing Modern Fashion Consumers

Using general dates of birth (many of which overlap) and lifestyle considerations, social scientists, journalists, and others now recognize the following consumer groups.

Generation Z

Generation Z is thought to comprise those born during the 1990s, particularly during the middle part of that decade. In short, this group is composed of those born from 1995 to present time, according to the American Marketing Association. These are consumers—perhaps you are among them—who have never experienced life without the Internet or without advanced communicative technologies in almost every aspect of their daily lives.

Generation Z has grown up using technology and members of this generation document many aspects of their lives using their cell phones. (Norman Pogson/Shutterstock)

Members of Generation Y, while interested in fashion, are by necessity more budget conscious than older generations. (Rex Rover/Shutterstock)

They have been called "digital natives" because their learning and cognition was shaped, even defined, by technology use. Consumers in prior generations might, for example, seek out a map to locate a store. Members of Generation Z probably would not even think of using one. They would opt, instead, for consulting with the map application (or app) on their smartphone. In all likelihood, they would receive voice directions from their phone to where they wished to go.

Fashion professionals are especially interested in this up-and-coming group. They appear to be more consumeristic and fashion and brand aware than members of older generations. After all, they have been exposed to such items through the extensive amounts of media they have encountered throughout their lives. Their parents were more attuned to fashion and brands as well and made reference to them in their own selections and purchases. Generation Z members, too, are thought to be more interested in self-expression over involvement with groups or teams.

Retailers, merchandisers, and practically every professional in the fashion industry seek to tap into this group. Extensive use of social media resources such as MySpace and Facebook, as well as tweets about new items, are now frequently used to inspire and sell to this group.

Generation Y

Generation Y, sometimes referred to as "Millennials," is considered to be made up of consumers born between approximately 1983 to 1994, aged 18 to 29, according to studies conducted by the American Marketing Association. As the dates of inclusion suggest, this group may not have been exposed to the Internet and other technologies their entire lives, but, certainly, for most of it. They, too, are savvy users of technology and of social media.

Generation Y is thought to comprise about eighty million members. Although possibly a larger group than baby boomers, there has been relatively little time to compare the size demographics of the two. As well, there is some discrepancy as to dates of inclusion for this group. At present, Generation Y has the highest levels of literacy compared to those before it; however, that may be eclipsed by members of Generation Z. Members of this group may have had economic challenges that led them to live longer at home (or to have to return home). Furthermore, they have had the experience of seeing others unhappy with early career and life choices and do not wish to make them until they feel they are ready to make ones that are correct and permanent for them.

Members of this group are interesting to fashion professionals. They are technologically proficient; they are highly literate and interested in fashion. Yet, economic obstacles including expenses of living compared to amounts of income earned, have forced this fashion-conscious group to be more budget conscious than previous generations. The fashion and retail industries have responded to this through such activities as developing masstige lines of merchandise, about which you studied in the previous chapter. Under this approach, clothing designed by famous designers such as Karl Lagerfeld and Stella McCartney, which can run into the thousands of dollars, is produced, marketed, and made available less expensively. As with Generation Z, this group may be reached by fashion professionals through social media and the Internet.

Members of Generation X consider value important and tend to be focused on family and career goals. (Norman Pogson/Shutterstock)

Generation X

Generation X is thought to include those born between 1965 and 1982, according to the American Marketing Association. Members are sometimes referred to as the "baby bust" generation. It is estimated to be the smallest of the recognized consumer groups with about twenty million members. This group has been shown to earn less than their parents (those of the baby boom generation right before it) when at the same age.

Change and diversity are two common traits of this group. It has experienced much in the way of shifting political leaders and policies. Furthermore, members of this group are more varied as to interests and orientations. Value is an important concern attributed to this group over brand awareness or desire. Overall, members of this group are thought to be focused on family and career goals over acquisitive ones. There are opportunities for fashion professionals with this group, however. "Nesting" and home life are important concerns, ones that can be addressed through merchandising and retailing practices that emphasize value, convenience, and enhancement of home life.

Baby Boomers

Over time and with so much scrutiny leveled at it, perhaps it is no wonder this generation has been more studied and discussed than any other to date. **Baby boomers**, those born between 1946 and 1964 (the post–World War II era), are notable for several reasons.

Boomers, as a group, are incredibly large with an estimated sixty-five to sixty-six million members. As well, it has considerable personal economic clout and much purchasing power. This group is believed to control about 82 percent of all noninstitutional financial assets and more than half of all total consumer spending. Physical size and economic power make this an impressive and highly important consumer group.

Baby boomers have considerable clout and demand both suitable styles and good customer service. (bikeriderlondon/Shutterstock)

Fashion and retail professionals, among others, are keenly interested in the opportunities provided by this group. Although boomers are generally fashion aware and conscious of fashion brands, they want them modified for them. This means, for example, garment design should focus both on trend awareness and adaptations for larger sizes; fit, appropriateness, comfort, and style are key issues with this group. Boomers are used to getting what they want, when they want it, and how they want it!

In addition to those attributes, boomers desire extensive amounts of assistance with purchases. This means that fashion professionals must find ways of integrating services along with product sales. Thus, providing services such as fashion consulting as well as alterations are all necessary components for making the sale to this group. Follow-up services are usually necessary as well, such as consideration of sales feedback and favorable merchandise return privileges. Stores and fashion brands that offer these kinds of services are sought out by this group with repeat business, as brand loyalty can be among the highest of any generational group. Vocal, active, and powerful, consumers of the baby boom generation are a significant influential fashion force.

Other Ways to Describe Consumers

Generational approaches such as those described above are highly popular. This is in part due to their multidimensional nature: they provide "snapshots," or summaries, of numerous people. This is not, however, the only way to describe consumers. Consumers may be grouped and defined by such characteristics as:

Gender: Male and female. As you have seen, studies by fashion brand Coach have provided insights into how and what different sexes want from that company and from fashion generally.

Educational achievement: Elementary, secondary, high school, college, postgraduate, doctorial levels of obtained learning. Often linked to income earned, educational achievement is another way of gauging consumer interests and expenditures.

Ethnic origin: African American, Asian, and Caucasian are but a few such groups that comprise important fashion consumers and fashion game players. Hispanics are currently the fastest-growing demographic group in the United States. Of note, this group has been found to significantly participate in fashion through social media.

Personally identified: Asexual, bisexual, heterosexual, homosexual, transgender, and transsexual are characteristics of interest to those studying consumers. Members of these groups often seek products and brands that are inclusive of such identifications in advertisements. In addition, they are more likely to patronize companies with similarly inclusive employment and other practices.

Household income: High, middle, and low are traditionally used, economics-based categories noted by consumer specialists. Yet, the growing interest in masstige suggests that such delineations may be less important. For example, Target's association with Neiman Marcus in December 2012, an arrangement that joined a mass-market retailer with a luxury one, was lauded as benefiting both stores' brand images.

Non-Western consumers: Those who inhabit non-Western areas—especially those where specific, defined cultural norms exist—present unique concerns and opportunities to fashion game players. This dynamic is so important that it is the subject of a later section.

As you now understand, there are many ways to describe consumers. The issue with using any one or even several measures is whether those chosen are useful. For example, multidimensional psychographic information would be helpful for identifying target markets for new fashion products. On the other hand, using one source of information, say, only men, for determining average sleeve length measurements for use in making garment patterns would likely be the most beneficial source of information for that task.

Consultants trained in gathering and interpreting information about the interests and preferences of men, women, or members of specific ethnic, cultural, or income groups are often sought by fashion game players. These third-party, or "outside," authorities are often able to identify ways of attracting and retaining members of these groups in sensitive, nonoffensive ways. For example, fashion promotions intended for Middle Eastern countries, or communities of peoples from such regions residing in the United States, require language awareness and an understanding of the norms related to public depictions of women.

What Influences Consumers?

If consumers influence fashion, what influences them to make the fashion decisions they do?

In contemporary times, as you learned in the previous chapter, no single trend or style prevails. Consumers are free to choose styles, designers, brands—everything—when it comes to how they dress. Long discarded is the idea that any person, such as one faraway designer, sets fashion's course for others to follow. Thus, there is no one source that may be thought to influence consumers. What, however, might be the most likely?

Think about magazines, television programs, and other media sources you have encountered. More often than not, these depict other people—some famous, others not—in their choice of outfits or showing their selection of accessories. Consumers seem most likely to look to others and what they wear for ideas about their own dress. Fashion influencers are as multi-faceted as "real" consumers, belonging to more than one of the groups noted here. However, in general terms, they may be described as:

Entertainment and sport celebrities: Those who have achieved recognition and fame through accomplishments in sports, music, and entertainment are sources of fashion inspiration for consumers. Some celebrities are "fashionistas," or the trendsetters of trendsetters; they take risks in what they wear and enjoy being known for doing so. Lady Gaga and Sarah Jessica Parker are examples of those known for their recognizable sense of style, of wearing one-of-a-kind garments, or of putting together different fashion elements in exciting ways. *Vogue* fashion editor André Leon Talley and musician Kanye West, in the United States, as well as presenter Graham Norton in the United Kingdom, are men recognized for their fashion presence and forward-focused attire.

Many celebrities leverage renown in one area for further popularity in another such as fashion. Madonna and the Beckhams, David and Victoria, are among examples of celebrities from music and sports who first established a personal fashion identity, then built influential brands.

One popular fashion trend has been for celebrity fragrances. These are perfume and cologne products bearing famous individuals' names. The Liz Taylor line of scents named after precious stones became and remains popular, spawning generations of fragrances as a result of its success. This is attributable to how well consumers associate celebrities with their eponymous products. Long known for a glamorous personal image and extensive jewelry collection, Taylor's "White Diamonds" and other fragrances made a successful impression on consumers, one lasting after the death of its namesake.

There are issues associated with the use of personalities and celebrities. When shown wearing recognizable brands, or garments of particular styles, celebrities further consumers' exposure to such items. This affects makers of such items in the following ways:

Use of products, or endorsement by celebrities for others' use, can **positively enhance brands and styles** in terms of their popularity and acceptance. In a process known as "seeding," those responsible for promoting particular fashion products, loan, or outright give, items they believe famous people will be photographed wearing or carrying. The thought being their respective lusters will brighten each other's: the celebrity's image of being fashion conscious; the brand or makers' of association with that particular celebrity. Celebrities attending "red carpet" events, such as awards ceremonies, programs millions of viewers will watch, are prime candidates for this practice. However, celebrities well regarded for their fashion presence are known to receive many items it is anticipated they will wear whenever they wish.

Celebrities may **negatively impact** brands, or styles, or at least, that is feared by fashion brand managers. Mike "The Situation" Sorrentino of the show *Jersey Shore* is routinely seen raising his shirt. This habit better enables him to show off his rocky abdominal midsection. Clearly visible in the process is an Abercrombie & Fitch waistband underneath. Entertainment and fashion sources report that Abercrombie & Fitch offered to pay him not to so visibly sport company products. They cited the brand as being "aspirational," one for a different target market than whatever might be the one Mr. Sorrentino represents. Whether done for publicity or not, this example underscores the extent to which celebrities are now seen as being influential—positively and negatively—with consumers.

After the many millions in revenue Nike earned from Lance Armstrong's association with that brand and his endorsements of their products, the company (and others) dropped him. This occurred within days after allegations proved true that he "doped" with performance-enhancing drugs to win his many Tour de France bicycle races. Celebrities are elements, components of fashion brands, and in the fashion game are managed accordingly. And there lies a dilemma for fashion game players. Celebrity spokespeople often generate many millions of dollars in sales revenues for companies. Yet, what should they do when concerns or outright scandals erupt involving celebrity spokespeople? Often, answers depend on the extent to which fashion game players balance the "rules" with which they work. Those rules are explored in the next section.

"Society" or wealthy individuals: Wealthy, socially prominent individuals have been emulated by those less affluent or less well positioned for centuries. The fashion choices of socially established women and men remain highly influential in our times. New York, Dallas, San Francisco, Washington DC, and other large cities have their share of individuals who serve as important sources of fashion influence in their areas as they shape and confirm the fashion preferences among those around them.

Royalty: You have discovered the influence royalty had on fashion in earlier centuries. Royalty "was" fashion, then, as rulers were the only ones able to afford and acquire such luxurious appointments. In modern times, royalty still retains a degree of fashion influence. The late Diana, Princess of Wales, established an appealing fashion presence during her lifetime and remains popular for both all-out glamour and easy, casual elegance. She did much to further awareness of British fashion designers and their businesses during the 1980s, a time when they were virtually unknown outside the United Kingdom. Fashion designers such as makers of her famous wedding dress, husband-and-wife team David and Elizabeth Emanuel, as well as hat designer Philip Treacy became popular through her patronage.

Catherine ("Kate") Middleton, now, after marriage to Diana's son, Prince William, known as Duchess of Cambridge, appears poised to be a fashion influence as well. Pippa Middleton, her sister, is followed, too, by the fashion press both in the UK and abroad. These siblings enjoy fashion and developing their own modern senses of styles combining costly items with more affordable ones, just as many "commoners" do.

Consumer Interaction with Fashion

However inspired, from whatever source, consumers' fashion choices and the timing of their selections, are, indeed, complicated. Three theories suggest how individual consumers are thought to make decisions about what they wear. What do you think?

Trickle-down theory: This theory holds that only after those who are high in a specific social hierarchy, or are in some way decision makers, accept fashion changes, will others accept them. This is probably the oldest theory of fashion adoption, referring back to the days when royalty and the wealthy were considered the prime sources of fashion guidance. This theory is not considered as powerful a means of determining consumer fashion acceptance today; there is no single, defining societal hierarchy or order. Yet this paradigm cannot be fully discredited. Clothing and accessories selected by Kate Middleton, Duchess of Cambridge after her marriage to Prince William of Great Britain, inspire the fashion choices of others. Fashion producers and purveyors report they sell out of styles that she has been seen and photographed wearing.

Trickle-up theory: "Grunge" fashions serve as examples of this theory. Under this approach, fashion change and acceptance occurs when **those of higher social and economic positions adopt the ways of dress of those considered less affluent or thought to be of lower social standing**. The Marc Jacobs 1994 collection of the same name for American fashion label Perry Ellis took inspiration from the urban homeless. So shocking was his collection that Jacobs was fired from Ellis. Yet, its presentation underscored how relevant this approach is.

Trickle-across theory: This is perhaps the most subtle of the three theories of fashion acceptance. Recall when you have been part of a group. At various times **what you wore may have changed based on what others in that group were or were not wearing**. For example, particular brands or styles of sneakers or jeans may have been popular with one or a few members of that group, which others soon took to wearing as well. You and others in that group may have been influenced by those few people to initiate and validate such changes. Now, imagine similar phenomena occurring in various different social groups from the very small to the very large, very poor to extremely wealthy. In that way, you will understand how this theory operates.

The Fashion Cycle and Consumer Choice

Have you ever encountered rack after rack of garments in stores and wondered why there were so many available of something you and obviously others do not want? On the other hand, have you looked for a particular favorite fashion item only to be told it has sold out? What you are experiencing is the fashion cycle. These occurrences come about because of consumers and how they perceive and want fashion.

Much of what is seen in retail store displays represents fashion ideas that are copied and varied for the mass market. (AXL/Shutterstock)

Introduction: During this first phase, designers and manufacturers only produce small numbers of items exhibiting the newest colors and trends. Retailers, reluctant to purchase large numbers of these untested items, usually purchase few of these to gauge consumer response. Only a few consumers, those interested in such items, take the risk of selecting and wearing them. These are fashion trendsetters, or "leaders."

Rise: As fashion ideas take hold among larger numbers of consumers, those ideas are copied at every price and variation. Makers are usually swamped with orders for these products as retailers seek to keep consumer demand and interest high during this phase. Fashion leaders may still exist during this time, as different groups of consumers learn about them. Likely, though, those who adopt fashions at this stage are considered fashion followers, after seeing others wearing and giving their tacit approval to such fashion changes.

Peak: Sometimes called the plateau or culmination stage of fashion acceptance, this stage is characterized by great interest in and demand for a particular fashion item. It is widely available at many more different prices and retail venues at this stage. What is interesting is that how long the item remains popular varies. The challenge those in fashion and retail have is ascertaining whether the style or item is a fad, one that they should curtail production and ordering of, or one that will enjoy a longer popularity with consumers. In such cases, they should continue making (perhaps with modification) and selling (perhaps, too, with greater promotion). Those who adopt fashions at this stage are probably best described as fashion "laggers," or those who are extremely slow to adopt new fashions unless a great many other consumers have accepted them previously.

Decline: After great demand for fashion usually comes great boredom: the fashion has been available for long periods of time and adopted already by those who would do so. Typically, the market for the item is considered saturated with many unsold products still available. In such instances, manufacturers attempt to eliminate their stocks of any unshipped goods though "jobbers," companies that buy such items to sell to other, often international markets, or use for scrap as with felt making. Retailers, too, seek to eliminate their stocks through drastic price reductions or sale to jobbers and deep discounter sellers. Those who adopt fashions at this point are primarily not concerned with or motivated by fashion, but by low price.

Rejection: Recall the 1970s-era midi skirt, which reached unflatteringly to about mid-calf. Such fashions, if available today, might well serve as examples of obsolete styles, those highly likely to be rejected by consumers. At this final stage of the fashion product lifestyle, the goal of makers and sellers is to eliminate all stocks of them as well.

The fashion cycle is influenced by economic conditions, both personal to the consumer and present throughout society. These factors can and do affect the speed of the fashion cycle. Sounds complicated? It isn't, really. As you know from your own experiences, when you have more money to spend on fashion items, you are more likely to do so than when you do not! Even those consumers who feel they are personally able to purchase fashion goods easily may not do so due to other factors. Can you think what those might be?

What Is "Consumer Confidence"?

The **Consumer Confidence Index**, prepared by the Conference Board Consumer Research Center, is one important measure of how consumers feel about the overall health of the economy. Often used by the fashion business press, this measure indicates how positively, or not, consumers perceive prevailing economic conditions; in other words, will times remain "good" or "bad"? High levels of consumer confidence are considered to bode well for continued interest in fashion and related retail sales. Low levels of consumer confidence often indicate sluggish, even unprofitable fashion seasons because consumers are reluctant to spend and choose to forgo purchasing and opt, instead, to save their money.

Section Finale summary

Consumers provide fashion's context, its reason for being. They are sought by all its players and, as a result, are the "goal" of the fashion game. Knowing them and their importance will make it easier to respond to the all-important question: "Who is your customer?" This section explored how consumers shaped fashion's development. It further provided means to describe consumers by motivations and interests, and noted how information about consumers is gathered and interpreted.

Review Questions: "What Did You Discover?"

1. Describe what it means to say that consumers are the "goal" of the fashion game.

2. Which members of earlier societies were able to indulge in fashion and why?

3. Distinguish "dress" and "fashion" as well as "style" and "fashion."

4. What were sumptuary laws and what was their goal?

5. Describe industrialization and some of the advances it brought about.

6. How did modern fashion respond to consumers of the nineteenth and twentieth centuries?

7. What was RFD and how did it bring fashion to consumers?

8. Describe the activities of Charles Frederick Worth, his contributions, and the meaning of haute couture.

9. Why were the designs of Christian Dior, especially his "new look," so influential with consumers?

10. What were the "baby boom" and "youthquake" eras and how did those consumers influence fashion development?

11. What was the "midi" skirt and how did it fare with consumers and why?

12. Who were "yuppies" and what was their influence on fashion?

13. Name two consumer interests that lead fashion and how they are manifested.

14. What is "masstige"? Where did the term come from and what elements does it entail?

15. Target marketing involves what actions?

16. Describe as best you are able how information about consumers is gathered and why doing so is important.

17. Describe several "generations" of consumers and give brief descriptions of each.

18. What are some sources consumers look to for fashion inspiration?

19. What are the "trickle" theories of fashion acceptance by consumers?

20. The fashion cycle is comprised of how many stages and what occurs in each?

terms

Terms to Know

Be sure you know the following terms from this section and can give examples:

Style

Baby boomers

Product customization

Questionnaires

Dress

Peacock Revolution

Fashion consumers

Focus group

Costume

Target marketing

Social media

Fashion

Demographics

Generation Z

Industrialization

Flops

Psychographics

Generation Y

Commodity

"Power dressing"

Analytics

Generation X

Mass production

"Hip Hop"

Primary data

Trickle-down theory

Ready-to-wear

Secondary data

Trickle-across theory

Haute couture

"Masstige"

Observation

Trickle-up theory

Fashion cycle: Introduction

Fashion cycle: Rise

Fashion cycle: Peak

Fashion cycle: Decline

Fashion cycle: Rejection

Consumer Confidence Index

Market Day Simulation Project Worksheet

Who Is YOUR Consumer?

Project Purpose:	Now that you have a general idea of what you want to provide for the Market Day Simulation, identify and describe your target consumer.
Step One:	Recall the working title for your project and record it here for reference:
Step Two:	Ask whether your proposed product, service, or combination of them would be better suited for use by OTHER fashion game players or by the public, the consumers you learned about in this section. For example, if you wish to make innovative, eco-friendly textiles, how might consumers use them, compared with another fashion game player, those able to incorporate them into finished garments?

Other Fashion Game Player(s)	General Consumer(s)
Which ones:	Which ones:
Why would it appeal?	Why would it appeal?

Step Three:	Describe in your own words how you might attract the consumer(s) you feel would be your ideal target. Might it be both or just one kind?

_____

_____

Section 2: Consumers and the Fashion Game (Optional Project)

TRENDMATCHING: What Trends Go with Which Consumer?

Step One:	Watch the crowd! Who are they and what are they wearing?
Step Two:	Record your observations and conclusions by stating WHY you think specific consumers find these trends appealing. HINT: Your observations may be used to support your reasons.

Person 1	Description
Person 2	Description
Person 3	Description
Person 4	Description
Person 5	Description
Person 6	Description
Person 7	Description
Person 8	Description

RULES OF THE FASHION GAME

FAST FORWARD

How—and why—do so many exciting things seem to happen in fashion? This section identifies four rules that fashion game players seem to follow, again and again, to attract and keep consumers and for their businesses to remain viable. Here, you will come to know better—much better—what goes on "at corporate" in the fashion and fashion retail offices you may be destined for.

WHAT YOU SHOULD KNOW ABOUT THIS SECTION:

- It introduces four straightforward rules used by fashion game players to attract consumers and run fashion businesses.
- It explains these rules with real-life examples to help you recognize similar rules that you will come across in your studies and work.

3

(Opposite page) Source: © Stefanos Kyriazis/Fotolia

Business principles may seem daunting to learn about, much less establish, and maintain once your career is underway. Getting to know basic ones—the rules you will discover here—and gaining general ideas about how they are used by those in fashion and retail companies need not be. Don't be surprised if after this section you are also better able to understand news and other media stories about what goes on in fashion businesses. You will!

Fashion in Four . . . Rules That Is!

The fashion game: it's about discovering how and why fashion and fashion retail businesses operate as they do. As with other industries, there are discernible, "knowable," rules they seem to follow. These are guidelines you can learn, apply, and work with, once you get to know them. Then, you can say you are a fashion game player, one who knows how to attract and keep consumers and remain in business.

Before reading further, think about what you know right now about fashion and businesses related to it. Compare two familiar fashion companies: a shoemaker such as Nike with a cosmetics company, say MAC Cosmetics, or a single luxury retailer, such as Saks Fifth Avenue, with a mass-market chain, such as Target. No matter how different the products or services each offer, don't they share similarities? Can you identify those? The rules that follow are about describing how fashion and fashion retail businesses are similar and why they operate in like ways. These are processes you can learn and learn to be part of easily!

Sideline:

In their daily work—in their careers—how do fashion game players "think"? Whether with large corporations, or perhaps the smallest boutique, why do they make the kinds of decisions they do? This section is about these issues as it touches on, introduces, and gives you a feel for the many terms, phrases, and concepts fashion players know about. As you progress in your studies and likely career in fashion, or fashion retail, you will glean other insights, your own unique perspectives, to add to the fashion game rules you discover here!

A fashion team, whether working in media or in the field, consists of several different people performing unique jobs. (Mangostock/Shutterstock)

Rule One: Be a (Big) Brand!

Rule One guiding contemporary fashion businesses is establishing a consistent, attractive identity, one to which consumers will respond. Put another way: Before talking about fashion products or services and what they will look like, or be, these entities focus on how consumers will come to recognize, understand, and appreciate the business and what it stands for. Next, modern fashion game players focus on what they will offer and how those products and services will reflect the image they have established for their brands. Subsequent sections will explore the relationship between product and service design and brand practices, such as discussions found in Section 5, "Producers: Designing and Manufacturing Fashion." Designers, for example, typically develop collections based on brand image and include colors, themes, even feelings consistent with brand identity. For now, get to know the basics of brands and what they are about. These brand concepts are the ones that fashion game players consider when building brands, big, small, and all.

According to the American Marketing Association, a **brand** is "a name, term, design, symbol, or any other feature that identifies one seller's good[s] or service[s] as distinct from those of other sellers." On the basis of just this description, do brands do nothing more than identify one maker's products from another's? From your own experiences as a fashion consumer, you know that there is much more. What does it mean to you to be "distinct"?

Certainly, different names, even label colors make manufacturers' products distinct. Again, from your experiences, you know that there are other aspects to being distinct. How do you feel when you wear your favorite pair of sneakers . . . that special item of clothing . . . a special sweater or dress? Think about why you select those items in the first place.

Brands build distinction among products on emotional levels with consumers. They build what might be referred to as "mystique," or the totality of thoughts, experiences, and emotions consumers associate with branded products and services. How did brands and branding practices come to be so powerful in contemporary fashion?

BRAND BACKSTORY

Brands themselves are not new. Whether on other products or fashion-related ones, makers have for centuries used some means to set their goods apart from others. Charles Frederick Worth, for example, is considered the first fashion designer to affix labels bearing his name inside garments. Later, another French designer, Jean Patou, in the 1920s, used his own "JP" initials, outside clothes, as both decoration and to identify his sportswear from that of other designers. When it comes to fashion, then, brands have been around a long time. What is new, however, is the degree of attention brands now receive from anyone interested in fashion.

A crowded marketplace of products and an ever more affluent (or creditworthy) consumer base occurred as the twentieth century advanced. As a result, mere retail bravado and sales acumen were no longer adequate to satisfy consumers, sell products, and earn profits. Marketing practices that combined attractive advertisement and promotional strategies began to motivate consumers more than ever. When faced with purchase choices, inevitably consumers were drawn to select those with appealing messages, seeming to speak personally to them and their lives. Brands are about consumers' lifestyles.

Although there are many examples, the reemergence of the French brand Chanel in the early 1980s (now one of the foremost fashion brands in the world) typified growing sophistication of brand management practices. Previously, it was a brand few considered at the forefront of fashion. How much has changed! Presently, the Chanel brand offers timeless and trend-focused

Much of the fashion industry in the United States is based in New York. (Songquan Deng/Shutterstock)

apparel and accessories equally successfully. In doing so, it finds appeal with teenagers, their mothers, and their grandmothers—generations apart in age and in lifestyles.

Products were not alone in benefiting from brand practices. Contemporary fashion-related services (think: Elizabeth Arden "Red Door" and "Aveda Concept" beauty salons and spas) gained a following based on associations that consumers held about those brands and what they represented. Thus, brands are what consumers look to ever more as representing stylishness, quality, value, special services, and other desirable attributes. What might you discover when considering brands themselves? How might they differ?

CLASSIFYING BRANDS

Fashion and retail professionals work with brands on a daily basis. Designers are charged with developing products that work within the context of a brand and its image. Retailers and merchandisers work to both build the brands of their stores and maintain the integrity of the brands they offer to consumers.

This is important: The following basic brand classifications are used frequently:

Industrial brands: These brands are attached to products used commercially to produce other items. As such, they are usually of limited interest to general consumers. Sewing and serger machines bearing the JUKI brand would be a fashion-related example of an industrial brand, as would be (Ralph) Pucci mannequins.

Consumer brands: These are the brands of products used in daily life. Think about how many you encounter. It has been estimated that, on average, consumers refer to about a dozen different brands a day, just in passing reference. General consumer brands are usually widely available from many different retailers. Right off the top of your head, you can probably name dozens of consumer brands such as Levi's and Gap.

Private brands: In contrast to consumer brands, which are widely available from many different sources, private brands are usually only available from one retailer. Many retailers, for example, offer their own brands of apparel and other items. They do so in order to reinforce the overall image of the store as being, for example, fashion forward or value oriented. As well, stores may be interested in keeping product costs down. By using vertical integration strategies (in which they own or control sources of products they sell), they are better able to accomplish that. With lower costs, retailers further have the potential to earn greater profit on "their" product brands.

Fashion brands: Take a look at the clothing and accessories you wear. Most have labels or some way to tell them from others. When brands are applied to clothing, accessories, cosmetic, nondurable home products, and even services, they may be considered fashion brands. Services, too, may form fashion brands when they are related to these items. Essentially, then, fashion brands are a subgroup of consumer brands.

Luxury brands: A term often encountered in fashion today is that of "luxury brand." It, too, is a subgroup of consumer brands and, when used with fashion and fashion-related goods and services, a further subgroup of fashion brands. Luxury-branded products are the "splurges" of many, the "staples" of few: highly expensive, exclusively distributed fashions, accessories, jewelry, cosmetics, and home goods. Such brands are aspirational; they tap into consumers' desires for affluence, for well-being, and for the perceptions of personal uniqueness.

IMPORTANT BRAND CONCEPTS

The classification of brands helps to describe them and the kinds of products to which they apply. How might you describe **ways** in which brands evoke the power they can have?

Brand personality: As with people, brands, too, have personality. With respect to brands, this means "how people feel about a brand as a result of what they think the brand is or does." Brand personality is part of the brand's overall image with consumers.

Brand salience: Awareness and recognition of a particular brand is at the heart of the brand salience concept. How, for example, are you able to tell one brand from another? For that matter, do you recognize any one brand at all? Brand marketers work to establish brand image and personality so that those brands have high levels of saliency with consumers.

Brand equity: Personality—salience—what do brand professionals seek by instilling such characteristics? Branding is ultimately about developing any one brand to be powerful enough that consumers will choose it over other competing brands, a concept known as **brand equity**.

WHAT MAKES A BRAND?

Brands are recognized by their constituent elements. These are the "building blocks" that brand managers, designers, and others use to attract and keep consumers' attention on their respective products. These important elements may be either tangible or intangible.

Symbols	Designs intended to represent a brand and what it stands for Example: The Nike "Swoosh" and Puma "Cat"
Logos	Usually a combination of initials signifying the brand Example: The interlocking "C"s and "G"s of Chanel and Gucci
Colors	Specific spectra of light used to signify brands Example: The bright red soles of Christian Louboutin shoes
Sounds	Tones, musical notes signaling brands to consumers Example: Commercials with jingles such as "Plop, plop, fizz, fizz," for Alka-Seltzer
Motion	Perceptions of activity, action occurring Example: Merchandising displays incorporating movement to attract attention to brands shown; MAC cosmetics' strobe-lit counters is one example
Scents	Olfactory sensations associated with particular brands Example: The aldehyde notes of Chanel No. 5 fragrance signal that brand's sophistication

Intangible brand elements

Services—Activities intended to add value to brands, products, other services (or both), as well as to those who provide them.

Example: Nordstrom has built its reputation as a fashion retailer that includes attentive customer service.

Policies—Practices, formally defined and intended to add value to brands, products, services, as well as to those who provide them.

Example: Liberal merchandise return policies among many fashion companies and retailers help to build the equity of those brands among consumers.

Amenities—Features that add value to brands, products, services, as well as to those who provide them.

Example: Sophisticated mirrors and video systems available in some stores and online that permit consumers to see themselves in clothes under different conditions.

Perceptions—Feelings and sensations that consumers experience about brands, products, and services.

Example: Retailers such as Abercrombie & Fitch rely on perceptions of sporty physicality to build appeal among male and female consumers alike.

This is important: Think of the branded fashion items with which you are familiar. What might those **brand elements** be that attract and keep your attention?

HOW LONG DO BRANDS LIVE?

Brands have a lifecycle, just like products, as you discovered in the previous section. A **brand lifecycle** consists of the following:

Introduction: Brand offered to consumers for the first time with much spent to promote it and gain acceptance; retailers are cautious to see whether consumers accept and stock in smaller numbers.

Rise: As brand gains traction with consumers, extensive advertising and promotion are required to further tap new consumer markets. Retailers increase inventories; discounts and incentives are usually not required to move inventory, because consumers actively seek out brand.

Peak: This is it! At this point in the brand's lifecycle, it is in great demand by target market consumers and other consumers, who become attracted to the brand they see everyone else has.

Decline: Consumers feel that they know the brand by now and either have decided it no longer suits their needs or have moved on to others. Sales decline sharply, and retailers mark down existing stock to reduce inventories and fail to reorder.

Exit: Consumer base has disappeared and the brand fails to attract new consumers. Retailers no longer order, and any existing stock is sold off, deeply discounted.

APPLICATIONS OF BRAND POLICIES

Brands are how many consumers come to know fashion. Several ways in which brands are developed and marketed underscore their prevalence and importance to consumers.

From shoes to shorts and shirts, even sunglasses and cologne, you may have noticed how many different products may all bear the same brand. What you are seeing is another brand concept of note: **brand extensions**. For example, many active apparel brands such as Nike, Adidas, and Puma entered the market with one product, such as shoes. As popularity of those companies' products grew and consumers became familiar with and liked them, those brands developed strong brand equity. Capitalizing off that, their parent companies offered hosts of items carrying names, logos, and other elements consumers would recognize, respond to, and, of course, purchase. Extensions have the benefit of increasing already powerful brand equity. Consumers make such brands their "go to" one for many kinds of goods, based on their positive perceptions of them. Yet, extensions are not without challenges. Successive products, if poorly planned or produced, can harm the brand and alter consumers' opinions.

With so much emphasis on building and extending brands, it seems logical that those responsible for them would want to protect them. **Brand management policies** are guidelines and practices that fashion game players put in place (usually with other players) to ensure that continued consumer appeal remains high. Brand management policies seek to prevent erosion of brand equity, so that it remains strong enough to keep consumers coming back time and again to **that** brand.

Branded products are expensive, not just for consumers, but for the stores that offer them. Usually, stores have to pay fees to obtain the right to sell particular product brands, and then must pay premium, above-average, wholesale prices to acquire inventories. That's one reason retailers develop their own private brands: it can be much less expensive.

Related to brand pricing policies are those rules stores must follow when it comes to marking down brands' products that do not sell. Under traditional retail practices, store buyers mark down slow-moving goods within thirty days after they first appear on the selling floor. Some brands, notably cosmetics, forbid stores to discount or put their products "on sale." Luxury brands in particular strictly prohibit any form of price adjustments of their goods by retailers to preserve their prestige image.

Stores are usually required to allocate specific amounts of retail and display space exclusively for brand merchandise. You've seen "stores in stores," those areas where only one brand is available? That's why! On top of all those incredible expenses, stores are required to spend additional sums advertising and promoting brands.

As a fashion game player, you will be responsible for developing or working with policies such as these related to preserving the image and equity power of brands. As part of the next fashion game rule—Be Legal!—you will discover that these rules are contained in contracts, or legally binding agreements between makers of fashion brands and retailers.

Brands are the powerhouse of fashion and fashion retail: the money makers, generating revenues for businesses by enticing consumers to continue purchasing. Be a (Big) Brand comes as the first rule, then, for without that process successfully in operation, there would be no fashion game!

Rule Two: Be Legal!

Rule Two is of concern to every legitimate business, including fashion and retail businesses. This entire text and many more could be devoted to how and why laws and legal guidelines relate to fashion businesses. However, you are here to get general ideas of how fashion game players operate and what it means to "Be Legal!" First for discussion is an overview of how fashion businesses may be organized and operated in legally recognized ways.

THE LEGAL ORGANIZATION OF BUSINESS

As you learn about another fashion game rule, "Be Profitable!," you will come to really understand the importance of knowing legal ways of establishing businesses. Some ways of doing so, such as organizing as a corporation, provide one way in which fashion game players and their businesses earn large sums of money. This is in addition to and totally separate from what they earn from making and selling their fashion products. Just think of designers Michael Kors and Ralph Lauren. They, among many other designers and fashion game players, are quite wealthy based on how they were legally permitted to set up their firms and what they could do with their businesses as a result. "Big brands" meet "big business"; together they have established the modern fashion game.

Business formations is a term used to describe ways of structuring commercial entities of all kinds, including those of the fashion industry. These ways, as you will see, may be quite simple or quite complicated. Reasons for selecting one way over another depend on the objectives business organizers have.

The most straightforward way would be for a business person to simply do nothing; just open for business! Referred to as a **sole practitioner**, the business owner is, essentially, the business itself: he or she assumes all responsibility for it. This means that the sole practitioner enjoys all the rewards that might accrue from the business. After payment of expenses and taxes, including federal income tax, the sole practitioner may keep the money earned from the business.

On the other hand, sole practitioners take all the risks, including assuming legal responsibility for virtually anything and everything that might go wrong. Because this is the easiest and least expensive way of doing business, it is popular with organizers who have little available cash to spend on more formal organizational plans. As you might suspect, the business terminates at the death of the sole owner. Individuals desiring to open a small fashion design studio or workroom might choose to operate in this form.

Partnerships, as the name implies, are those business organizations comprised of two or more individuals. Like sole practitioners, these can be easy to establish and operate. Nothing in writing is required to establish partnerships (as is also true with sole practitioners). In general, the operation of partnerships can go smoothly as long as all members are in agreement about such issues as their respective responsibilities to the business. This would include agreeing about the kind and amount of expenditures they will accrue in the name of the business, how profits will be divided, and how other internal decisions about the business will be made.

As with the sole practitioner form, the partnership format has some serious downsides to consider. For example, the partnership is considered dissolved, legally, upon the death of one partner. Furthermore, each partner in the arrangement is liable for all legal and financial obligations of the business, regardless of responsibility or any separate, written agreement to the contrary. The partnership form of business organization is one method by which two or more individuals may go into business with each other and with a minimum of cost and outside assistance, with each paying federal taxes on their earnings from the partnership.

The partnership format is realistic for small fashion businesses. Say, you and a friend wanted to run a store, but do not have much in the way of operating funds available. Both of you might choose this way to organize. The sense you should have after learning of the first two forms of business organization is that one or a few individuals "are" the enterprise. This is the primary difference between them and corporations.

Corporations are legally considered to be separate "identities," entirely apart from those who organize and control them. Corporations are noted with an "inc" designation at the end of the name, or in the English manner, as with American fashion designer Michael Kors, "Michael Kors Holdings, Ltd." Unless special kinds are formed (known as "C" corporations or "S" corporations), the corporation itself and those earning money from them are both subject to taxes. This is called "double taxation" and is an additional and often considerable business expense of corporations.

These are complicated forms of business organization, requiring much in the way of expertise and expenditures. There are two reasons for choosing this form: protection and longevity. By working in the corporate form, principal members are largely shielded from personal legal and financial obligations. Of course, being a legal "person" itself, the corporation may have to assume these in order to continue operation. In addition to protection, operating in the corporate form permits the business to continue after the death of any of its principal members, including its founders.

Corporations are difficult to establish correctly, but they do offer advantages. Corporations, being entities separate from those who start and run them, may be owned by others. For example, there is no realistic way to divide ownership of a sole practitioner. On the other hand, with corporations, percentage amounts of ownership may be possible. This idea is important when considering the third rule of the fashion game, "Be Profitable!," since those percentages may, just like a pair of shoes the corporation makes, be sold!

One person could own almost all or almost nothing of a corporation, as would not be true in a partnership. When only a few people have ownership of a corporation, it is said to be a **private, closely held corporation**. Few outside the founding family would likely be interested in owning a portion of such a business. The corporate structure in this case protects ownership interests held in the business. Many family businesses, such as local retail stores, are operated as closely held corporations. But there are exceptions and big ones at that in fashion! Chanel, a colossal fashion concern if ever there was one, is "private." Only a few members of the very wealthy Wertheimer family "own" interests in Chanel.

Limited liability company (LLC) is another business formation. Like corporations, laws govern establishment of these businesses, which combine traits of sole proprietor and partnership forms with corporations. Notably, LLCs protect organizers from the extensive financial liability they would otherwise have operating under a sole proprietor or partnership.

Large corporations have become principle players in the fashion industry. These complex organizations operate in the corporate form for all of the above reasons. Yet, there is another to consider. Recall the ability for percentage ownership possible with corporations: it is possible to own a "piece" of a corporation. Many large fashion houses rely on this feature and offer shares of stock, or ownership interests, to the public. These are legally considered **large, publicly traded corporations**. Establishing these business entities and offering **stock** (known as "securities") to the public are very complicated and expensive processes. There is much governmental oversight (i.e., there are many laws) about how stock shares are sold. Stringent criminal penalties, including large fines and imprisonment, exist for failing to adhere to securities-related laws. These exist to protect investors, both individuals and other businesses, from unscrupulous activities and practices.

"Going public" is done so that corporations may raise money. Perhaps the corporation is considering an expansion and needs funds to do so, or perhaps a principle (such as Kors or Lauren) desires money for personal reasons. By doing so, public companies may earn revenues from product sales and from the first time they sell shares of ownership in the company, in a process known as an **initial public offering** (IPO). This, of course, has an important implication: how to maintain control of the corporation after selling stock shares. Although publicly traded corporations earn revenue from the first time they sell shares of stock, they lose some amount of control of the business at the same time, possibly forever. That could mean that jobs, or even the entire business itself, might disappear, because the company chose to "go public." Nevertheless, doing so can earn the business and its "name" designer many hundreds of millions of dollars.

Once sold, shares of stock are considered "outstanding." As you might suspect, those who own those stock shares want to have some ability to affect company decisions, or at least have an opportunity for their opinions to be heard. Corporations have to answer to these investors. They can—and often do—become extremely powerful forces with which company managers have to work. Depending on how much in the way of percentage ownership of a corporation is sold through stock, investors have been known to take control of publicly traded corporations. They are able to do so because they have gained a majority ownership in the corporation. In such instances, investors typically remove members of upper management in the corporation (even the chief executive officer) or completely disband the business. They may then "sell off" the business, piece by piece. This means that investors sell production facilities to other businesses, close retail stores, and sell remaining inventory at deep discounts. They may even sell the company brand. As you can see, corporations offer many advantages to business organizers as long as they are careful about how they operate it.

Stocks are but one form of security. Another important one is **bonds**. These represent not percentage ownership but financial obligations. Corporations, indeed any business, can issue bonds or bond-like interests, although those of corporations are generally thought more desirable because they have assets, or property, of greater value available to pay them. Bonds are, at their core, written promises made by businesses that they will repay sums of money investors have loaned them at particular, set times in the future. In addition to repaying amounts borrowed, investors usually receive additional amounts known as interest. Think of bonds as being companies' "credit cards."

Companies issue bonds when they need capital, or "money," for such things as building new factories or buying new equipment, although reasons may vary. As you might suspect, bonds issued by certain businesses are more desirable than others. Some companies are soundly operated and able to repay bond obligations easily. Other businesses may have greater problems and, therefore, their bonds are not considered as desirable. Investors in the latter case may require more in the way of interest in order to purchase those entities' bonds. On the other hand, some company bonds are so desirable (because they have a strong likelihood of being repaid) that investors are willing to pay more for them. Some fashion and retail companies quite easily earn money based on the financial soundness of their business, whereas others struggle.

You probably know the H & M of fashion, but do you know the "M" and "A"? Other legal topics of note include **mergers and acquisitions** (M & A). Simply put, a merger is the joining of two or more businesses into one, larger entity. An acquisition involves one business "buying" (with either cash or shares of stock) one or more others. These may run separately, and even have completely independent identities. Essentially, mergers and acquisitions are legally orchestrated consolidation activities: They bring businesses together to form a new, stronger enterprise, one more competitive than the previous, individual ones. A term you will often hear is "economies of scale." This usually refers to the greater profitability some companies have because of how well they operate. Mergers and acquisitions seek to instill better economies of scale to assist better profitability. Many retail stores were affected by these activities in the 1970s and 1980s, as you will discover in the next part of the text.

The M & A process is quite lengthy and involves great legal expertise and financial acumen on the part of those involved. Numerous fashion and retail companies are currently seeking to either buy, or be bought by others, as duly noted in the fashion trade and general business press.

Stocks . . . bonds . . . corporations . . . mergers . . . acquisitions . . . wasn't this supposed to be a text about fashion?

It is!

Sideline:

*Discussions about these very topics happen daily among fashion professionals. Much of **Women's Wear Daily** and other fashion industry news sources are devoted to these very topics. As a result, everyone—from fashion designers to students—is affected by how these issues develop and are resolved. For example, a fashion company that is acquired through a merger or acquisition might either gain or lose jobs from factory line workers to well-paid executives. The above summary of legal concepts is just the beginning of your understanding of what fashion—as a business—is really like!*

GETTING TO KNOW CONTRACTS

What might be next to consider as part of "being" legal? Fashion game players, indeed almost all in business, enter into contracts. There are agreements "with a kick," meaning that they are legally recognized and provide financial penalties (called "damages") when their conditions and terms are not fulfilled. Did you ever wonder why merchandise got into stores? Have you thought about why you see some stores in one mall and not in others? These arrangements came about through the use of contracts. To be a fashion game player means to know about at least the very basics of contracts!

Contracts may be thought of as the language of all businesses, the means by which professionals communicate with each other to get things done. As such a necessary part of business, understanding contracts is important. Like business formations, much could be discussed about contracts. However, for you and the work in fashion and fashion retail you might pursue, two concepts about these legally enforceable agreements are important.

When the topic of contracts arises, the first question you should ask is what the **subject** of the contract is. Are you working with an agreement that is about services, for example, or does it involve the sale of "moveable, tangible property" merchandise? Perhaps it is about renting an apartment or store space in a mall. Such leases are examples of non-sales agreements. Depending on what your answer is, then, two different sets of laws apply. These laws are similar—after all, they are about agreements; however, they are entirely separate in use. A few basics will help you get started!

Contracts for anything other than the sale of goods are governed by the laws of the state in which the agreement originated (or by laws in another area agreed upon by those involved). Those laws provide necessary elements for an agreement to be legally recognized and enforced. Such elements include an offer, acceptance, and consideration.

An **offer** is an invitation given by one party to another to enter into an agreement. **Acceptance**, of course, would be an indication of willingness to join into such an agreement. **Consideration** in the legal sense is not quite what you might imagine from the name. It refers to the presence of an exchange, meaning that both parties to the contract are giving up something, such as money, time, or service, to receive something from the other. Before there can be a "contract," there must be discussion of what its terms will be. Lacking any "meeting of the minds," no valid contractual agreement exists. Negotiations, the "back and forth" of business discussions, are necessary to reach such mutual understandings.

Contracts have been defined as legally enforceable agreements. Simply put, that means should one party to a valid contract fail to do as previously agreed, the other party may seek what is referred to as "damages." These are financial penalties, monies they are owed as a result of the other's inaction or incorrect action. Almost every aspect of fashion and fashion retail hinges on contractual agreements, from how much counter space a retailer will provide to payment of advertising costs and rent amounts. Multinational treaties concerning trade relationships between countries are examples of contracts as well. As a fashion game player, you may be responsible for negotiating, carrying out, and complying with provisions, or terms, of contracts.

Another area in which contracts are used extensively is the sale of **goods**, or merchandise, from one fashion game player, a **merchant**. Recall that this area is subject to a separate set of laws. Retailers, store buyers, clothing manufacturers, and many others (such as shipping and warehouse services) usually follow **Uniform Commercial Code (UCC)** provisions. Its provisions operate in all states, except Louisiana. This series of laws is complex in scope and application. At its core, however, it intended to make buying, selling, and transporting goods more convenient for those to which it applies. It also provides for damages when one party does not perform as agreed.

The effects of business formations and contractual relationships permeate the fashion business world. However, it may surprise you to know that you are already familiar with the interplay of law, contracts, and even the UCC under discussion here. Recall the "5 Rs" of fashion merchandising, otherwise known as "the right merchandise, in the right quantities, at the right time, and in the right place, and at the right price." These very issues find their origins not in fashion or retail, but in provisions of the UCC, which are present in virtually all contracts fashion game players enter into and affect all of their professional interactions. "Be Legal!" It means being aware of legal requirements and how they may be met. More and more, being "legal" requires fashion game players to be aware of laws and regulations affecting quality of life and preservation of the environment. Of course, laws are complex, as is how they apply to real-life practices. Fashion and retail businesses face special legal challenges. Many of these relate to protecting the "big brands" that form the basis of the first rule. Subsequent discussions in this text will explore topics related to that concept, such as fake or counterfeit products and "intellectual property" such as trade and service marks.

Fashion companies need to be mindful of how production methods can affect the environment. (wonderisland/Shutterstock)

Rule Three: Be Fair!

Today, consumers all over the world seek out more fashion items and more quickly than ever before. Think about how many pairs of jeans or shoes you may have. As well, recall how quickly you seek out others when those are no longer of interest, when their appeal passes. You are not alone—a great many other consumers feel the same way. To accommodate such demand, fashion and fashion retail businesses produce and offer ever newer, innovative, exciting, and ever **more** items. It is this aspect of fashion that gives rise to the next rule of the fashion game.

Fashion and fashion retail businesses are now asked by consumers and their respective industries and required by governments to address how to employ people and use resources in thoughtful ways that are less harmful to those workers and the world in which they—and others—live.

A concise way of stating these requirements is simply: "Be Fair!"

Considering the fast pace with which fashion travels now, with the demand for so many new products so quickly, **sustainability**, or the prudent production of new fashion items and continuation of the lifecycle of those already made and used, is crucial.

In efforts to satisfy consumers' demand for fashion items, the human and physical environment in which they are produced can be minimized, even entirely forgotten. Laborers still toil in deplorable conditions and production pollutes air and water resources. **Ethics** in fashion—the "Be Fair!" rule—means establishing better working conditions and preserving the world's ecology.

"Be fair," then, is about actively pursuing and furthering sustainable, ethical practices, not inducing consumers to believe something untrue. How, then, does such "fairness" come about? It includes operating ethically with others and sustainably with respect to the environment. Although neither of these concepts is new—for over a century, working conditions have been subjected to scrutiny and recycling was part of the daily life in previous centuries—what is of modern origin are discussions about how these may be incorporated to an even greater degree in contemporary fashion businesses.

Today, of course, integrating ethical and sustainable elements is much more difficult than might have been so in previous generations. This is not to say they were, or are, any less important then or now: need for them was and remains necessary. Rather, ethical and sustainable practices must now work within the contexts of highly competitive brand practices, more pervasive laws, and greater profitability pressures.

Much of fashion is built on promotion of images of luxury, status, and fashion savviness. Whether its source is a boutique or Wal-Mart, think of the number of fashion and fashion-related products suggesting to consumers that their purchase will enhance these impressions. Ask how those impressions might be reconciled with those related to ethics and sustainability. The disconnect lies in what current consumers perceive as being "luxurious" and "fashionable." Usually, these include pampering, as with cosmetics, or being "on trend" with fashion items, not feeling guilty about such purchases. How might the gap between responsibility and fashion be better bridged?

Consumers have been noted as being the goal of the fashion game. Their interest and ultimate purchases are what keep it going. They are the power driving the fashion game. For the "be nice" rule to become more fully integrated into the fashion production process, consumers, perhaps more than laws, will need to play referee of industry practices. One recent example includes the ban by the fashion house Versace (following such nonluxury brands as Levi's and H&M—Hennes & Mauritz) of sandblasted denim textile fabrics. Production of this fashion component, in which raw denim is "sandblasted" with silica particles, is highly dangerous to both workers' health and the surrounding environment. With respect to health, the practice can result in silicosis, a deadly respiratory disease.

Many companies go beyond the basic requirements to establish inclusive, safe offices, factories, warehouses, and other workplaces. (Zastolskiy Victor/Shutterstock)

The particles are pollutants that do not dissolve. Versace not only discontinued that practice, but even went so far as to ban fabric finishing contractors who use the practice from supplying the company. Versace also actively promotes elimination of the practice throughout the industry.

What caused this fashion brand, identified with both luxury and fashion-forwardness, to go to these lengths? Consumer awareness and outcry about them. Though only one example, the Versace denim issue, nonetheless, shows that when consumers are aware of these issues, they can be instruments of change. On the other hand, those in the fashion industry who understand how such responsiveness to consumer concerns can be incorporated into their brands' images can further "nice" practices. Profitability, again, remains the challenge.

Often, ethical and sustainable practices are more expensive than others to identify and to locate suppliers that practice them. Consumers, long accustomed to seeking low prices as part of their fashion experience, may not see the value in paying more for ethically produced items, especially when others will not know they have done so. Thus, for real inroads to be made in "fair" practices, more brands should consider incorporating these and related practices into the image with which consumers associate them. "Oh, yes, that's the brand that protects consumers and the environment!" is the sought-after result as much as instilling images of luxury and status. How the fashion and fashion retail industries are including sustainable and ethical practices into their production and the new trends related to those are included in Section 9, "Consumers and Sustainability Concerns."

Rule Four: Be Profitable!

Without profits—what's financially left over from earnings after expenses are paid—there is no business! This is true whether a small boutique or a large fashion production company is involved. What, then, does it mean to "Be Profitable!" within the context of fashion businesses? Put a more straightforward way, how and why are some fashion companies so successful and the designers who helm them so wealthy? Does such success come from what they make, such as dresses and purses, or some other aspect of their businesses—or some combination of these? Here you will gain insights into the **functional environment** of fashion businesses and how those activities are conducive to profitability.

Fashion businesses are challenged to remain externally competitive, internally operational, and profitable. No matter the size of the fashion business—large, small, or in between—these are the basic function areas required to operate them in an effort to "Be Profitable"!

Business functions may be classified into the following groups: accounting, finance, legal and regulatory, management/human resources, and marketing. Typically, in large organizations separate departments are devoted to each. In small ones, such as sole proprietorships and partnerships, business owners are usually responsible for carrying out these functions, or engaging specialists such as accountants and attorneys to do so.

ACCOUNTING

How should businesses handle their income? Why might it be important for companies, large and small, to break out in such detail the amounts and sources of their businesses' incomes? There are several reasons to note.

First, income, from whatever legal source, is the lifeblood of any company. Without income businesses ultimately fail. In addition, investors (those seeking to own a portion of the company through purchasing shares of its stock, or those interested in owning rights to receive repayment of monies lent through bonds) are interested to know that the company is able to continue its operations and pay its obligations. Corporations pay taxes as well. They must account for business income to satisfy reporting requirements imposed by taxing authorities.

Accounting practices internal to fashion businesses, despite the fact that they remain unseen to most consumers, nevertheless, influence fashion. Failure to comply with accounting rules, both legally and practically, can seriously affect the longevity of fashion businesses and consumers who rely on them.

FINANCE

It might surprise you to know that fashion companies do not only "make money" from sales of products to consumers. Rather, large corporations (and small businesses) seek **income streams** from different sources. Sometimes called "lines of business," income streams not from sales typically come from financial practices. These are mostly activities focused on how the company may invest in itself, or in other businesses. Issuing stock or, bonds—company debt, to the public—are examples of company "self-investing." Fashion companies may invest in other businesses whether fashion-related or not.

As you might imagine, these are highly complex financial undertakings, ones requiring business analysts and attorneys. Financial investing in these ways is done primarily to maintain company income levels. Income amounts are cyclical, variable from fashion season to fashion season, year to year. The finance function of such businesses seeks to "smooth" those cycles and develop a more staple income stream upon which fashion business might rely over time.

There are other reasons fashion businesses engage in financial activities. These might include obtaining monies to fund employee pension and benefit plans or company acquisitions. Financial operations and their effects, as you can see, hugely influence fashion businesses. Their outcomes determine whether businesses can respond to consumers and their needs and to the needs of the business itself.

LEGAL AND REGULATORY

You are already familiar with two aspects of what it means to "Be Legal!" To "Be Profitable!" fashion—really, all businesses—devote attention to how they are legally regulated. In this context, to be profitable means being legal, as laws passed by Congress (and signed into law by the president) and government rules interpreting them regulate, or control, business operations extensively.

Some regulations concern how individual businesses conduct activities in this and other countries. When questions arise about trade relations, production issues such as pollution and work conditions, relationships with foreign and our own government, and what happens when businesses falter (as when they approach bankruptcy), among many matters, businesses must respond. Failure to defensively address or being found to have violated these requirements can—and does—result in severe penalties for the company and personally for those involved.

Businesses may seek to influence Congress and the laws that it passes through legitimate "lobbying" efforts. Many join together to form **special interest groups** (SIGs) for that purpose. These are proactive ways of working within the legal/regulatory framework of business. In the fashion industry, the Council of Fashion Designers of America is one such SIG. Perhaps you enjoy fashion, but feel more drawn to the excitement of working to develop the industry. Careers as corporate lobbyists, or with an influential SIG, may allow you to combine both. Any option you pursue, though, will put you and any business square in the middle of the quest to "Be Legal!" and "Be Profitable!"

Companies need to be very careful with how they manage consumers' personal information. Target recently had a security breach where personal information was obtained from the credit cards of customers, which has negatively affected profitability of the corporation. (leolintang/Shutterstock)

MANAGEMENT

If you had a choice, would you follow the directions of those who owned a portion of your business through stock ownership, as discussed above, or those who purchased your fashion designs? In business terms, that means, would you answer to shareholders or consumers? Each can have widely different concerns.

Shareholders are fractional investors in companies; they own only portions of it, but they can wield great power over the decisions that company managers make. Through such events as annual meetings, they can, if so inclined, "vote out" upper-level managers when they no longer are confident those executives will work in the business's best financial interests. Ultimately, investors desire monetary returns, those "rewarding" them for purchasing company stock.

Marketing strategies develop advertising, promotional, and sales campaigns to support a product. (Nejron/Shutterstock)

Consumers, on the other hand, may be more concerned about "feeling good" with the purchases they make. How would you feel about a garment hanging in your closet knowing that it was made by incarcerated workers in a modern-day sweatshop? Investors may applaud management's ability to lower production costs (and raise profits) through selection of "cost-efficient" contractors, ones who might have such workers. Consumers may not be so impressed. Much of fashion production remains "behind the seams," but consumers, retailers, and workers' rights groups continue to raise awareness about how to find ways of balancing financial and social concerns related to production of fashion items.

MARKETING

Who are your customers? What do they like to do? What do they like to wear while doing those activities? These are but a few of the questions marketing professionals ask of designers, of stores, of anyone interested in selling fashion products. In the previous section, you learned of the importance of marketing to specific consumer groups, target markets. Here is how tasks related to that are performed in fashion businesses.

In general, marketing practices first identify a Target Market, or highly specific, identifiable group of potential users to which products or services might appeal. They then develop marketing strategies. These focus on ways to provide goods, including fashion-related ones, in sufficient quantities, at appropriate prices, in stores or in other venues that appeal to targeted consumers at appropriate times, such as according to fashion seasons. Marketing strategies then develop advertisement, promotional, and sales campaigns to support the product. Much of modern fashion is based on marketing, particularly on finding new consumer groups and satisfying their needs and desires. Marketing practices, therefore, can have a major influence on fashion and its direction, assuming that consumers adopt what is being offered!

Section Finale summary

This section has identified four "rules" informing the activities and players in the fashion game. Yet, rules are one thing—how they work together to affect outcomes—that's more complicated! None of the four rules noted here "stands alone," each has an impact on the others. That, ultimately, is what this is all about!

Previous generations of business leaders might have thought the rule related to profitability should be paramount, especially in the ways management practices furthered that result. Today, as always, profitability and management remain important. However, business people working in every industry would suggest that brands and practices related to them are critical. In many ways, this is justified: think of how many thousands of new products, including fashion ones, are introduced each year. Somehow, they must stand out from others and continue to attract consumers. Given the amount of interest in brands currently, the first fashion game rule is, logically, build "big brands." With the power that comes from having established a popular brand, it is easy to see how other rules apply.

Because legal guidelines inform so many business practices, they are noted next. Simply, every legitimate business must follow specific laws and be subject to their powers. "Be fair" is listed next as a hybrid rule, somewhere between legally required (which many are becoming) and a function of good business practices (which many companies are realizing is critical to attracting consumers). One challenge for future fashion game players is finding ways to produce items as ethically and as profitably as possible.

Ethical challenges remain to be resolved in fashion production. Fashion, by its very nature, encourages consumers' consumption of resources. As populations continue to increase throughout the world, demand, too, increases for such components as cotton. Another challenge for future fashion game players is finding ways to incorporate sustainable practices, ones that preserve resources, into their brands permanently without harming brand image and financial profitability.

Are you beginning to see, none of these four rules stands alone; each is intrinsic to individual fashion businesses and interrelated and interconnected within the industry of fashion!

Finally, "be profitable" is noted last, because without compliance with the first three, it would be difficult for any business to achieve it. To be sure, that is an important rule. However, ask this: would many businesses be able to follow such a rule if they had not built a "big brand" in the first place? Could "big brands" even be established and operated without businesses following necessary legal requirements? Some legal requirements, too, overlap the remaining rule: "be fair." Fair labor practices and workplace safety are laws, but many companies go beyond their basic requirements to establish inclusive, safe offices, factories, warehouses, and other places. Even so, ask how likely it would be for a fashion company to build big brands (and, hence, be legal and profitable), if it engaged in unfair practices?

To be sure, this is neither a business text nor one on ethics, law, or brand marketing. Its intent is to give you a "mental model," a way of thinking about why fashion businesses operate as they do. Perhaps you are thinking about how you might work within the rules suggested here in your own fashion career. Ideas about how to do just that follow in the next section.

Review Questions: "What Did You Discover?"

1. Identify the four rules of the fashion game and briefly describe each.
2. What are the different classes of brands noted in this section?
3. Differentiate consumer brands from fashion brands.
4. What are private brands and why might they be important to fashion game players such as retailers?
5. Define brand elements and note differences between tangible and intangible ones.
6. What are phases of the brand lifecycle?
7. Why might a once highly popular brand disappear completely from the marketplace?
8. Brand extension practices are responsible for what kinds of products and why?
9. Explain what you believe brand management policies are and how they are used.
10. Which two aspects of law were explored under the rule "Be Legal"?

11. What are business formations? Give a few examples of them.
12. Contracts may be described as agreements of what kind, with what kind of characteristics?
13. What is required for forming an enforceable contract?
14. What do the initials "M" and "A" stand for when it comes to legal and business activities?
15. Why is it important to know about legal and business matters in fashion?
16. What are some results of "going public"? How did fashion designers such as Michael Kors benefit from doing so?
17. What are "bonds" and how, briefly, do they differ from "stocks"?
18. Why might a fashion business offer bonds to the public?
19. What are "damages" when it comes to contracts? What kinds are there?
20. What do the initials UCC stand for? Briefly describe its application.

Terms to Know

Be sure you know the following terms from this section and can give examples:

Brand
Business formations
Sole practitioner
Partnership
Corporation
Stocks
Bonds
Industrial brands
Consumer brands
Private brands
Fashion brands

Luxury brands
Brand personality
Brand salience
Brand equity
Brand elements
Brand lifecycle
Limited liability company (LLC)
Brand extensions
Brand management policies
Offer
Acceptance

Consideration
"Public" and "private" businesses
Uniform Commercial Code (UCC)
Goods
Merchant
Sustainability
Contracts
Business functions
Special interest groups
Ethics

Making the Fashion Game Your Own:
Build Your Brand

Project Purpose: Develop your Market Day project further by establishing a brand identity for it!

Step One: Recall the working title for your project and record it here for reference:

_____

_____

Step Two: What words and images do you want others (whether they are players or target consumers, even the general public) to think of or recall about the product/service/combination you would like to present?

Step Three: What brand elements (described in the section) best reflect what your brand is about? Use as many as you need; include words, images, and colors—anything you think will help us get to know your brand better!

_____   _____

_____   _____

_____   _____

Step Four: Put the pieces of your brand together! This will be the name and identity of your idea. This will become part of your presentation at Market Day!
(Note: Address what you and your brand will stand for ethically, as well. Scan the Table of Contents and note issues discussed in Part Three. At this point, just give a general explanation of your position on these issues. You will prepare a more complete description and report later.)

Section 3: Rules of the Fashion Game (Optional Project)

Know the Rules . . . Know the Fashion Game

Project Focus: In this section, you have explored the fashion industry from a highly unique, but highly important perspective: what its rules are and how they apply to so many different aspects and players. In this exercise, you will conduct research by finding examples of each of those rules.

Steps: Below are noted the "rules" of the fashion game.
1. Describe in writing what you think each rule means.
2. Locate in various media examples of each rule.
3. Explain in your own words how or why the examples relate to the rules.

Rule One: Be a Big Brand

Rule Two: Be Fair

Rule Three: Be Legal

Rule Four: Be Profitable

Making the Fashion Game Your Own:
Growing Your Brand

Project Purpose: Where do you see your brand in the future? How might it grow to include a range of different products? You might surprise yourself by how well your brand might "translate" into a lifestyle. This development might well be used in your Market Day presentation to show others the scope of yours or your group's vision!

Step One: Initial or Current Product Service or Combination and Name

_____

_____

Fashion Accessories

_____

_____

_____

_____

_____

Step Two:
Take it away! How might your brand be applied to any number of different products/services?
(These are just examples. You can add others you feel are more applicable!)

Cosmetics/Fragrances

_____

_____

_____

_____

_____

Home Goods and Other Products

_____

_____

_____

_____

The essence of the brand—its DNA—are the following ideas, feelings, and emotions sought to be evoked, no matter the specific product/service or combination to be presented:

_____

_____

_____

_____

Building a Brand Tree

Project Focus: Describing the growth/development of a fashion brand. Some outside research through periodicals may be required.

Name of Brand: _____

Brand Information: _____

_____

1st Generation

| Original Fashion Product: |
| Date Introduced: |

Fashion Accessories | Cosmetics/Fragrances | Home Goods

2nd Generation Product(s)

| Date: | Date: | Date: |

3rd Generation Product (s)

| Date: | Date: | Date: | Date: | Date: | Date: |

Other Generations

Product:	Product:	Product:	Product:	Product:	Product:
Date:	Date:	Date:	Date:	Date:	Date:

Product:	Product:	Product:	Product:	Product:	Product:
Date:	Date:	Date:	Date:	Date:	Date:

Product:	Product:	Product:	Product:	Product:	Product:
Date:	Date:	Date:	Date:	Date:	Date:

Product:	Product:	Product:	Product:	Product:	Product:
Date:	Date:	Date:	Date:	Date:	Date:

Product:	Product:	Product:	Product:	Product:	Product:
Date:	Date:	Date:	Date:	Date:	Date:

PART TWO PREVIEW
THE FASHION GAME PLAYERS IN ACTION

FASHION IS ABOUT CHANGE! ARE YOU?

The four sections making up this part of the text describe the working life of fashion game players. These are the fashion professionals who embrace and thrive in change. Coming up, you will get to know better the four types of fashion game players to which you were introduced previously. Providers . . . producers . . . purveyors . . . promoters . . . . you will find out what they do in "real life," what information they need to know in their work, issues they face, and many more details concerning how they anticipate, even encourage change.

SECTION 4: PROVIDERS: SUPPLYING FASHION COMPONENTS

Providers are those fashion game players responsible for making available textiles and other items used in garments and accessories all of us wear, use, and enjoy.

How might you discover what providers offer and why characteristics of those things are important? To answer such questions, you will explore who providers are and items they make available as well as what kinds of related trade associations and careers there are. Of course, how and why rules of the fashion game apply to providers and those who patronize them are topics described as well.

SECTION 5: PRODUCERS: DESIGNING AND MANUFACTURING FASHION

Producers are those professionals such as designers, pattern makers, fabric cutters, sewers, finishers and many others who plan, construct clothing, and finish fashion items.

From first drawing to finished garments, the sequential process of putting fashion items together, melding creativity, interesting components, with technical know-how, and business acumen, is exciting! This section offers, truly, "behind the seams" perspectives of fashion design and production processes for those curious about careers in fashion and accessory design and production. Of note, this section returns again to "fashion game" rules and their application to fashion production.

SECTION 6: PURVEYORS: BRINGING FASHION TO YOU

This text distinguishes two kinds of purveyors, or sellers, of fashion and related items: wholesalers and retailers. Wholesale purveyors make available fashion and fashion related items to retailers throughout the

world. Retail purveyors are responsible for identifying and obtaining attractive merchandise, items they prepare for profitable resale to end-users, consumers.

You will encounter . . . and work with . . . both throughout your fashion studies and career. Whether involved with wholesale, business-to-business (B2B) selling to stores, or working with retail business-to-consumer (B2C) stores, purveyors are responsible for putting fashion on yours and the world's back! You will look inside a wholesale showroom, explore what occurs there, and discover how such activities are part of the fashion game and applications of its rules. As well, you will walk through a "typical" department store and "see" it not through the eyes of a consumer, but from the perspective of a fashion game professional.

SECTION 7: PROMOTERS: MAKING FASHION EXCITING

Fashion game promoters are professionals responsible for getting the word out about what's current in fashion as well as suggesting what future direction fashion may take.

Editors, bloggers, visual merchandisers, educators, any number of others working in fashion and fashion-related retail, publishing and education are included in this section. What's exciting is how the very idea of fashion promotion is changing, thanks to social media. Consumers play active roles in fashion promotion through their participation. Also, changes in fashion promotion happen faster than ever before, at the speed of technology. Promotions professionals are responsible for keeping up with and working with such advances. Get to know the fast-paced world of fashion game promoters in this section and how they, too, employ and benefit from fashion game rules.

Turning from action to thought, the next part of the text explores current issues raised by the fashion game and its rules and how these concerns might be addressed by the next generation of game players . . . . yours! The terms, concepts, and ideas you explore in part two will prepare you for those provocative discussions.

PROVIDERS: SUPPLYING FASHION COMPONENTS

FAST FORWARD

You are now able to describe the fashion game concept and identify its players. What about the daily work they perform? What are the items, ideas, and interests with which they are involved? Before exploring fashion design and production with this text, take a step back. Consider fashion's most basic "things." What are they? Who among the fashion game players is responsible for them? This section focuses on **providers. These are the fashion professionals who make available textiles and other components out of which clothing and accessories are constructed.** Sometimes referred to as fashion's "primary sources," or the "primary level" of fashion, these suppliers and the products they make available for fashion use are always important!

WHAT YOU SHOULD KNOW ABOUT THIS SECTION:

* It introduces you to providers and the textiles, leathers and furs, and other items they develop and offer for fashion use.
* It offers the perspective that fashion components, including items as small as buttons, have helped form the identities of many famous fashion brands.

4

(Opposite page) Source: © krsmanovic/Fotolia

Recall what you may have seen, touched, or perhaps even purchased during a recent shopping trip. How did their "stuff," the very things of which they were constructed, make them "dreamy" enough for you to want?

Fashion Components and the Fashion Game

How many times do you get dressed scarcely concerned about *what* the items you wear are made of? You might be concerned with how warm or cool you will feel based the fabric of your shirt, pants, or skirt. Other than that, you may not give the components of your garments, shoes, or accessories another thought. The purpose of this section is to change that! Its goal is to make you aware of how interesting and important even the smallest constituent of what you wear is.

How do fashion components help "build big brands"? Whether your clothing budget might be described as student-like "cautious," or socialite-level "couture," a quick survey of fashion brands shows how closely associated many are with components of their well-known products:

Sideline:

The components described here are necessary for clothing and accessories to function as needed and appear as desired. As well, from the fashion game perspective, these "raw materials" serve as important ways to distinguish fashion brands. Before identifying and describing such items as textiles (what many call "fabric," "cloth," or "material"), leathers and furs, and trimmings such as zippers and buttons, think about how much you know about fashion and fashion brands based on the components for which they are most closely associated.

- Levi-Straus is known for the deep indigo blue denim textile it uses for its "501" and other jean styles.
- Merona's colorfully dyed jeans are another brand known for denim textiles.
- Nike uses the "Dri-Fit" fabric it developed in its workout and leisure garments.
- Burberry—now a multiproduct, multi-extended brand at many different price ranges—began with one item—the trench coat, made of tan, waterproof "gabardine," a cotton twill-weave textile (a term you will soon know more about)—that company founder, Thomas Burberry, developed in 1879 and patented in 1888.
- Whether found at Neiman Marcus or Target, boldly colored, zigzag Missoni textiles stand out. Beginning in Italy after World War II, the brand initially built its highly distinct, recognizable identity with intricate, "warp" knit textiles (a term you will also come to know), which were then fashioned into sweaters and separates for men and women and now children.
- Another innovative knit, "Santana," was developed by and is identified with St. John Knits of California. This wool yarn with a polyester-core is knitted into versatile finished textiles and then designed and made into suits and dresses.
- When many consumers think of leather "fabric," the high-fashion brand Bottega Veneta comes to mind. The component of plain-woven leather strips, referred to as "intrecciato," is as much a recognizable brand element as any other company's logo. Dramatically colored, cleverly constructed fur garments and accessories signal another Italian brand, Fendi.
- Tory Burch, Milly, and Anthropologie are fashion brands that incorporate vintage-inspired trimmings such as buttons into their products, making those brands unique and recognizable by consumers.
- Miu Miu (a division of Prada) and Marni (also from Italy) take their respective brand cues from vintage, too. Using textiles adapted from designs of the 1960s, 1970s, and 1980s,

these brands are recognizable for the fabric and decorative elements used to make styles seem "old" yet altogether "new."

- Current fashion brands with highly distinctive textile components include Herve Leger's "bandage" dresses of knitted rayon, nylon, and spandex. As well, Issey Miyake pleated polyester fabrics are key brand elements. Jhane Barnes, Robert Graham, and Arnold Zimberg are fashion brands known for boldly textured, detailed textiles. Although no longer in operation, Mary McFadden Couture fashions were instantly recognized by their deeply pleated, Japanese "Marii" polyester textile in every color imaginable. Fashion historians study the silks of Venetian Mariano Fortuny from the 1900s to try to discern his still-secret pleating and dyeing techniques!

These examples point out how much fashion and fashion brands depend on the very elements you will explore in this section. They are necessary in forming the substance of garments and accessories and building distinctive, recognizable brands. Going forward, continue to think about other brands and the ways you recognize them based on their components. You may be surprised how long your own list will become!

Advancing Technologies Advance Fashion

Before exploring fashion components, think about how the all-important textiles developed. Thanks to eighteenth- and nineteenth-century technological advances, natural, or "raw," textile fibers such as cotton, wool, and silk became more easily processed and better able to be modified into usable textile products. Perhaps long ago and far away, the actions of early providers brought about other changes. Ultimately, advancing technologies served to advance fashion and its ability to flourish:

1733—The **flying shuttle**, invented in England by John Kay, enabled quicker, better-quality cloth weaving.

1764—The **spinning jenny**, also from England and invented by James Hargreaves, allowed production of many separate yarns at a time. By **1769**, Englishman Sir Richard Arkwright invented an even faster spinning machine powered by water.

1785—Between 1785 and 1787, English reverend Edmund Cartwright invented and patented a fast weaving **power loom** run by steam engines.

1790—Englishman Samuel Slater left England and began the **American textile industry** by opening mills devoted to carding (separating and lengthening) and spinning cotton fibers into high-quality threads and yarns in Rhode Island.

1793—American inventor Eli Whitney (1765–1825) invented and patented the **cotton gin**, a device that mechanically cleaned cotton fibers and substantially increased the amount and quality of usable cotton fiber that could be produced in less time.

1813—Francis Cabot Lowell developed a **highly efficient loom**, one that produced high-quality textile fabrics more easily and less expensively than others.

1846—American Elias J. Howe, Jr., received the first patent issued for a **hand-powered sewing machine**. Today, he is considered the inventor of the sewing machine. Others, such as Walter Hunt, had invented similar devices around 1832, yet had failed to claim official recognition for it. Howe's machine, unique among his rivals, produced a lockstitch that prevented fabric from puckering and sewn seams from unraveling.

1858—Isaac Singer produced a foot-powered sewing machine, one with a better lockstitch. Easier to use and widely available through installment sales, **Singer sewing machines** became among the best known in the world.

The sewing machine was one of the technological advancements that enabled textiles to be mass produced for more accessibility to the marketplace. (© Levent Konuk/Shutterstock)

Gaining Perspective on Early Technological Developments

What do all these developments from so long ago mean? Why do they remain important enough to mention today? They set in motion a series of circumstances enabling, supporting, and encouraging contemporary fashion and, ultimately, establishing the fashion game concept:

- **Providers** in the eighteenth and nineteenth centuries developed cheaper, better-quality cloth.
- These innovations enabled the **producers** of those times to make better garments faster and less expensively than ever before.
- **Purveyors**, wholesale and retail sellers, were able to sell clothing items between themselves and to consumers profitably, enabling both to flourish and continue.
- As industrialization spread, workers became able and interested consumers. **Promoters** tapped into this growing affluence and sophistication by creating demand for newly evolving fashion ideas.
- Ultimately, availability of fashion products and interest in them worked to expand the idea of "fashion" to include seasonally changing accessories, cosmetics, men's and children's fashions, and decorative items for the home attuned to color, theme, and holiday trends.
- The fashion game concept emerged among these four player groups, complete with discernible rules governing their interactions.

Introducing Fashion's Fundamental Elements

The most commonly used fashion elements include textiles, leathers and furs, and other items referred to as "trims," or "trimmings."

These fabrics are made from many different yarns using various techniques to achieve a desired effect. (© OlegD/Shutterstock)

Textiles

Consumers tend to refer to textiles, very generally, as being "fabric," "cloth," or perhaps just "material." Although finished textiles may be called these, **textiles are, as well, the fibers and yarns from which such finished fabrics are made**. Fibers may be from naturally derived sources; think: cotton and silk. They may also come from manufactured sources, such as rayon and polyester and others synthetic fibers. **Yarns are combinations of fibers, either natural, manufactured, or combinations of them held together through such means as twisting.** Fibers and yarns may be dyed or otherwise treated before other textile manufacturing steps occur.

As you will come to discover, fibers and yarns may be joined together through several means, such as interlacing (weaving) and looping (knitting), to form textile fabrics. These are often dyed, printed, and finished in ways that impart characteristics you see, feel, and experience. Colorful men's dress shirts that are "no iron" are examples of these processes. **To recall: any fiber or yarn capable of being**

formed into fabric through any physical means as well as fabrics themselves may be considered textiles. As you know and have seen here, many famous fashion brands became and remain sought after by consumers on the basis of their unique textiles, or highly identifiable ways they are used in garments and accessories.

Leathers and Furs

In addition to textiles, leathers are crucial for the construction of many fashion items, especially shoes and accessories. **Leathers are the "dermis," or outermost skins of animals processed in ways that preserve, enhance, or impart particular characteristics.** Glossy, smooth, or textured in appearance and feel, even colorful, and waterproof, these are among many other possible attributes leathers may have, thanks to preparation, processing, and finishing methods. Artificial leathers exist, too. It may surprise you to think of these as being textile, not animal, products, as many are made by pressurized compression of fibers!

Along with leathers, furs remain popular among fashion followers who dream of wearing fur coats or having fur accessories, such as scarves and hats. **Furs are the hairy outmost dermal layers, or skins of animals (usually those of mammals) used for their appearance, texture, color or color variations, or other physical characteristics.** Fur is widely present in fashion: the glossy look and sleek feel of wild or farm-raised mink in jackets and coats, the tactile plushness of beaver hats, and the dramatic look of long-haired fox collars are just some examples. As well, thick sheep hides, shearlings, are sought for thickness, warmth, and durability especially for rigorous, outdoor wear. Many famous—"big"—fashion brands have been built around skillful, distinctive uses of leathers and furs.

Trimmings

Take a look at your clothing and accessories. To be sure, textiles and perhaps the leathers and furs of which they are constructed are important. Of course, you know there is something else about them other than just their primary component. You have probably noticed those "somethings," those items enabling what you wear to fit and function as intended. What, for example,

The coats shown on this display are made mostly of leather and fur. (© Pavel L/Shutterstock)

would hoodies be without zippers and drawstrings to make them work? Then, there are some items just "for looks." These might be patches on jeans or metal studs like the kind covering Lady Gaga's sky-high shoes. Zippers, drawstrings, patches, metal bits and pieces . . . what are these functional, decorative, even occasionally both kinds of things? **Trimmings (or "trims") are items that add function, decoration, or both to clothing and accessories.** Some in the fashion business distinguish "notions" as being trim elements that add function and support to garments and accessories. Thread, lengths of tightly wound textile fibers holding together clothing and accessories, is one kind of notion, as is elastic used in undergarments.

Valentino handbags sport pyramid-shaped stud trims. This is one of the subtle, but known to those in the know, ways to identify that brand. As well, the very obvious "MK" medallion seen on purses and totes signify the Michael Kors brand. Trims can be and often are used as much for brand identification as for decoration and function.

Importance of Fashion Components

Now that you have some idea of fashion's basic components, how they developed, and their relevance to the fashion game perspective "Be a Big Brand," consider how important they are from the standpoint of contemporary consumers, fashion game "rules," and, importantly, other players:

- Selection of one textile or other fashion component by a designer means jobs for others. After receipt of factory orders, **producers** such as fabric mills (sources for components like denim fabric for thousands of pairs of jeans) are able to hire workers.

- Understanding fabrics and other elements and their use means that **producers** are also able to plan correctly the manufacture of many hundreds, often thousands, of garments with fewer production problems and potentially greater profits. Both actions of producers are explored in more detail in the next section.

- Similarly, knowing textile characteristics and those of other components enables **purveyors** such as wholesalers to offer retailers finished garments constructed in trend-aware, season-appropriate fabrics, leathers, and trims and findings. Retail stores then offer such garments and accessories when, where, and how consumers want to buy them. Both kinds of purveyors seek profitable returns from these actions.

- **Promoters** get the word out! Whether they are touting a seasonal trend color for clothing and accessories or the features of an innovative textile (such as those having greater stretch for comfortable wear or providing a medically recognized sun protection factor, SPF), the more they know about fashion components the better able they are to generate excitement. Whether through cutting-edge technology or "old timey" print advertisements, promoters get consumers interested in such things as new textile products.

- Learning about textile properties and the characteristics of other components enables **consumers** to make better informed, more satisfying purchases. Even knowing just basic concepts as the "weave" of a textile or recognizing whether a trim such as a zipper is metal or plastic can make a great deal of difference in the appropriate selection, enjoyment, and, certainly, care of fashion purchases.

These are just a few ways that "little" things, the kinds many outside of fashion really don't give much thought to, in fact, are of "big" concern to those who are in fashion businesses. Given the importance of fashion components for so many different reasons, what do you think might be among their most important characteristics? What are details about them that those involved in fashion know and may assume others with whom they work understand as well?

Fibers to Fashion: Textiles

Fashion—yes, it's about trends, being in the moment, but it is also about feel, fit, and function! Think how much you like, dislike, or are just indifferent about articles of clothing you have just because of how they feel when you touch them. Think, too, how much a garment has meant to you based on its ability to retain its original, bright colors or fade in both color and your estimation of its quality over time. These characteristics as well as many others are mostly due to the textiles from which those garments were made. Why might fashion legend Yves St. Laurent have admired jeans so much? Perhaps the denim textiles from which most are constructed were responsible for the characteristics he so hopefully described. Up next: a primer of this important fashion component and its sources, characteristics, and role in the fashion game.

Cotton is the most common raw material used to create fabrics. (© mexrix/Shutterstock)

Before Fabrics: Fibers and Yarns

Fibers are single-strand textile components, often referred to as "practically invisible," "hairlike strands"; these are both found in nature and made artificially in a laboratory. They have important, distinguishing characteristics. Cotton, for example, produces short, textured, wavy fibers, known as **staple fibers**. High-quality cotton textiles, those with a glossy "sheen" and smooth, cool touch are often made from long-staple cotton, which has fibers of naturally greater length and less texture. Textiles of coarser surface texture (textile feel is often referred to as its "hand") are usually made from shorter cotton fibers. In contrast, silk as well as many manufactured fibers produce **filament fibers**. These fibers are long, continuous, and smooth. Silk is the only naturally produced filament fiber.

Contrast the appearances and tactile, or touch-like, qualities of a cotton tee shirt you own with that of a silk dress or necktie. The matte, dull-like finish of the former differs from the shiny look of the latter mostly due to the physical characteristics of the fibers forming the fabrics from which they are made. **Microfibers**, a term you will come across, refers to fibers that are much smaller in diameter than others. These fibers are exclusively manufactured ones, such as acrylic, nylon, and polyester. They typically have a thickness only one-half or one-third that of human hair,

Commonly Used Natural Fibers	Characteristics and Production Methods
Cotton	From smooth and glossy to thick and textured, cotton is fashion's versatile textile fiber. Cotton is picked from cotton "bolls" and then ginned, a process that removes seeds from fibers. It produces staple fibers of varying lengths, which determine quality. Fibers are then spun into yarns and woven or knitted into textile products.
Silk	Strong, lustrous with a smooth "hand," or tactile touch, silk may also be roughly textured. Filament fibers are produced from the cocoons of silk worms; usually cultivated on farms. These filaments are often very long. "Wild" silk refers to that which is not cultivated, often with shorter, coarser fibers. Silk may be spun into threads and yarns with other kinds of fibers before being woven or knitted.
Wool	Wool consists of absorbent fibers from the fleece of sheep, lambs, or goats such as angora and cashmere. Fibers are shorn, or cut, from animals, graded for quality, and then processed. Processing includes "carding" and "combing," steps that separate long and short wool fibers. Fibers are then spun into wool or wool-blend yarns, and then woven or knitted into textile products.
Flax/Linen	The earliest discovered textile fiber, flax's fibrous nature requires lengthy processing to produce textiles that range from smooth to crisp textured; it wrinkles if not blended or treated. Flax plants are harvested, then "retted," which separates fibers; it is then "scutched," "hacked," and "combed," all of which produces long lengths of fibers. These fibrous strands are then spun into yarns and usually woven into textile products.

making them smaller than such natural fibers as cotton, silk, or wool. "Human-made" filaments are produced by a showerhead-like device known as a **spinnerette** through which liquids are forced at high pressure. The resulting filaments harden after doing so, forming lengthy strands.

You are now familiar with the basic fiber types. Just from your own experience with clothing and the textiles comprising that clothing, you know there must be something more. After all, when you look at the textiles closely, you can see "something." What you are seeing are **yarns** made up of those fibers. Yarns are of two kinds. They may be multiple strands of fibers combined in ways that ensure they remain together and impart particular characteristics. These are **spun yarns**, or groups of fibers mechanically twisted together tightly to form continuous "lines." Cotton, linen, and silk are examples of fibers usually spun into yarns. On the other hand, filament yarns are manufactured, like shorter fibers. Filament yarns, however, may be programmed to be produced in any length and thickness.

Textile Construction

Weaving and knitting are the two primary means of constructing textile fabrics. Think "interlacing" for the former and "interlooping" for the latter, and you have an idea of what occurs during each process. Both weaving and knitting are centuries old. Technology first brought fabric construction from time consuming—it previously took days to produce even small amounts of usable textiles—to timely. It still continues to do so. Hundreds of years since the early textile production innovations noted in this section, "industrialization" continues. Now, it centers on developing ever-faster looms and knitting machines. These have enormous capacities, producing thousands of feet of textile fabric each minute. As well, the fashion components that these looms produce may already be on their way to becoming full-fledged garments. Items such as underwear and socks are now produced almost complete from today's fast, computer-driven, "seamless textile" looms.

The basics of fabric construction include recognizing "warp" and "weft" strands. Both apply to weaving and knitting processes. The first term refers to lengthwise yarn strands, those that "go up and down." "Wefts," or fill strands, go "left to right." Both warp and weft strands meet at right angles to each other to form the fabric. Weft strands are the stronger of the two, meaning

Weaving uses "warp" and "weft" strands to create fabrics. (© pavelgr/Shutterstock)

that they are less subject to puckering and unraveling. **Weaving refers to how these strands "meet" on looms producing textile fabrics.** From simple to complicated, weaving processes include:

Plain weaving: The simple, "over-under" means of textile construction in which one weft yarn is passed alternately by one warp yarn is called plain weaving.

Twill weaving: Take a good look at your jeans. Notice the faint diagonal lines. Those indicate twill weaving. In contrast to the one-up-and-over plain weaving method, with twill weaving warp strands may cross the surface of several weft strands before "going under." The diagonal line you see occurs because the interlacing moves over one warp strand after each completed row.

Satin weaving: To achieve smooth, shiny surfaces on fabrics, the satin weave is usually used. With this method, one strand (it may be either warp or weft) is "floated" over a number of strands before interlacing. Although appearing beautiful and sleek to the touch, fabrics produced through this method are usually weaker in strength and less durable in longevity than those produced through other means. Filament-yarn fabrics produced by this method are referred to as "satin," whereas those constructed of staple yarns, usually cotton, are called "sateen."

Jacquard weaving: Highly detailed, textured fabrics such as brocades (think rich-looking upholstery fabric) are produced through jacquard weaving. Specialized, highly complicated looms follow patterns that guide the placement of warp and weft strands. This may be done manually with punched cards as design guides, as originally occurred when these looms were developed in the early nineteenth century. Today, many jacquard looms are computer guided.

Pile weaving: How are "fuzzy" fabrics made? The loops found on the surface of terry cloth, for example, come about because of three sets of strands: warp and weft ones plus an additional strand. That "new" strand may be either warp or weft and forms loops found on fabric surfaces. These loops may be cut, as with velvet, or left intact.

Knitting is another means of fabric construction; however, unlike weaving, basic knitting only requires one strand of yarn. Recall that this method involves "interlooping," or **the process of continuously joining loops of yarn together**. There are two kinds of knits: weft and warp,

Knitting uses one strand of yarn to loop together fabrics. (© Drozdowski/Shutterstock)

produced through two different methods. Knitted textiles with horizontal (left-to-right) rows are referred to as weft knits. Warp knitting is more complicated, requiring more than one yarn strand, often a great many. These are then looped together to form detailed designs.

Textiles, as a final note, may be constructed in other ways besides weaving and knitting. Those produced by felting are comprised of textile fibers pressed to a backing and held with glues. Bonded fabrics (or even leathers) are those in which textile fibers, or skin pieces, are joined together under high pressure.

The Textile Production Process

Once woven, knitted, or produced in other ways by **fabric mills**, textiles may not yet be useful. Known as **greige goods** (say: "grey" goods), these are unfinished textiles. Such products are then purchased by **converters, businesses responsible for finishing raw fabrics** by dyeing, printing, or otherwise treating them. Mills may offer finished or greige goods, depending on production capabilities and business profitability.

The brilliant color of a new T-shirt makes clear how important color is with textile products. Color is imparted through a dyeing process. Dyeing may occur at any stage throughout textile construction. Fibers may be dyed in a process known as **stock dyeing**. As well, **yarns** may be dyed, referred to as **yarn dyeing**. Textile products such as **greige goods may be dyed**, too, **known as piece dyeing. Garment dyeing** refers to the practice of **coloring entire, completed items of clothing and accessories**. In general, stock and yarn dyeing produce colored fabrics less likely to fade.

And what would those T-shirts be without a design on them? Textiles may obtain decoration on their surfaces through **hand painting**, or printing. **Applying brush to fabric produces one-of-a-kind designs for which hand painting is sought.** For large-scale production, fabrics may be printed through such means as screen or roller methods. With **screen printing**, designs are printed using a pattern, held tightly by a frame that permits color to adhere to portions of the textile surface and not to others. There may be one or many "screens" used to complete the final design with the printed design allowed to dry before another one is included. **Roller printing uses a different cylinder for every color in a design.** Each has a design pressed onto them. Textile fabrics are passed through one roll at a time and allowed to dry before going through the next. In this way, designs on the textile are completed. **Heat transfer** is another means of printing textiles. In this, **designs are printed onto a medium such as paper then pressed against textiles using heat and pressure**. After dyeing and printing, textiles may be **finished** in any number of ways. Usually, these treatments are done to **add desirable characteristics to textile products**, such as wrinkle-resistance and shrink-proofing. At once an old industry while at the same time new with technical developments, production of textile products is crucial for fashion and consumers.

Textiles and the Fashion Game

Think back to the previous part of this text where you came to know fashion game rules. All four are applicable to textiles and their role in fashion. As noted, being a "big" brand is one of those rules. By now you are familiar with fashion brands, big and small. How is it possible for such things as fibers to become big brands? Aren't brands just for completed things? Getting to know more about manufactured fibers and how they are marketed shows just how important it is to "brand" even the most fundamental fashion component.

Screens are pressed into color dyes to create patterns on textiles. (© burnel1/Shutterstock)

Many manufactured fibers have two names. They may be referred to by generic names, often derived from chemical origins: polyester, polyamide/nylon, acrylic, rayon, spandex, nylon, and lyocell. They may also be known by such "brand names" as Dacron (polyester), Supplex (nylon), Acrilan (acrylic), Modal (rayon), Lycra (spandex), Antron (nylon), and Tencel (lyocell). Chemical companies such as E.I. DuPont de Nemours & Company, Inc., Monsanto Chemical, and others devote many millions of dollars and company resources toward developing ever-newer fibers and faster, more efficient textile production capabilities. One way to both "be a big brand" and "be profitable" is to patent these innovations. During the time of patent protection, usually seventeen years, originating companies own their technology exclusively. Others cannot legally use the same means to produce fibers. Having the technology is one thing. How do you think businesses get consumers excited about such things as the very fibers of which their clothing is made? Branding puts names to fibers. With brand names and marketing, consumers can more easily identify specific fibers out of the many generic ones. Think how many times you may have said that something was made of Lycra or Tencel, even described a jacket as being "Polartec," and how extensively these fibers have been marketed to get consumers to do just that! Textiles are marketed to fashion and retail professionals just as diligently at such **specialty trade shows as Premiere Vision**, held every year in New York City.

Patent protection is one way in which fiber manufacturers may "be legal" as well as use other fashion game rules. The remaining one, "be fair," is notable. That rule involves not just careful use of natural resources, but human ones as well. Fiber and textile production have long histories of resulting in environmental pollution and worker exploitation. From early on, waterways were polluted with textile production wastes and workers (sometimes children) toiled in deplorable conditions.

Sideline:

Fiber innovations have been made by such companies as Dow Chemical, DuPont, and Polartec. Dow, for example, has introduced Silvadur antimicrobial, a textile fiber "that provides long-lasting freshness and reliable protection against bacteria that can cause unpleasant odors, decay, rot, and discoloration in fabrics." In addition, DuPont has developed Sorona fibers intended to give greater stretch (and comfort) to cotton, wool, or rayon. As well, the fiber is extremely colorfast, ensuring that brightly colored garments, even swimsuits subject to harsh water conditions, remain so. In addition, Polartec has developed a synthetic insulation Polartec "Alpha," developed to be both breathable and lightweight all while providing wind and color protection superior to "puffy" style garments. Heeding consumer needs, fiber innovators continue to develop fibers intended to further garment sophistication.

Caveman to "Au Courant": Leather and Fur Components in Fashion

Leathers and furs have been determined to comprise the earliest known garments. Prehistoric-era "wraps" made only of raw, untreated animal pelts were precursors of today's leather and fur garments and accessories cut into exciting silhouettes and shapes, vibrant with bold colors or sophisticated with subtle shades, complete with remarkable features and attractive textures. Thousands of years since their first uses for spiritual reasons, group identification, and personal physical protection, leather and fur components now contribute to fashion's exciting trends and identify its unique brands.

Leather Fashion Components

From shoes to hats and almost everything else that might be worn or carried, **leathers, or the prepared and preserved skins of animals,** are popular components for use in fashion.

BASIC LEATHER INFORMATION

Cow and cobra, elk and eel, and don't forget goat, pig, sheep, ostrich, alligator, or any number of other mammals, reptiles, fishes, and birds—these are among the many legally available sources of leathers in the United States. In general, such components are available as by-products of edible meat production and would be wasted were it not for use as fashion components. As different as sizes of these source animals are, specific terminology has arisen to classify by weight the **raw, unprocessed pelts** rendered from them. Usually, the term **"skins" refers to pelts of less than 15 pounds**. Of note, **"kips" are pelts ranging from 15 to 25 pounds**. The commonly heard term **"hides" refers to pelts of more than 25 pounds**. Leather products are marketed to other fashion game players via trade shows held throughout the world. These include shows in Russia and many in China, an area where much of the world's leather is now processed.

GETTING TO KNOW LEATHER PRODUCTION

Raw pelts require extensive treatment before the resulting finished leathers may be cut and sewn into garments and accessories. These steps may be done directly by tanneries, fashion game providers in the business of preparing leather components that they then market and sell to purveyors or consumers. There are converters for leathers as well as for textiles. These converters buy pelts that they then sell to others as finished leathers after they have contracted with tanneries to prepare them.

Typically, pelts are first cleaned of hair. They are then tanned, dyed, and "finished." Tanning involves applications of oils or toxic chemicals that soften them to make them flexible enough to work with in production and, ultimately, wear with comfort, or use as intended. As well, tanning waterproofs skins, kips, and hides. Dyeing may enhance the natural coloring of these or may impart of-the-moment, trendy colors. The finishing phase usually involves applications of other chemicals and processes done to add such characteristics as lustrous shine, matte, or suede-like appearances and textures or special effects and designs. Western wear and related accessories such as boots and belts are often recognizable by their embossed designs,

Leather is a popular fabric used in fashion. (© Shkvarko/Shutterstock)

pressed into leathers during finishing processes. Leathers are then ready for construction into garments and accessories. As a precursor to textile garment making described in the next section, finished leathers are cut according to patterns, or guides. The resulting pieces are then assembled into leather items found in wholesale showrooms and retail stores, and sought by consumers.

The high-gloss, high-fashion patent leathers of Gucci, the luxuriously understated Hermes leathers, Louis Vuitton's textured "Epi" leathers—these are among the truly "big" fashion brands known for the quality of leather components used in their products. The rough-hewn appeal of Andrew Marc's "Marc" leather jackets and coats and the glossy leather handles and trims of Longchamp's nylon "pliage" totes and bags are examples of other big, accessible fashion names relying on leather components for product function and brand identification.

Fur Fashion Components

Love or loath it—the use of **fur, or the hairy skins of animals, usually mammals**, remains "in fashion." Consumers continue to purchase fur-based products, and demand appears to be increasing as new markets expand throughout the world. Like leathers, furs are important components not just for garments and accessories, but also for building fashion brands. To that end, understanding the origins of furs, how they are processed, and how they are worked into fashion items gives way toward understanding the roles that furs play in the fashion game.

FUR SOURCES

Many "think mink"! Consumers also consider fox and many other kinds of fur desirable. However, furs of any origin are described first according to how they are obtained. **Furs may be hunted in their natural habitats.** These are referred to as **wild furs**. Other fur sources are **ranch facilities devoted to breeding, developing, and harvesting specific types of fur**, such as mink and chinchilla. These produce **"farmed" furs**. With these basic distinctions in mind, fashion's frequently used furs and their animal origins include:

Species of Origin	Representative Kinds of Fur
Canine	Fox
Feline (Cat)	Lynx
Rodent	Chinchilla Nutria
Ungulate	Persian Lamb Broadtail
Weasel	Mink Sable

FUR PROCESSING

Wild fur pelts are usually sold by hunters and trappers to agents. These brokers then auction them to fur garment manufacturers. Fur auctions are held throughout the world in such countries as Canada, Denmark, and Russia, as well as New York City; these are the countries of origin for furs and centers of manufacture of fur items. Sable, lynx, and fox pelts, those prized for their natural coloration and marking, are examples of the kinds of furs usually hunted in the wild and auctioned. A majority of fur pelts, however, are farmed, and these are not auctioned. Rather, they are sold in large lots to garment manufacturers from source providers. Each year, trade shows such as NAFFEM (North American Fur & Fashion Exhibition) held in Montreal highlight fur fashion trends, showcase innovations in the industry, and provide opportunities for exhibitors and participants to share information.

Like leathers, furs must be processed in ways that prevent them from decomposing and make them easier to work into garments and, ultimately, comfortable to wear. Usually, they are first "dressed." This process cleans and softens skins, kips, and hides. Phases of this include "leathering," which effectively "tans" their underside portions making them useful for later production into fashion items. Long "guard hairs" may be cut, or plucked, to give furs uniform surface textures. Fur components may then be dyed in fashion-themed colors such as deeply saturated reds and blues, or always in style, blacks and browns. As well, some furs may be stencil dyed with patterns such as geometric stripes, V-shaped chevrons, or any number of other designs printed onto the actual hairs. Other furs may be "bleached" of their natural coloration, or "lifted" to lighter shades. Usually, all furs—whether natural, bleached, or dyed—are finally glazed. This is a conditioning process adding visual shine, luster, and tactile smoothness.

PREPARING FUR PRODUCTS

Garments and accessories require thoughtful planning and skillful construction. Those constructed of fur, however, require detailed attention to function and appear as intended. Typically, treated skins are laid out on a pattern and **matched** according to fur characteristics such as color, texture, and hair length. Fur matching is crucial to obtaining a final product of uniform quality. It requires extensive knowledge of and experience working with furs. As with leather and textile-based items, prepared skins are then cut according to the pattern using a variety of techniques. As with textile and leather items, the amount of "hand work" such as manual cutting and sewing necessary for construction adds greatly to the cost of fur garments.

Constructing fur garments can become quite complicated. Fur products may be cut and sewn by the **whole-skin method** in which the entire processed skin is cut according to a pattern. Another construction technique is referred to as the **skin-on-skin method** in which **skins are sewn to each other**. This method can produce a "blocky" appearing garment, one with highly visible seams, a feature that may be sought by the designer. The **letting-out method** of

Fur is a controversial fashion fabric. (© Yevgen Romanenko/Shutterstock)

construction is much more sophisticated. This method of constructing fur garments requires skins to first be split lengthwise, down their middle. Then, each skin is cut diagonally no more than one-eighth-inch wide. This produces hundreds of narrow fur "strips," which are then sewn together to form one continuous-appearing skin with few if any horizontal seams. The "let out" skins are then matched again and sewn into the shape of the garment, or, if a complicated design, portions of it. The form is dampened, stapled to a board, and allowed to dry. This step effectively stretches the fur, giving the garment its shape. After these steps, the garment may be cleaned and glazed, and have trims such as closure hooks and textile linings sewn into it. Other methods of constructing fur coats and the like include the **split-skin method**. This is similar to "letting out" and **involves inserting leather strips between skins to make less expensive fur garments**. These are some of the truly "behind the seams" processes that go into the construction of fur garments and accessories such as hats and even handbags.

Leathers and Furs and the Fashion Game

"Big" brands have not only legal and ethical concerns, but also, as with all aspects of fashion, profitability concerns; in short, leather and fur products touch on all aspects of the fashion game just like textiles. Leathers are part of "big" brands and their identities as you have seen. Furs, too, form the basic element of fashion brands. They may do so in two ways. For one, brands such as Dennis Basso and Fendi rely on high-quality skins and construction techniques to produce trendy, exciting garments and accessories truly worthy of red carpet entrances.

Another way to build fur fashion brands is through design and styling. Providers of fur components "brand" their products with trademarks as well. "Blackglama," for example, has been promoted to consumers so they will seek out that brand when looking for black mink fur products. African "Swakara" broadtail lamb is another example of brand marketing applied to fur components. These and other companies often put in place strict animal care, breeding, and harvesting standards as well as skin selection criteria before fur components can claim they come from such sources, or finished items bear brand-identified labels. Some, such as Blackglama, go so far as to print numeric authenticity codes on brand labels, tags that also carry brand confirmation information only seen under special ultraviolet lights. Why these security measures? Quite simply: furs can be faked! Thanks to greater technology, it is possible to dye and trim less desirable furs in ways that make them appear more luxurious and costly. Consumers unfamiliar with such techniques might be duped into buying fur garments of inferior quality. As well, it can be difficult if not impossible to tell exactly the countries of origin of furs just from physical inspection of them.

Because of issues such as these, individual fur providers put in place consumer protection measures. From above, you are familiar with aspects of Blackglama's approach. As well, fur industry trade groups promulgate other consumer protection guidelines, as do federal laws. The International Fur Trade Association (IFTA) and several prestigious fur auction groups have developed the **"Origin Assured"** program. This series of standards accompanied by group oversight protects consumers by effectively guaranteeing the true country of origin of furs bearing the "OA" label. The **Fur Products Labeling Act of 1952**, in its present form, requires that consumers be informed clearly of furs' names, their countries of origin, and whether they have been dyed or made out of "junk" pieces, not entire skins.

In addition to consumer protection measures, animal welfare regulations control leather and fur and their providers. Invoking the fashion game rule "be fair," notably its aspect of sustainability, or preservation of existing resources, federal laws exist to protect designated animals and species. These laws prohibit hunting, selling, and transporting into the United States hides of lions, tigers, leopards, or products made from them. Elephant tusk ivory and rhinoceros horns are examples of other protected animals and prohibited products derived from them. Fines, imprisonment, and confiscation are penalties for those found guilty of breaking these laws. The **Endangered Species Conservation Act** is an example of a government-mandated form of animal protection.

Other kinds of animal protection activities, this time intended for all species, are carried out by special interest groups such as **People for the Ethical Treatment of Animals** (PETA). This and related groups throughout the world do much to promote awareness among consumers about conditions under which leather or fur-bearing animals are hunted or raised. As well, it vocally and actively seeks to convince consumers that wearing leather and fur in any form is unfashionable. Picketing stores and disrupting shows or other events where such products are offered for sale or shown are some of the tactics used to get the groups' message across. These measures and announcements by celebrity spokespeople that they would "rather go naked than wear fur" were highly effective, dissuading consumers' fur purchases during the 1990s.

As such efforts had an impact on fur providers' abilities to "be profitable," they mounted promotional campaigns aimed at attracting consumers to fur products. Countering PETA's arguments and informing the fur-interested public about industry practices, as well as rising affluence, especially from new world markets, worked to increase demand for leather and fur-based products. Results of both groups' efforts have established what appears to be the current fashion industry position. Right now, selling or wearing leather or fur-sourced products is framed as being a business or personal decision. Sell it . . . don't sell it . . . wear it . . . don't wear it—the choice lies with fashion businesses or consumers.

Whether you agree or not with that stance, several considerations arise. One, of course, is that the demand for fur remains. It may be easy for individuals to decide the issue for themselves. They likely do not operate businesses depending on fur products to generate revenue and contribute to profitability. The choice to engage in the fur trade has financial consequences few in business can afford to ignore. Thus, decisions about providing, producing, purveying, and promoting fur products may well hinge on whether doing so affects the "bottom line" and the ability to become a "big" brand with consumers.

Fashion's Substance and Style: Findings and Trims

Without something other than the denim textile from which they are constructed, your jeans could only be wrapped haphazardly around your body. If you could find a way to wear them, they might even appear boring! Those "something others" are trimmings. They give fashion its functional substance and visible, tactile style. Trimmings, or "trims," are other items offered by fashion game providers, along with textiles and leathers and furs. To recap: fashion professionals typically refer to **trimmings as being those items that add function, decoration, or both to clothing and accessories**. Some trims serving purely functional purposes, such as **threads, "plain" fasteners, snaps, and unseen interfacings and pads giving garments structure, are known as "notions."** Because trimmings are so important to the fashion industry, they even have an organized industry trade show, **Trimmings Expo**, held each year in New York City.

Consumers depend on information about fashion components when making such decisions as whether to purchase items made of fabrics requiring dry cleaning instead of those that may be washed at home. Separate from the garment's textile, trims have their own care

Trimming on jeans makes them something other than just plain denim fabric. (© DAN SCANDAL/Shutterstock)

requirements. They have lives of their own! What that means, of course, is that care must be taken by producers to obtain components that not only perform functional and decorative needs, but also are compatible with the garment fabric, leather, or fur they accompany. Can garments and their components be dry cleaned together? Decorative buttons, for example, often have to be removed or covered before chemical cleaning to prevent damage to both. Failure to consider these issues often results in unsatisfied consumers, those who return items with faulty trim elements. With these thoughts in mind, consider the characteristics of threads, buttons, and zippers, as these are among the most frequently encountered trimmings.

Threads

When you think about how many garments and accessories rely on threads for their very existence, you get some "notion" of thread's importance. How might you describe something so obvious, something you likely do not think about every time you dress? **Threads are textile fibers and/or filaments spun and twisted into continuous lengths.** Threads may be comprised of cotton, silk, nylon, polyester, or any fiber or filament capable of being manipulated into long, thin strands. Threads may also be comprised of combinations of these. Cotton and polyester, for example, is a popular thread type in which polyester filament is wound with cotton fiber.

Basic information to know about thread includes understanding its various sizes, physical structure, and processing technique. Thread "size" refers to its thickness. Denier and TEX systems are ways thread size may be measured. In the United States, for example, the denier system is used as a common way to express thread size. Denier refers to the linear mass density of a thread strand. It is defined as the mass in grams per 9000 meters. The basis for measurement, "1-denier," is based on the weight (1 gram) or 9000 meters of silk thread. Thus, "micro denier" threads are those that weigh less (i.e., are less thick) than silk, whereas those of higher numbers are thicker. The TEX system is similar but is phrased as the mass in grams of per 1000 meters. Used in many European countries, it is another weight-based measure of thread thickness.

"Twist," refers to the direction and tightness with which threads are wound; threads with tight twists are less likely to fray and unravel. Thread weight and twist are two important characteristics along with fiber or filament content. These characteristics determine whether a thread will be appropriate for the manufacture of a garment and how it will wear and withstand care.

With denim jeans, where sturdiness and durability are sought, heavier weight threads with polyester "cores" surrounded by cotton casings are used. For items intended for light use, in contrast, such as wedding gowns, a fine "core spun" polyester thread may be used.

A commonly encountered term refers to threads as "mercerized." This refers to cotton threads that have been subjected to mercerization, a chemical process that makes threads more lustrous (shiny) and physically stronger. Cotton fabrics may be mercerized as well. Fashion game producers use thread from large cones with lengths up to tens of thousands of yards for large-scale garment and accessory construction. Consumers such as home sewers usually use thread supplied on "spools" holding anywhere from 125 (114 meters) to 500 yards (457.2 meters).

Buttons

Functional, often colorful, but perhaps a bit illusive to describe until now, **buttons are any nonpermanent means of joining segments of garments and accessories, usually to open and close them**. "Snaps" are metal or plastic garment closures that must be pressed together in order for them to function as similarly nonpermanent closing devices.

Buttons may be used for practical purposes and/or decoration of the same items. Buttons can—and have—been made of almost any physical material, either natural or human-made. Only imagination or presently unavailable materials limits the kind of things from which buttons may be made. Plastics, synthetics, and metals are the most common materials from which buttons are now made.

Buttons are usually round, flat objects, although options for shapes they may take appear infinite: "half-moon" and other forms are common, as are novelty shapes such as animals. However, there are specific configurations of note. Buttons may have obvious holes intended to aid application onto garments. These are referred to as **"sew-through" buttons**. On the other hand, some buttons have no holes and are known as **"shank" buttons**.

Many buttons are comprised of two parts. With these, plastic or metal fronts are inserted into a shank-type back. The fronts of these buttons may be of any material, but usually when these kinds of buttons are used, they are covered with some kind of fabric. A **"self-covered" button is one covered in the same fabric as the garment on which it is applied**.

Other information to know about buttons includes button sizes and how they are noted. Standard button sizes range from 9.2 millimeters (.362 inches) to 25.4 millimeters (1.00 inch), although, of course, there are examples of buttons of larger and smaller sizes. Button size is noted in "lignes" with an "L" following the size notation. One ligne is equivalent to 0.635 millimeters (0.025 inches). Thus, a 9.2 millimeter button would be referred to as "14 ligne," or "14L"; one of 25.4 millimeters (1.00 inches) would be "40 ligne," or "40L." Sizes of commonly used buttons include 16L (10.5 mm, or 0.413 inches) on shirts and 32L (20.5 mm, or 0.807 inches) for jackets.

ZIPPERS

Think how many fashion items close or are decorated with zippers. Given their predominance, have you ever thought about how to define them? **Zippers are the mechanical means by which two edges or end pieces may be nonpermanently joined until separated.** As you know, those "edges," or "end pieces" may be comprised of textiles, leathers, or even furs. What we would mostly likely recognize today as the "zipper" appeared around 1913. Until the 1960s, zippers were made with metal components. After that date, nylon zippers began to appear. Both tape and "teeth" of these zippers could be dyed to match clothing color. They also did not rust as did most early metal ones, which were made of inexpensive base materials. Today, zippers can be custom made in virtually any configuration to further garment design and function. Recent advances allow zippers to work "both ways." This permits two sliders to function together or separately on the same zipper.

Understanding zipper selection criteria or evaluating those used in garment construction are important aspects of fashion buying and evaluating garment quality. Thus, the selection of zippers, as with all trim and finding elements, depends on intended use and appropriateness. For example, heavier, thicker zippers are usually used with correspondingly tougher textiles, sturdy leathers, perhaps furs—items intended for hard use in harsh climate conditions. Some designers have been known to use heavy zippers for decorative contrast on light, even sheer fabrics. In such cases, the underlying garment fabric is reinforced with cloth tapes to accomplish that effect and prevent garment puckering.

Zippers are an important trim in fashion. (© Ruta Saulyte-Laurinaviciene/Shutterstock)

Other Trims

The exciting world of trimmings knows almost no limit as their producers work to make garments ever more fashionable, functional, and in tune with consumers' desires and needs! To the most commonly used ones described above, other interesting, useful trims include:

Beads—These are spherical, or cylindrical objects, cut internally, or so made that they may be sewn onto garments or grouped together on threads, strings, or cords. They are used primarily for ornamental purposes. Larger ones may be used functionally as closures.

Embroideries—Decorative needlework and ornamental stitching techniques comprise embroideries. These may be completed by hand or by machines. Two terms to know: **Schiffli embroidery**, where individual designs are repeated, separated, and sewn to other items, and **framework embroidery** of individual pieces such as patches and badges.

Ribbons—These are decorative, sometimes functional strips of cloth or other textile product available in a wide array of colors, textures, patterns, lengths, and widths. When employed as belts and other closures, ribbons offer functional capabilities to clothing and accessories. Four ribbon styles to know: **satin** (those with a smooth, glossy appearance and "hand," or feel), **velvet** (having a napped, "fuzzy" surface due to the use of pile weaves that leave small loops or strands on their surface), **jacquard** (highly ornamental ribbon with designs and thread placements determined by computer programs), and **grosgrain** or **faille** ("file") ribbon (characterized by raised "ribs" on both sides, due to weft strands that are thicker in width than opposing warp ones).

Rhinestones—Tiny pyramid- or dome-shaped pieces of cut or faceted glass, crystal, or plastic disks backed with metallic foils or paints intended to imitate diamonds and other precious stones denote rhinestones; they are often called "strass" in European countries and are used almost exclusively to decorate garments and accessories.

Sequins—Flat, often round objects attached to clothing and accessories largely for decorative purposes are sequins; "paillette" usually refers to large sequins used to decorate clothing and accessories by imparting color and texture to them.

Section Finale   summary

Here, you have gained an introduction to the sometimes unsung, but always necessary fashion components. Primary ones noted here include textiles, leathers and furs, and trimmings. As described, **textiles** are constructed through combining fibers, yarns, and other elements by weaving, knitting, and fusing. **Leathers and furs** are the skin and hair products of animals used for warmth, durability, and sensuality. **Trimmings** are among the fashion components described as well. These are items that give decoration, function, and excitement to garments.

Review Questions: What Did You Discover?

1. List the major fashion components and briefly describe each. You may use a chart-style format for easy reference later.

2. Describe how early advances in textile technology enabled the modern day fashion game to come about.

3. What characteristics distinguish the major kinds of textile fibers?

4. Briefly recount the means by which fibers become finished, usable textiles.

5. What are the different kinds of textile "weaves" and how do they differ?

6. How might leathers and furs be described, according to this section? What kinds are there?

7. Briefly note the leather or fur production process.

8. Describe trimmings, or "trims" and note their basic functions.

9. Why might knowledge of fashion components be important to consumers as well as to fashion professionals?

10. In what ways do fashion components enable professionals, "players," to "build big brands"? Can you find examples other than the ones noted in this section of how components do so?

Terms to Know

Be sure you know the following terms from this section and can give examples:

Flying shuttle
Spinning jenny
Power loom
American textile industry
Cotton gin
Highly efficient loom
Hand-powered sewing machine
Singer sewing machines
Providers
Producers
Purveyors
Promoters
Textiles
Yarns
Leathers
Furs
Trimmings
Staple fibers
Filament fibers
Microfibers
Spinnerette
Spun yarns
Weaving
Plain weaving

Twill weaving
Satin weaving
Jacquard weaving
Pile weaving
Knitting
Fabric mills
Greige goods
Converters
Stock dyeing
Yarn dyeing
Piece dyeing
Garment dyeing
Hand painting
Screen printing
Roller printing
Heat transfer
Finished
Skins
Kips
Hides
Wild furs
"Farmed" furs
Whole-skin method
Skin-on-skin method

Letting-out method
Split-skin method
Origin Assured
Fur Products Labeling Act of 1952
Endangered Species Conservation Act
People for the Ethical Treatment of Animals
Threads
Buttons
"Sew-through" buttons
"Shank" buttons
"Self-covered" button
Zippers
Beads
Embroideries
Schiffli embroidery
Framework embroidery
Ribbons
Satin
Velvet
Jacquard
Grosgrain
Faille
Rhinestones
Sequins

Assessing Your Brand Using SWOT Analysis

Project Purpose: You will need to know how your proposed fashion brand of products or services stack up against others!

Step One: Proposed Idea for Market Day Presentation: _____

_____

_____

Step Two: Research similar ideas that are ALREADY available to professional, or general consumers. Which did you find? Name them here and collect images, advertisements, other media explaining them.

_____   _____   _____

Step Three: Describe how your proposed idea is different so that you can differentiate it when others ask for comparisons:

_____

_____

_____

_____

Step Four: What does all this mean? If you were to present your idea to the "real world," how might it be received, how successful might it be, what concerns might there be about it? A SWOT analysis should be a helpful way to answer these concerns! How do the following apply to your idea?

Strengths of Idea	Weaknesses of Idea		Opportunities Presented by Idea	Threats to Success of Idea

Describe Fashion History from Your Perspective!

Focus: Fashion history is a fascinating exploration into the lives and times of others through what they wore. Throughout, there were always "players" of the fashion game. The purpose of this project is to identify them, then demonstrate importance of their contributions. You will conduct research to complete this project.

Step One: Select an Era or an Inspirational Period
Find a decade, or a specifically defined time of interesting occurrences ("Hip-hop" of the 1980s–1990s, for example).
The time I am most interested in is: _____
I like it because: _____

Step Two: Identify Several Players of the Fashion Game and Importance of Their Contributions

Player	Contributions and Importance
Providers	
Producers	
Purveyors	
Promoters	

Step Three: Take Us There!
You are now something of an expert on fashion of a particularly unique time and those, then, who made it so! Describe what was going on and what the fashion mood of that time was based on your research about its players.

_____

_____

_____

_____

_____

_____

PRODUCERS: DESIGNING AND MANUFACTURING FASHION

FAST FORWARD

This section goes "behind the seams" to explore the actions of another kind of fashion game player: producer. You know, by now, that producers are but one group responsible for bringing fashion products to consumers. Here you will see what they do and how their activities relate to the concepts and rules with which you are familiar. Many outside of fashion are fascinated by fashion designers. Yet, they have scant idea of the work producers actually do, how they use creative skills in very businesslike ways to build "big" brands and big businesses. This section explores that process and garment production processes.

WHAT YOU SHOULD KNOW ABOUT THIS SECTION:

- It describes the fashion design process and its relationship to building fashion brands.
- It outlines the manufacturing steps required to produce fashion apparel.
- It relates these processes to the rules of the fashion game.

5

How do fashion ideas become finished, recognizable, branded garments? The very things reflecting your lifestyle—your interests—you! Be prepared to learn many new terms and concepts, including ways in which brand elements (with which you are already familiar) are incorporated into fashion design and production processes. Fashion's "real purpose" may be to tell us who we are, but it takes us, as fashion game players, to define the process by which it may do so.

Fashion Makes the Lifestyle Connection Early

Ancient history or precursor of today's world? No matter your perspective, there can be no denying that the past has much to do with shaping fashion—its inspirations, practices, and future. Modern fashion designers and brands are but the latest in a long history of fashion game producers to promote, even further the "lifestyle" concept. Now, anyone with the financial means can purchase and wear what they want and define what they want others to believe their lifestyle to be!

In the eighteenth-century world of France's King Louis XVI and Marie Antoinette, however, opulent, costly clothing and accessories defined individual social status, and access to finery was limited to all but royalty and those elites who depended on them. Enter Rose Bertin (1747–1813)—acknowledged to be among that era's foremost fashion and social "gatekeepers."

Known as a "marchande de mode," Bertin gained fame for the elaborate dresses with skirts of gigantic proportions that she designed and whose construction she oversaw. Trimmed with all manner of ribbons, laces, feathers, and jeweled ornaments, she sold her rich wares to an aristocratic clientele, only those she deemed of appropriate social standing. By doing so, Bertin reinforced then-current norms of dress determined by position. Yet, she did something more.

In an era when women, even aristocratic ones, had limited opportunities, Bertin (who, in fact, was legally prohibited from actually cutting and sewing clothes; those jobs were reserved for male-only members of tailors guilds) gave women physical presence with her sizable, commanding gowns, ones that took up large amounts of physical space, that demanded deference, and, through choice of decoration, gave women the means to express their own opinions—politically and socially—as strongly as men might through speech. A woman might, for example, make known her political leanings—monarchy or democracy—simply through the color of dress she chose to be seen in. The only "voice" she had in her rigidly defined lifestyle was through a means made possible by Bertin, among fashion's earliest producers!

Forgotten or fashionable? Designers such as Alexander McQueen have found inspiration from such medieval garments as these. (© Hein Nouwens/Shutterstock)

Methods of Garment Production: Couture

Garments may be made individually, or in quantities ranging from small in number to astronomically large. Single garment production is usually referred to as **haute couture**, or **custom-made** for women's wear. For men's wear, the term **bespoke** denotes tailored clothes made for just one person.

Whether for women or men, one-of-a-kind items are begun usually when ordered by purchasers. Orders are turned over to appropriate workrooms in the couture house. For example, *tailleurs* or tailored garments are produced by one section of the house. Garments with draped, softer lines (usually dresses) are executed by a team of workers responsible for *flou*. Both ateliers produce garments whose sizes are determined from clients' actual body measurements, not predetermined from "sized" patterns. As well, clients may decide certain garment features such as color, trims, and other details. Because incredibly expensive fabric, trims, and time-consuming labor traditionally go into making women's custom clothing, **toiles**, or **models** in inexpensive muslin are made first from those specifications. Men may be offered by bespoke tailors opportunities to try on prototypes as well.

For women, toile "garments" may be tweaked with adjustments made for flattering fit and comfortable wear after clients try them on. Often, designers or makers will suggest at this point how fabrics may be best utilized to take advantage of weaves, prints, or other textile features. A couture-made "little black dress" might be constructed, for example, with fabric cut from particular sections of a large bolt to better ensure that the final garment has a "clean," harmonious look, even if the dress is of just one color! As well, a bespoke man's jacket may have fabric cut in ways that, when sewn, one-dimensional pinstripes and plaids appear to align, giving completed garments a three-dimensional appearance. Attention to details such as these as well as near-exclusive use of hand labor, not sewing machines, defines women's and men's custom-made clothing.

Fabrics chosen for final garments are then cut according to sizes and features determined from adjusted toiles and initial fittings. If garments are complicated, such as wedding dresses or those requiring highly skilled sewing or tailoring techniques, clients may be asked to try them on several times throughout the production phases. Body measurements and personal preferences are noted and kept for future reference for both female and male custom clients. When completed, these finely made items are delivered in gigantic boxes wrapped in an avalanche of tissue paper or on hangers in luggage-like garment bags.

Costs for haute couture garments, especially from well-known French fashion companies helmed by equally famous fashion designers, are incredible! In general, couture garments cost in the mid to high five figures; those with special features such as hand-beaded trims or furs may go for much more. It is not unusual for elaborately beaded wedding dresses to cost $100,000 or more. Costs of men's bespoke suits from recognized firms in England and Italy depend partially on fabric quality selected, but tend to run in the five-figure range as well.

The tradition of haute couture continues in the United States with hundreds of custom dressmakers specializing in one-of-a-kind work. They may make custom orders for wedding, debutante, and other special-occasion wear. Men in the United States, as well, have available bespoke tailors offering their services. Usually, these businesses have retail outlets or regularly send representatives to the hotels and offices to take custom orders. "Bespoke" is sometimes used to describe men's clothing first made from producers' standard patterns (i.e., not based on one person's measurements), then extensively altered to approximate full custom-made garments. These are more correctly referred to as "made-to-measure" and usually feature less hand labor in their construction than true bespoke clothing.

Often, the term "couture" is used to mean expensive, high-quality women's ready-to-wear of the kind found on the racks of such stores as Saks Fifth Avenue, Neiman-Marcus, Nordstrom, and many others. Couture clothing, technically speaking, is a hand-made, one-of-a-kind garment, made for only one client upon her order, using her specifications.

To describe haute couture as legendary, especially when it comes from France, would be an understatement. Images such as the one opening this section capture only some of the

Sketches are often the preliminary step in creating haute couture garments. (© Shutterstock)

excitement each season's new couture collections generate. Perhaps because of the attention it garners, or how integrally linked it is to national cultural identity, or for any of a number of reasons, French couture is highly protected by a governing body. Begun in 1886, the **Chambre Syndicale de la Couture Parisienne** controls the powerful Fédération Française de la Couture. This organization controls use of the name "haute couture," which kinds of businesses may use it, rules such "houses" have to follow, and other details.

Methods of Garment Production: Ready-to-Wear

In contrast to custom-made is **ready-to-wear** fashion production. As the name suggests, this process results in **fully prepared garments consumers can instantly put to use**. Except for alterations or slight changes (such as moving buttons for better fit), ready-to-wear garments are "good to go" once they leave final production finishing. High-fashion lines may produce only a few hundred "ready" garments for specialty retail stores and exclusive boutiques. Ralph Rucci (formerly Chado Ralph Rucci) is one brand producing relatively small numbers of highly influential garments each fashion season. On the other hand, Inditex Group (otherwise known as Zara) produces many thousands of garments each day. It is estimated that the company made 835,000 garments in 2011, or over 2,000 a day! Whether the result is a few garments or almost a million, production of wear-to-wear usually follows a series of steps. Broadly speaking, those steps may be grouped accordingly: preproduction, production, and postproduction. These steps suggest what occurs, details of which are for further discussion. Part of that will include noting how rules of the fashion game apply and how they are interpreted.

Ready-to-Wear Preproduction

Fashion begins with ideas. Brand building relies on those ideas to establish indelible impressions—moreover, unified ones—from fashion season to season that represent brand image. The design process beginning ready-to-wear preproduction has the twin goals of starting off the process for one season and establishing a context for others that follow.

Sketches are the language of fashion. It is through drawings—some formal and highly artistic, others rough and functional, or yet others now generated through computer-aided design (CAD) programs—that designers or teams of designers communicate inspiration. **"Croquis"** is the term for drawings realistic enough (usually printed with head, shoulders, and legs for ease) for others in the fashion development process to understand. From them, they perform their own work such as making patterns. Drawings are important, but there are other means of communicating design intent in fashion. **Draping** is the process of applying textile products to model forms in order to express fashion creativity. Draping techniques offer designers of all skill levels the abilities to express fashion creativity. Often, drawings are made of draped designs for production practicality.

From idea to drawing or draped model to seasonal fashions what happens? Usually, designers come up with many ideas, sometimes tens, even hundreds. Designers set out ideas for separates, suits, day dresses, dinner or cocktail dresses (late day into evening apparel), evening wear (often, long gowns), and, sometimes, wedding gowns. Men's wear designers might sketch a range of items from casual sportswear to shirts and trousers to suits and

Designers make collections of garments that are all based around a particular theme. (© eddie linssen/Alamy)

tuxedos, updated for the upcoming fashion season. Children's wear fashion designers set out designs for youngsters of different ages. Preparation of designs for different kinds of garments — men's, women's, or children — is usual practice for most fashion companies. Specialty fashion companies, those offering seasonal style varieties of one kind of garment, such as swimwear or wedding gowns, would likely only produce designs for those items. In established fashion businesses, designs are not always "original." Rather, ideas from past fashion seasons (especially those that sold well) are reintroduced but modified in some way. For example, garments may be designed for production in updated colors or fabrics. Designs of this origin are called "carryovers," or "anchors."

Taken together, these design ideas form the product line, or "line," the fashion company will produce for a particular fashion season. Sometimes this assortment of designs is referred to as a "collection." Usually, there is a theme to lines or collections. This concept is based on their initial inspirations. Themes can be a unifying color, design element (such as patterns or motifs), or even feelings. Recent fashion themes have included such colors as orange and such evocative times as the 1970s. Once themes are established, garment designs are organized into groups or product categories.

Production of Ready-to-Wear: Cutting, Sewing, and Finishing

Technical dimensions of the human form, especially those related to bodily proportions, are used to produce patterns for ready-to-wear. **Patterns are paper or cardboard "blueprints," or guides, enabling users to construct three-dimensional, wearable clothing items from one-dimensional fabric textile products.** A pattern, however, only produces one garment in one size at a time. How are patterns for other sizes of clothing made?

Through a process known as grading, one pattern can become another pattern, and another, and still another, for garments of all sizes. **Grading**, then, **is a process of adjusting dimensions contained on one apparel pattern to produce multiple patterns for**

variously sized garments. A skilled pattern "grader" can draw and cut a series of different-sized patterns for making small- to large-sized garments that, when laid on top of each other, resemble a "nest." Although much of patternmaking and grading is done by computers, designers still find it necessary to know basic differences in apparel size characteristics.

Production of Fashion Garments

The fashion production process may occur "in house" or be contracted to others. Fashion producers may determine that it is profitable and timely to keep manufacture in their factories. In general, the steps include cutting fabric, organizing their assembly, and obtaining necessary items (such as zippers and buttons). In only very expensive, in-house production is garment production accomplished by just one person. Rather, it is completed by several people, each completing a specialized task. Afterward, semi-completed garments are passed on to others. This continues until the garments or portions of them are completed. This is known as unit production.

Fashion Design and Production

Is it mystery or mastery that makes for fashion? Fashion design and production processes seem shrouded in mystery to those not in the fashion game! On the other hand, to its players and informed consumers, there are discernible, sequential activities that occur, tasks that bring about the fashion garments available for purchase in stores. The previous portion of this section focused on couture, the one-of-a-kind, headline-stealing garments worn by celebrities and socialites. What about ready-to-wear, or what the French term "prêt à porter"? The various phases required to bring about these items, part and parcel, demonstrate fashion game producers in action.

Ready-to-wear fashion producers work in all sizes of businesses, from gigantic corporations to small, fledgling businesses. Thus, an exact template, a "set" procedure, for how a fashion idea becomes an item available on a store rack can be difficult to delineate. The process can be somewhat fluid depending on company resources and abilities. A designer at a small fashion house may have only himself or herself, or perhaps one or two other workers, to carry out processes defined here. As well, they may only informally discuss ideas before putting them into action. On the other hand, in large to very large fashion companies, entire teams are devoted to researching trend and color ideas as well as locating production sources in far-away countries. Many meetings and presentations usually are required to put together a seasonal line of fashion items, certainly one with many different styles and variations on them. These conditions noted, ready-to-wear fashion does begin with ideas. But where do those originate?

Current inspiration alone may not be the only element at work behind the development of a fashion collection. Rather, past successes may be influential. **Carryovers** are fashion designs that have earned a record of commercial success and are continued ("carried over") from one fashion season to another. Of course, those "hits" may be modified as to fabric and color selection to be appropriate for the current season being planned. They are, nevertheless, familiar, popular designs, ones for which retailers and consumers clamber.

Carryovers are common, but new styles are what stores and consumers really seek. To make such garments available, producers engage in all manner of detailed research to find out what their target market consumer really wants. What, for example, are the trend-aware colors that will find favor with that group? What newer, better (and hopefully less expensive) textiles and trims are available, components that may form the basis of entire garments? This kind of research is undertaken and necessary toward formulating at least the initial designs making up a seasonal fashion collection. Research, inspiration, and hard work—all these come together to form the creative and commercial approach of the line. Actual designing occurs next!

Steps consumers most likely associate with working as a fashion "designer" usually occur only after the kinds of preparations noted above are completed. Using the principles of design, such as **silhouette** (garment shape or style, such as "strapless" gown or "double-breasted" jacket), **color** (specific ranges of perceived light rays), **texture** (tactile sensations of touch caused by physical contact or as perceived when seen), **pattern** (recurring design motifs such as stripes or dots), or other attributable characteristic (such as those available with high-tech textiles such as sun protection), fashion designers devise their arrangement using one-dimensional drawings or computer-generated images. Whatever their ephemeral inspiration, perhaps a film they saw or emotion they felt when listening to a particular piece of music, it is through these means that those feelings become fashion! As well, it is through these means that researched trends, colors, and components become tangible, touchable, purchasable fashions.

Sketching fashion ideas for fun is one thing, doing so for commercial reasons is more complicated. In general, once inspiration strikes for one garment idea, professional fashion designers then form entire **lines, or groups of garments** based on those ideas. This means, practically speaking, that other fashion items are planned, ones that coordinate with the initial garment designed. For example, a blouse is designed to work with a skirt design, or a slack style is planned for a jacket. Research continues once these items are designed. Are acceptable fabrics available to produce parts of the line? That is one such common question the answer to which determines whether the design will actually make it from the drawing board to the selling floor.

As designs are finalized and at least tentatively planned for production, a technical designer, or (usually with large companies) a team of designers, step in to write the garment details known as "specs." These **specification sheets** include information about the exact dimensions the proposed garment will take when finished. For example, the length of garment sleeves according the planned **size runs**. Within each style, as you are aware, garments of different sizes are planned and offered to accommodate consumers' physical sizes and shapes. At this time, preproduction, garments in the line are tentatively "costed," that is their cost of production is estimated. Garments determined to be too costly (i.e., unprofitable) to produce for the maker are dropped from the line at this point. This can occur, for example, when research reveals that increased fabric, trim, or production costs render the garment too expensive to actually produce according to budget allocations.

As well, garments that might be cost effective to produce are nonetheless dropped when it is determined that **wholesale prices** (amounts purveyors such as wholesalers and retailers would be willing to pay for the proposed garment) would not be within the ranges associated with the fashion brand or company. During the costing process, producers' own profit percentages—that amount above the actual costs to produce the garment—are figured in. In general, retailers "mark up," the amount they paid wholesale purveyors.

Designers often plan groups of garments based on the original garment's style, colors, and fabrics. (© Professional photography/Shutterstock)

Garments constructed from expensive fabrics cause the cost of production to rise. (© anghifoto/Fotolia)

From the technical specifications, a **first pattern** for the garments is produced. Very high-end fashion ready-to-wear houses often employ a patternmaker, whereas large-scale fashion businesses use computer-generated patternmaking systems, such as Gerber. In short, **patterns** are the paper, cardboard, or computer diagrams that set the exact dimension of every part of a garment. That means that it details not a sleeve, for example, but each and every part required to form that sleeve. Think of it this way: patternmaking is the process of diagramming ways of cutting and sewing a one-dimensional length of textile and signifying where to apply appropriate, necessary components such as zippers or buttons, so that the fabric becomes multidimensional, capable of being worn on the body.

After the initial pattern is made, it is applied to a fabric. Depending on the producer, the pattern may be "cut" in the fabric intended for the final garment, or, if too expensive, one of lesser quality. This prototype garment is checked for appearance, fit, and other standards such as newly estimated costs. Rising costs during the design and production of fashion garments is a prevalent concern. Usually, these involve fabric and labor costs that go up for any number of reasons.

Designs produced in fabrics intended for use in making the final item are often referred to as **first samples**. Once all samples are completed, the entire line is reviewed for continuity of theme, "flow" of designs from one kind of garment to another. For example, does the design of a cocktail dress intended for inclusion in a seasonal line relate to a daytime suit also proposed? Designs that stand out negatively are dropped from the line at this point; their samples are later sold off at "sample sales." Once the final components of that season's line are determined, costs are estimated further. A balance is sought. Some designs are more expensive than others to produce, while some are relatively inexpensive. Will enough of both sell such that the producer operates profitably, or will one overly expensive design take too much of the producer's resources? Individual garments are, of course, important, but at this point the issue is how to produce the entire seasonal line cost effectively. Once all garments proposed for the line have been developed, approved, and their costs determined, fabrics, trims, and work orders are generated and issued to third-party vendors such as fabric and trim houses.

Behind the actual production scenes, promoters and others are preparing press packets highlighting features of the new collection to entice the interests of purveyors such as wholesalers and in some cases retailers, those who purchase "direct" from the factory or have "private label" brands the producer is making just for them. In terms of actual garment production, the initial pattern is "graded" from the sample size pattern. **Pattern grading** is the process of increasing or decreasing dimensions of sample patterns to correspond with at least somewhat standardized garment sizes. One common complaint voiced by consumers is that specific sizes do not "translate" from one maker to the next: a size six dress by one maker may feel tight when tried on, whereas one of the same purported size by another producer feels loose. Producing garments in multiple sizes, while necessary for any producer to remain in business, presents a conundrum. Within a style run, consumers expect to pay the same amount for garments no matter their size. Yet, larger-sized garments require more fabric and trim to produce and, in general, are more costly to make as a result. This is another demonstration of the importance of costing procedures.

Production markers are guides used in the actual cutting and sewing of garments. These may be as "high tech" as a computer program or as fundamental (and historic) as those made of heavy cardboard. From these, the pieces of the garment are cut. Cutting may be done by hand, or, most commonly, by a powered "saw" able to cut through many layers of fabric at a time. These pieces are then bundled and sent to sewers and finishers for assembly and preparation for shipment. As you might suspect, at each step along the way, fabric and workmanship is inspected to ensure that quality standards are maintained.

Actual garment production may occur as close by as New York City's Garment District or as far away as the other side of the world. Wherever chosen whether for cost or convenience, **production orders** accompany bundles of cut garment pieces. These orders state conditions and times under which the production facility agrees to operate. Commonly included provisions of these contracts include dates when garments are to be completed and shipped as well as the ability of the design house to inspect finished goods at specific points, such as after the first run or series of garments are produced. In this way, design houses are able to ensure quality control and that the finished goods comply with sample ones that manufacturers may have shown as an indication of the kind of work of which they are capable.

Assuming all goes well, an entire collection awaits at the end of production. But something more remains. The garments must be finished, inspected, pressed, and prepared for shipment, including sewing in the maker's label. From there they are sent on to purveyors, to be, it is hoped purchased by consumers.

Postproduction: Making Ready-to-Wear Ready for Wholesalers

Anyone who has shopped for clothing, or for that matter any other kind of merchandise, has seen them: the series of little black lines on labels and tags. Their presence makes checking out a series of fast-paced "beeps" as they make their way across merchandise scanners. Besides convenience, what other purposes do these fulfill? These are **Universal Product Codes** (UPCs). Below a series of vertical lines, there are ten or twelve numbers; the first six of which identify the seller, or maker of the item. The remaining numbers identify the exact product by numbers assigned to represent styles, colors, and sizes. The lines are "read" as the numbers and the information they contain.

If they have not already been assigned to the garments at some point earlier in the production phase, they are assigned at postproduction. As well as manufacturers, retailers may apply UPC or SKU codes to merchandise, the latter representing "shop keeping unit." With the use of UPC codes, vendors know exactly what "units" of merchandise are selling. Using that information, they may then develop replenishment strategies with manufacturers. Some of these, like JIT, or "just-in-time" methods, keep track of inventory as it is sold (or if it is sold) so that retailers have on hand, as nearly as possible, only merchandise customers want when they want to purchase it.

Postproduction tasks also consist of reviewing items for quality and noting deficiencies. With that information, internal production practices may be changed or other outside contractors considered for use. This is formally referred to as **"quality control"** and is usually evidenced by small stamps, or little pieces of paper with the notation "QC" and the inspector's identifying number or even name. "Traditional" QC is important; however, other forms of quality assurance are notable. **Benchmarking** is a process by which finished merchandise is judged by standards set by other companies. The quality of finished cut-and-sewn apparel and the processes by which it is produced and distributed are often subject to benchmarking in order to produce as good a quality garment as possible as quickly and as cost effectively as possible. Using methods developed by others, garment

This series of numbers identifies the maker and specific product.
(© sdmix/Fotolia)

manufacturers are able to remain competitive. Often, consultants with current knowledge and expertise about benchmarking in particular industries such as textiles and fashion are hired by fashion producers to advise about how to better their merchandise and their production and delivery. **Total quality management** (TQM) refers to the ongoing process of improving the character of merchandise produced, the way in which goods are made and how they are distributed and sold. TQM is a process involving the entire fashion company and its workers who remain vigilant as to implementing it. Consultants are available for this as well.

To be sure, fashion production is a detailed, expensive process. Fashion game players of every category—provider, producer, and others—seek ways to keep costs as low as possible. Whether those costs are related to making, selling, marketing, promoting, or distributing fashion goods, maintaining as low an overhead as possible is one way to "be profitable," as the rules of the fashion game contemplate. However, such measures cannot come at the expense of overall product quality. For success, brands depend a great deal on consistency: the elemental colors that define brands—for example, Nike's "Varsity Red"—must remain constant over time and over successive products made by many different vendors. Postproduction practices related to quality garment manufacture seek to ensure that consistency while maintaining the possibility of profit for the maker.

Many students become interested in fashion because of fashion designers. And why not? Successful designers are celebrities; in many ways they are the most noticeable representatives of the brand or brands bearing their names. But what does it take to go from "upstart" to outstanding as a fashion designer? In a number: twenty-five million dollars. No, not in designer earnings, but in sales volume. As has been noted by fashion industry commentators, such as *Women's Wear Daily*, it is at that sales volume, a brand is on its way to going corporate. Even then, of course, that's no guarantee of success—the road is ragged. Many brands lose money and very few designer businesses ever get to anything close to twenty-five million dollars in sales.

Now, perhaps you see why the idea of the fashion game paradigm and its various rules came about. There had to be some way to bridge a gap. So many think fashion design and designers are just about visual creativity. At the same time, they know fashion is an industry, big business. But there appears to be disconnection about how the two meet. Visual creativity: yes. But that skill, must be "focused" on ways that build fashion brands. For example, design or brand elements that were not popular one season, say a collar or logo style, are usually not repeated for brand building (and profitability) reasons.

Fashion designers sometimes face the mirror-image problem: they want to move on, to try new styles, even though consumers still clamber for them to repeat old ones. Carryovers are these kinds of styles and established fashion brands return them to the racks, just in slightly different fabrics, or new seasonal trend colors over and over. Avant garde fashion designers, feeling the need to move on, to challenge themselves creatively, may want to drop good sellers, perhaps to the financial peril of their brands.

Think about what these differing thoughts really mean: with $25 million in sales, margins (differences between sales earnings and expenses) of 40 percent would leave $10 million after goods are made and shipped. Of that, $6.25 million might go to selling and general administrative expenses and $3 million to hold two glitz fashion shows, leaving the company with a $750,000 profit. But it doesn't stop there! From that profit, expenses would be deducted. These numbers are gleaned from fashion industry source *Women's Wear Daily*. That reference then considers $60 million to be the next threshold number designers should seek to meet! Then designers can expect to receive the attention of private equity firms willing and able to place large sums of money into businesses. They are willing to do so because the designer has established a successful record of sales in an industry in which it's difficult to even get the attention of new consumers. Designer businesses not only have done so by the time they reach this level, but also have a core of clients who return season after season to purchase from the brand. As a result of those two factors, designers at this level have contracts with stores extending for several seasons in the future.

$25 million—then $60 million—then what? How does over $100 million sound? Design businesses at that level are candidates for "going public." You are familiar with that concept from Section 3, "Rules of the Fashion Game." When they do so, design businesses sell shares of stock to the investing public. That can generate revenues with which to fund future growth of the fashion business. As well, it can result in very large paydays for namesake designers. Michael Kors, for example, made over $100 million in personal income from doing so in 2011. Granted, for every Kors there is a "could have been" fashion designer, one whose business fell by the wayside due to the inability to generate sufficient sales revenues to continue.

Section Finale summary

At the fashion show opening this text's first section, you were focused on identifying those in the audience and, perhaps, less on the show itself and what was being presented. Here, however, you had an opportunity to consider the clothes and learn how they made it to the runway. More specifically, you explored how they came into being in the first place. You saw, for example, that the creative nature of fashion design is tempered by practical production considerations. As well, it is driven by the need on the part of fashion businesses to establish and reinforce the identity of their brand. And to be profitable!

Couture clothing for women and bespoke gentlemen's garments are those custom-made for their wearers. The process by which both are made can be painstakingly detailed and painfully expensive. From initial sketch through pattern and sample (or template "toile" garment) to refined, finished piece, couture and bespoke wear produce truly one-of-a-kind articles of clothing for discerning clients.

Most people wear ready-to-wear! Whether costly high-end "designer," reasonably priced middle-market wear, or inexpensive mass-produced clothing, the production processes for most of those garments is remarkably similar:

Preproduction involves originating designs for garments, organizing the making of patterns from which successive items will be made, and coordinating production of samples. These are prototype garments that may be shown to potential wholesale

purchasers or presented in runway presentations. Not all designs make it from designer drawing board or computer to department store racks. Initial garments may be "tweaked" or removed from the line altogether. When final decisions have been made about the number of items that will be in the line and what those garments will be, fabric and trims are purchased for their manufacture and patterns are prepared for production of garments in a range of sizes.

Production of garments may occur "in house" by the fashion company itself. As well, it may happen in contractors' factories. These may be domestically located within the United States, or they may be (and often are) located in foreign countries. Individual garments may be produced in their entirety in outside "shops," or pieces of garments (such as sleeves) may be made by one and assembled in another.

Usually, garments are then "finished" and made ready for delivery. This may be to the design house itself, or to wholesalers or retail vendors, depending on what has been arranged, or on computer-generated "re-orders" of depleted merchandise stocks.

If not otherwise sold and sent, garments awaiting sale move to **postproduction**. This phase involves distributing finished garments to distribution centers where they will await shipment upon receipt of orders from wholesalers or retailers. The subject of distribution and wholesale purveying, selling of fashion, is discussed in the following section.

Review Questions: "What Did You Discover?"

1. Describe the process of producing haute couture garments. What are some of the historic highlights of this process of note?

2. What is draping and how does to compare to other ways of garment production?

3. Identify the stages of the ready-to-wear garment production process and state in general terms what occurs during each.

4. What is meant by the term pattern "grading" and how does it relate to fashion production?

5. What do the initials TQM stand for and how do they relate to fashion production?

6. Define "carryovers" and note how they affect the establishment of a seasonal fashion line.

7. State how rules of the fashion game, such as being a "big brand" affect the fashion production process.

8. What is one way a fashion designer may be judged "successful" according to this section? Do you agree, or might other criteria be used instead, if so, what other means?

9. What are "benchmarks" and how do they impact garment production?

10. What is involved in the postproduction stage of garment manufacture? How are other fashion game players such as wholesale purveyors involved?

Terms to Know

Be sure you know the following terms from this section and can give examples:

Haute couture	Grading	First pattern
Bespoke	Carryovers	First samples
Toiles	Silhouette	Pattern grading
Chambre Syndicale de la Couture Parisienne	Color	Production markers
Ready-to-wear	Texture	Production orders
Sketches	Pattern	Universal Product Codes
Croquis	Lines	Quality control
Draping	Specification sheets	Benchmarking
Patterns	Size runs	Total quality management
	Wholesale prices	

Planning Market Day Products or Services
Presentations

Purpose: This part of the market day simulation project is devoted to explaining **WHAT EXACTLY** you or your group will present. By now you have explored what kind of game player appeals to you, what trends and consumers are relevant, and how you will form a brand. Will that be a product, a service, or some combination of the two? Here's where you bring all the "components" of the previous parts of the text together.

Step One:
What have you or your group determined to be the product/service/or combination of these you would like to present?
This is the idea around which the remainder of this project will be oriented.

Step Two:
Describe generally how you are going to present your idea. Will you create a display of some kind showing it?

Diagram/Sketch of Presentation

Describe in words what visitors to Market Day will encounter when they approach your presentation. Will you have actual samples of your branded idea, for example? Will there be posters, something explaining your brand? Tell us about your presentation!

_____

_____

_____

_____

_____

Section 5 Supplying Fashion Components (Optional Project)
Garment Components Analysis

Purpose: Putting the pieces together in this project means taking them apart! A garment that is. For this project you will need to obtain an article of clothing that you are able to disassemble and evaluate. Ideally, several different kinds of garments should be selected so that their components may be compared and contrasted in class. Follow the instructions on this worksheet to complete.

Method:

Step One:
What is your garment? Identify it and describe its purpose.
Garment: _____
Purpose: _____
_____
When/Where Worn: _____

Step Two: Carefully disassemble the garment using scissors, or threadpullers, or another tool selected by your instructor; isolate its individual components as best you can.

Step Three: Identify as best you can the following components; note of what they are made.
Answer the questions about those items, again, as best as possible. Use your own experience with clothing, or your sensory impressions.

Textile #1: (The one comprising a majority of the garment)

Textile #2: (Linings or other secondary fabric)

Textile #3: (Interfacings, or those giving strength to the garment)

Thread #1:

Thread #2:

Zipper/Fastener #1:

Zipper/Fastener #2:

Trimming #1

Trimming #2

Other:

PURVEYORS:
BRINGING
FASHION TO YOU

FAST FORWARD

Stores—real or virtual—are probably the venues where most people encounter fashion, even where some start to think fashion might be their career. Today, "multichannel" retailing means that fashion professionals must be attuned to how best to use different selling channels to drive sales. Behind interesting storefronts, exciting interiors, and experiential Internet sites, however, very practical, very real concerns exist for retailers. How does any kind of store really work? Here you will come to understand ways successful stores use rules of the fashion game to become "selling machines" through their organization and operation.

This section describes the activities of fashion game **purveyors**. These include **wholesalers, intermediate representatives between producers and retailers**. You will enter their world of markets, marts, trade shows, and "insider" showrooms. But that's not all. **Retailers are another group of purveyors** you will explore in this section. They, and the stores they operate, function as the most visible, accessible ways in which you and others get to know fashion, what it's about, and changes that occur in it. You will find out how and why wholesalers and retailers—those that ultimately bring fashion to you—are part of the fashion game.

WHAT YOU SHOULD KNOW ABOUT THIS SECTION:

- It identifies ways completed fashion items go from producers to wholesale and retail purveyors.
- It describes the basic attributes of "business-to-business" (B2B) fashion selling.
- It notes major centers where wholesale markets are located, their schedules, and how they operate.
- It gives an overview of retail's exciting beginnings and surveys different kinds of stores.
- It explains "business-to-consumer" (B2C) fashion selling by surveying retail store layout.

Fashion Wholesale Distribution

The seasonal line is designed! Hanging in rows, wrapped in plastic are samples, models of garments. Processes have been organized from their production and manufacturing facilities are waiting for orders. There may even be ready-made goods available for delivery as well. Just waiting. If you were a fashion **manufacturer**, or in "rag-trade" language, a **vendor**, how might you get hundreds, potentially even thousands of garments or other items into stores, into the hands of consumers? How would you do so while styles are still timely and freshly reflect current trends? More importantly, how might you accomplish such tasks profitably enough to remain in business? These are the kinds of questions manufacturers—fashion producers, as noted in the previous section—face and must answer throughout the year.

Fashion producers have these concerns. Likewise, **fashion retailers** (about whom you will study in more detail in the following section) have opposite kinds of issues with which they contend: where to find merchandise for their stores? Not just any items, of course, but trend-focused, reasonably well made goods, ones that will arrive when consumers want to purchase them. Many merchandising students imagine careers as fashion store owners or retail buyers. Those in both careers encounter and must know how address these questions. Like manufacturers, they must also work profitably to ensure the ongoing success of their respective businesses. With those concerns in mind, to whom do you think retailers—and manufacturers—might turn?

Intermediaries bring manufacturers and retailers together. In doing so, they provide opportunities for all three to build businesses and prosper. These "middlemen" go by a variety of different names: sales representative (sometimes shortened to "sales reps" or just "reps"), "vendor's representatives," or "manufacturer's representatives." Some work out of their homes, traveling by car to meet with retailers at their stores. Others have elaborate "stores" of their own, known as showrooms. These wholesale selling venues are often found in trade marts or other special areas where other wholesale purveyors may be found as well.

No matter the location, these are the fashion game professionals responsible for presenting and selling perhaps one or even many makers' lines of clothing and accessories to retailers. Very large or highly prestigious manufacturers may have their own "in-house," corporate sales representatives and control their own wholesale operations. Typically, though, producers leave selling to others. That's where showrooms, representatives, marts, and markets come into play. This is the world of fashion wholesale distribution: the selling to and buying from professionals of fashion goods before consumers ever see them.

Fashion Wholesaling

Fashion wholesaling relies on the concept of "business-to-business" selling. Unlike retail selling, where retail stores are open to and sell to general consumers, like you, wholesaling involves one segment of the fashion industry selling to another. There are several approaches fashion wholesaling may take. The "people" and "places" involved distinguish wholesale operations from retailing ones.

Some fashion producers retain control of their wholesale operations, usually by establishing separate business units, or company divisions devoted to that function. These corporate areas are run independently of others and have specific places and people devoted to it. These "places" are showrooms devoted to selling items by that one maker. When fashion production businesses operate their own showrooms, these are referred to as **exclusive corporate showrooms**. There, only merchandise made by that one vendor is offered. Sometimes that may be just one line of goods or many different ones; however, all merchandise is that of the one maker. Sales representatives, the "people," found in such venues represent that one company. To that end, they usually work on a combined salary and commission basis paid by the business. This means that they receive a "base" pay and a percentage of sales they generate. Commission percentages vary, as do whether corporate sales reps are reimbursed for expenses they incur.

Multiline showrooms and sales representatives contrast with their exclusive counterparts. These "places" are where several, even many, noncompeting manufacturer lines may be found. The "people" there are known as multiline sales representatives.

As part of the changing nature of retail buying, stores are effectively delegating wholesale purchases to technology. For example, very large retailers have **automatic replenishment programs**. With these computer programs in place, vendors send merchandise to store accounts as soon as informed store stocks are low. Merchandise items with a high volume of sales are candidates for this type of purchasing.

Business-to-business fashion wholesaling may be done in ways other than those described previously. These specialized methods are typically used to conserve the financial resources of neophyte fashion businesses or to maintain merchandise exclusivity. They may be used, as well, to ensure the availability of quantities of goods, or to produce private-label, store-brand merchandise.

Wholesale showrooms may contain products from several different competing manufacturers. (© Pavel L/Shutterstock)

Corporate selling by fashion producers bypasses representatives and showrooms entirely. Through this approach, manufacturing companies sell directly to their retail accounts. Usually, one or several people make up the corporate sales team. They are employed by the fashion business itself and may be in or near corporate headquarters. Often, especially with very young fashion and accessory businesses, they may be close to production facilities. With corporate selling, manufacturers retain almost total control of the entire process of selling to retailers. They are, however, responsible for all costs such as salaries, sales commissions, overhead, and other expenses. Companies choosing this approach include:

New fashion businesses, as noted, rely on corporate selling. Typically, such businesses are not able to make goods in large enough quantities to make working with intermediary wholesalers cost effective. Mostly, then, such producers engage in corporate selling in order to make careful use of what few financial resources are typically available to "start-ups." An employee or even the designer/business owner performs such selling functions as sending out style books, DVDs, and e-mails with merchandise descriptions and images to prospective accounts. They also consult with interested retail buyers about merchandise availabilities and negotiate item costs and payment terms. In some instances, the new fashion business may be able to produce limited special orders (such as styles in different colors) for individual retailers or expedite shipment of popular styles, due to the one-on-one nature of small-scale corporate selling and production.

In short, through this method, small fashion producers and retailers are better able to communicate mutual needs. Young or small producers can inform retailers whether and to what extent they are able to modify their merchandise to better suit stores' consumers. Since items bear makers' names or brands, not those of the stores carrying them, they are able to grow their own businesses in the process.

Highly exclusive fashion businesses also use corporate selling as the chief means of getting their goods into the (few) retailers allowed to carry their merchandise. Many of these producers are financially able to hire third-party wholesalers, but choose not to engage such services. Fashion businesses using this approach are often high-quality, certainly high-priced, "designer" ready-to-wear and accessory lines. Like new fashion businesses, one person, or perhaps several, has responsibility within the fashion company for selling its merchandise to retailers. As with new fashion businesses, the more interpersonal nature of small-scale corporate selling allows these manufacturers to change styles' specifications and production schedules to better serve retail account needs. As part of negotiating with retailers, exclusive producers selling merchandise on their own may agree to accept custom orders from store clients, because they have the ability to modify production processes. Unlike new fashion businesses, however, which may not have the ability to produce large quantities of merchandise, these businesses may be able to make more items than they do. They use this approach to maintain the exclusive nature of the few goods they offer each fashion season.

Large-scale manufacturers with large retail accounts are candidates for corporate selling as well. "Volume" producers, those manufacturing huge quantities of standardized goods throughout the year, have corporate staff specifically devoted to selling merchandise to large-scale retailers. Typically, these wholesale clients are entire store systems or their divisions. These accounts purchase thousands to tens of thousands of items over the year. These may be staple items (the classic white T-shirt). This is merchandise consumers always expect to be readily and cheaply available in stores when they wish to purchase replacements. Whereas the first two examples of corporate selling at the wholesale level were indicated for businesses that make few garments for small numbers of accounts, these makers routinely devote entire production runs to making the same items. Selling done this way enables makers to plan production well in advance. Retailers, too, benefit from having an established, controlled replenishment merchandise plan: stores remain stocked with salable goods. Without third-party representatives, this method has the further advantage of keeping distribution costs lower than if they were used.

Internal selling occurs when manufacturers produce a large number of customized fashion goods exclusively for one retail account; in this case, third-party vendor representatives are not usually used. Without these middlemen, again, distribution costs remain lower than if they were used. This is, in essence, another form of corporate selling as discussed above, since it is done "in house" as in the other instances. What distinguishes internal selling here is that retailers have a great deal of control over the entire process. Store brand and private-label goods are made to the retailer's specifications and delivered on their schedules. Usually, designers will develop a collection appropriate to the client-retailer's needs. This may be a seasonal line, such as fall or spring garments, or specialty ones such as swim or active wear. These are not replenishment goods, as above, but specialty items for which the store—not the maker—seeks to build its image and grow its business. Merchandise managers, allocators, buyers, and other decision makers edit these selections to determine their "buy" from the particular vendor. Based on that, they then devise plans for how and when goods will be made available to consumers.

Markets and Merchandise!

You began your study of the fashion game at a fashion show. What happens after the show? Now, samples have been prepared and even vast amounts of salable merchandise waits ready. Producers about whom you learned in the previous section now need to take orders for those goods and sell them. For those tasks, many turn to wholesalers once they release their seasonal line. Some makers, as you discovered, have their own in-house selling operations. Most do not. These producers rely on wholesale purveyors and fashion market weeks to sell their merchandise.

The New York fashion markets open selling. Because fashion production and distribution take so much time, what buyers see in shows, showrooms, and markets is seasons ahead of

Some smaller retailers sell products that are a store brand or made to the retailer's specifications. (© vadim kozlovsky/Shutterstock)

Many buyers attend fashion shows to determine what lines to promote. It takes about six months for the products to reach consumers. (© Hill Street Studios/Gifford Sun/Alamy)

its intended selling time. This means that buyers in January are reviewing goods for summer-time delivery to stores. "Back to school," first of fall season, goods are shown in February. In this advance-of-season way, merchandise for delivery around Thanksgiving is shown to buyers in April. Holiday and gift garments and accessories are available in markets by August. In November, before the Thanksgiving holiday, goods for spring store delivery are presented.

After the New York markets, regional markets open. These are in such cities as Los Angeles, Dallas, Chicago, Atlanta, and Miami. As well, there are smaller markets in Denver and Kansas City. Markets may be for virtually all kinds of fashion and home merchandise. Men's wear, children's wear, and bridal dresses are examples of specialized markets. Market weeks, as they are called, are held at **marts**. **These are places of wholesale business not open to the general public**; only to those with the legal ability to resell merchandise and collect sales tax from consumers are permitted to enter.

At these marts, retail buyers from the region, or those who have a particular interest in certain types of goods offered at the market, see products and place orders. Stores such as Dillard's, based in Little Rock, Arkansas, send buyers to the Dallas Apparel Mart and its markets for merchandise such as mid-priced women's wear. Large retailers such as this one, of course, are present at other regional markets as well. Similarly, stores looking for trend-focused, contemporary apparel and accessories visit Los Angeles–based marts and attend markets there.

At these markets, buyers "leave paper," or place orders. This is where contracts and the Uniform Commercial Code come into action. You discovered concepts related to these as part of learning about the fashion game rule "be legal." At markets, buyers write orders for merchandise, noting details in their orders such as item style numbers, colors selected, and sizes. Critical is mention of numbers of merchandise units ordered. Production of high-quantity sales needs extensive planning on the part of manufacturers. As well, high-quantity sales give leverage to retailers to ask for better terms. Showroom staff and vendor representatives are available to assist buyers in preparing orders.

Payment terms are noted in orders. Often, discounts are arranged after negotiation between wholesaler and retail buyer. Percentage discounts such as 8 percent is commonly offered to stores paying for goods by set times, such as receipt at stores. "Chargebacks" are also negotiated. Retailers do not want unsold goods at the end of fashion seasons. Manufacturers do not want such items either, as they cannot be sold "as new" or made up into other garments. However, to attract and keep retail business, some makers will agree to pay back retailers some amount of money—effectively to reimburse them for having bought the goods in the first place—and also agree to accept returns of unsold items. The chargeback approach permits stores to share the risk of buying goods with their producers.

Delivery dates are another important consideration when retailers place orders. Goods received too late are goods likely to remain unsold, requiring unprofitable markdowns. Goods that are available for immediate, or near so, delivery are advantageous for retailers. On the other hand, goods "on the water"—that is, merchandise that will be shipped or is somewhere in transit—may arrive late. Whether wholesalers will discount or accept as returns such goods are terms negotiated between the parties as well. Time, money, and so many details affect the wholesale process.

How Retail Rose to Prominence

Origins of modern fashion retail stretch back to ancient marketplaces, trading bazaars, and small shops. Yet, what most of us would recognize as a "modern" style store, such as a department or specialty store, came about by the mid-eighteen hundreds. The "department store" concept was a then-new way to bring myriad different products and services under one (sometimes very big) roof. Today, vestiges of these first stores survive in the United States and Europe: New York City's "Macy's," begun by R. H. Macy between 1840 and 1850, London's "Harrods" (1849), and Paris's "Au Printemps" (1865) and Galeries Lafayette (1895). What was it that led to the establishment, proliferation, and, indeed, continuation of such retail arenas?

Using concepts from previous text sections, the rise of retail **purveyors** was made possible by successes of other, earlier fashion game players. Innovations by eighteenth- and nineteenth-century **providers** of textile products, had, by the 1800s, made fabrics cheaply and plentifully available. Furthermore, contributions made by the era's **producers** (which advanced sewing and manufacturing technologies) made finished garments equally prevalent and much less costly. Increasing numbers of **consumers**, interested in and able to afford fashion purchases, were influenced by advertisements and other efforts of **promoters** (whom you will discover more about in the following section). Wholesale and retail principles and operations, the work of purveying, or selling goods were well established by the mid-1800s. All of these combined to give fashion retail stores a relevance and importance in post–Industrial Revolution societies.

Identifying Traditional Kinds of Retailers

Sometimes referred to in modern times as the "retail segment" of the fashion industry—the last step between consumers and other fashion game players such as providers and producers—there have been different kinds of stores, operating in different ways, for as long as there have been recounts of them. Referred to now as **retail formats**, their characteristics have changed but little over time.

SMALL STORES

Perhaps the simplest kind of retail establishment of the early era—even still found—was the **mom-and-pop store**. Usually run by a family (hence the name), these offered limited

Personal attention to consumers' needs has historically contributed to retailers' success. (© Everett Collection/ Shutterstock)

selections of general merchandise, everything from chewing gum to household items. Though small in size and scope, these kinds of retailers remain important sources of goods and services sought by communities as well as functioning as informal meeting places.

SPECIALTY STORES

Specialty stores offer focused assortments of merchandise within particular product categories, such as only men's and boys' wear. Ladies' specialty stores were common as well. Both specializations remain popular with today's consumers: "Jos. A. Banks" and "Men's Wearhouse" specialize in men's apparel; "Chico's" and "Ann Taylor," women's.

Early specialty stores were more sophisticated than their small store counterparts. They were run by individuals often acknowledged in their communities for their expertise. In particular, this meant that store owners knew their customers, often personally. With such knowledge, they were able to provide them with appealing fashion items, appropriate in style and price for their lifestyles. This was an example of early **target marketing**, the practice that now largely defines branding practices, as discussed earlier. The scope of influence wielded by early specialty stores might range from neighborhood to citywide and even further. Specialty stores carried **narrow assortments** of merchandise, limited to one or several categories of goods, such as jewelry, housewares, or men's and boy's clothing.

Services offered by specialty stores often included alterations, deliveries, and extension of credit, all intended to enhance consumers' positive experiences with and favorable impressions of the store. In business terms, these contributed to the **goodwill** of such stores, its intangible value to those it served, apart from that of store real estate and physical inventory.

CONTEMPORARY SPECIALTY STORES

Today, specialty stores remain widespread and popular. There are retail venues for highly specific kinds of items such as fashion forward, luxury apparel, maternity clothing, running and yoga wear, or specific lines of cosmetics, to name a few. "A Pea in the Pod," "Expecting the Best," "Foot Locker," and cosmetics brand "LUSH" are examples. One advantage of this format should be familiar within the fashion game paradigm: It enables companies to "build big brands" by highlighting only their branded products. Specialty stores usually have highly visible brand elements such as colors, logos, and slogans that consumers will recognize and to which they will be drawn. Specialty stores keep brands in front of consumers, so that even if they do not purchase items, they will gain salience, or recognition, of the brand.

Additionally, they often offer exclusive products available only in those stores, further adding to brand image and excitement around the brand. "Puma" and "lululemon" active wear are brands that use specialty stores in these ways. Specialty stores typically offer the services of highly trained staffers. Fashion-related items such as cosmetics are a case in point. "Bare Escentuals," a brand of natural mineral color cosmetics, offers its stores' customers personalized instruction about how to best use its neutrally toned products.

Have you stopped to think about what it means to be a "specialty" store, especially to survive as one? Considerable financial expenditures and management expertise are required to open and continue to operate specialty stores. Expenses include where stores are located. Mall owners charge store tenants rents based on

Specialty stores sell specific types of products, such as cosmetics. (© Johner Images/Alamy)

square footage used and percentage of sales earned. Being in a popular mall, though, is no guarantee of success. Specialty stores depend on consumer awareness and interest, how much and what kind of advertising are allocated by its parent company to support it, as well as how well it receives timely deliveries of new, different kinds of merchandise, where stores are located, even where in particular malls or selling venues they are located. Consumers expect specialty stores to be just that: special! When stores offer uninteresting brands and products, are poorly promoted, seem out-of-date, or are inconvenient to find, they are no long so special.

Countless specialty stores have come and gone because of these factors. Managerial cost-cutting decisions based on the expense and maintenance required to run specialty stores have resulted in the shuttering of some. Too, changes in brands and their management have resulted in closures as well. Specialty stores "Ruehl," run by "Abercrombie & Fitch," and "Martin & Osa," operated by "American Eagle," had little appeal among young professionals who wore the latter brand during college. As a result, "Ruehl's" distinctive "townhouse" style stores, modeled after urban brownstone dwellings, were closed when the brand was eliminated. Tangible and intangible factors, past and present, contribute to the success or spell the demise of fashion specialty stores.

DEPARTMENT STORES THEN AND NOW

Specialty stores were and remain popular, as do **department stores**. Traditionally, department stores offer many different kinds of merchandise at an array of prices as well as many services. In retail parlance, they are known as "general merchandisers." First found in commercial centers, such as downtown areas of large towns and cities, retailers such as Macy's opened **flagship stores**. These architecturally imposing, multistoried edifices were thought to be signs of their respective communities' economic "progress" during the nineteenth and early twentieth centuries.

In contrast to specialty stores' narrow range of goods offered for sale, traditional department stores carried **wide assortments** of merchandise. This meant stores stocked with all kinds of goods from the most mundane to the most extraordinary. In some instances, both specialty and department stores could afford to carry **deep assortments** as well. This meant offering either much of just a few, selected types of merchandise (as with Tiffany's and Brooks Brothers), or, to use a phase from an earlier time, "much of a muchness"—a gigantic amount of many kinds of goods. Department stores added to their draw and financial overhead as well by offering amenities and services intended to keep shoppers doing so for as long as possible. Restaurants, luxurious lavatories, theatres, and more skilled services such as watch and then-necessary saddle repair were common features.

Today, department stores are classified into two broad kinds: **full-line department stores** and **limited-line department stores**. The former kind of store offers "hard" lines of merchandise such as housewares, even appliances, in addition to "soft" lines such as clothing and accessories. "Macy's" and "Kohl's" are examples. The latter store format, with such stores as "Saks Fifth Avenue" and "Neiman Marcus," offers upscale clothing and accessories but usually not appliances.

As populations moved to the suburbs after World War II, established department stores opened **branch stores**. These were secondary stores, operating under the same name and senior managerial control as "downtown" flagships. Branches might be found in large shopping malls, or groups of stores. In these venues, they functioned as **anchor stores**. Typically, there were two such stores at opposite ends of a mall: one thought of as an "upscale" retailer; the other, a more budget-conscious one. Radiating from these anchors, other, smaller stores were situated with a park, or other feature, as an attraction. Suburban stores offered shoppers the conveniences of not driving far, not having to find available parking, and not carrying packages any distance.

Suburban stores proved successful, to the detriment of flagships. In all but the very largest metropolitan communities, downtown flagship stores suffered as consumers shopped closer to their homes. Demographically, this practice contributed to entire central business districts languishing, ultimately vanishing in some places. By the 1970s, certainly the early 1980s, after twenty or more years of eroding customer support, many retailers closed once-prominent flagship stores.

The loss of many flagships came to symbolize more systemic problems plaguing the department store concept itself: "old-line" stores were unable to keep up with changed consumer tastes and increased competition. The story of Scarbrough's, formerly located in Austin, Texas, exemplified this trend. An icon among that city's several department stores, Scarbrough's offered a wide (but usually narrow) array of goods. The store offered personalized shopping and other services and further enjoyed much community goodwill. These, however, were not enough to withstand the incredible growth the city experienced on the way to becoming the "Live Music Capital of the World." More and more retailers sought to establish an Austin presence. A downward spiral ensued for Scarbrough's, the store that used to offer everything from mothballs to ball gowns.

"Open-to-buy" money was cut just to keep stores open and meet payroll. This resulted in broken arrays of merchandise remaining, as replenishments were not ordered. The long-time Scarbrough's shopper could no longer depend on it to have expected items. These included "basics," or "replacement" items, such as household supplies, general-interest books, and sewing notions among other goods. Fashion-seeking customers gravitated to specialty stores with trend-focused merchandise, the kind Scarbrough's carried little of. Bargain shoppers, furthermore, gravitated to the large number of discount retailers that had sprung up. No one, it seemed, had a reason to shop at Scarbrough's.

The store's major assets became leases held on substantial amounts of mall space where its two suburban mall stores were located. Dillard's, Inc. acquired the Scarbrough's leases in 1989 and put in stores under its own name. Only a small Scarbrough's women's apparel boutique remained until 2009. Scarbrough's, however, is not lost to history. The dramatic Art Deco black granite façade of the former flagship, sited at the corner of Congress Avenue and SXSW concert venue East Sixth Street, downtown Austin's busiest corner, may be seen still as background in many television commercials, films, and music videos.

Acquisitions, or purchases, as in the Scarbrough's example, and **mergers**, the joining of two or more retailers, were common during the 1980s and 1990s. Why? By then, assets such as leases or buildings were more valuable than the businesses holding them. Selling off assets or combining them was more cost effective than keeping stalwart, but unprofitable stores open. These practices included large-scale, chain store merchandisers as "Woolworth's," now gone from the U.S. market. Today, there are significantly fewer local and regional retailers because of acquisitions, mergers, and consolidations among those remaining.

Getting to Know Basic Retail Practices

Stores of long ago did more than establish the modern retail format. Their business practices remain relevant, even to those selling through then-unimaginable means of the Internet. At their core, these fundamentals echo one fashion game rule: profitability. It seems obvious to say all businesses must earn profits, or economic surpluses beyond expenses, to remain "in business." Yet, how do retailers accomplish that?

Stores rely on **margin**. Simply put, this is the difference between what the store pays for items purchased at wholesale and what remains, financially, after it is sold and store expenses paid. Professional retailer buyers typically seek as low wholesale costs as possible for items purchased for their stores. To those items, they apply initial "markup" percentages (usually they double wholesale cost of items). This difference, or margin, is critical; with what they earn from sales of goods at retail prices, stores earn revenues they can then apply toward "overhead" or selling expenses. Margin also enables stores to "mark down," or "put on sale," slow selling or older items. In addition to margin, sales volume is also necessary for store profitability.

Think of margin as being the means of store profitability and stock turn, the method by which it is achieved. **Stock turn** is the number of times stores sell the same kinds of items to which margin percentages have been applied. Retailers monitor stock turns closely. Some items such as jewelry or furs, those costly for stores to obtain and for which they may have few of, may be projected to "turn" only a few times until the store's inventories of such items are depleted. Other items are expected to turn more frequently, perhaps several hundreds of times a week as with low-cost merchandise. Revenue (gross earnings) obtained through the joint efforts of margin and stock turns is critical to continuing store operations.

"Same store sales" is a term you will encounter frequently related to revenue from sales. This term refers to how much revenue an existing store earned during one week, usually, compared with how that same store performed at the same time in the previous year. Expressed as a percentage, same store sales numbers show whether any given store is performing above, at, or below previous levels.

The Fashion Game in the Retail Environment

Now that you know what kinds of stores were traditionally considered retailers and basically how they function, how do these stores fit into the fashion game? Take a look, floor-by-floor, of a "typical" department store. Notice its layout and features. By doing so, you can gain perspective about how and why the fashion game works. As you know, retail establishments can and do take many forms: some comprise one, two, three, or more levels of selling space, but consider a usual multileveled, mall-based retailer. In this familiar venue, what might you find? Why are certain areas of it designated as they are and why are they important to fashion game players?

THE GREAT SMELLING GROUND FLOOR

Stepping from the mall into a store's ground level, take a deep breath! Smell the fragrances wafting from the cosmetics area. Usually, this department occupies space near what is considered stores' main entrances. Cosmetics, skin care products, color makeup, and fragrances draw shoppers to stores. These are "**destinations**." This means, consumers go out of their way to obtain such products. This is the result of the cosmetics makers, truly, building "big brands" with their target market of consumers.

With such interest and demand created for their products, it should come as no surprise that cosmetics companies tightly control their selling "**doors**," which stores in which markets (geographic areas) they permit to sell their products. Some brands limit the number of retail accounts to one or only a few stores in any place. The ultra luxurious French cosmetic, skin care, and fragrance brand Sisley-Paris is an example. One, perhaps two, stores have that firm's account per city. Other brands are less exclusive. The Estee Lauder and Clinique brands may be found in many different retailers in the same market.

As you recall, the fashion game paradigm includes the provision "be legal." This means working in ways recognized by various laws, such as those pertaining to enforceable agreements or contracts. These documents determine the business relationship cosmetics companies and retailers will have with each other. Often, they contain such terms as which stores in which locations will carry particular brands (often referred to as the number of "doors" out of which the brand sells), how many square feet of counter space will be allocated, and the kinds of support the cosmetics company will provide by way of training sales associates and product return policies. Difficult-to-find brands, stale products, out-of-season colors, lack of trained staff—all these factors result in lost sales and tarnished images for both stores and brands found in them. Because of the importance of such issues, these are spelled out in contracts entered into between stores and cosmetics brands. Sales associates and counter, or department managers, all must be keenly aware of what is expected of them based on these agreements.

OTHER GROUND FLOOR MERCHANDISE

There is much more to be found on the ground floors of department stores. In addition to cosmetics, there are usually seasonal accessories. Scarves, gloves, and knitted caps in winter; sunglasses and hats in summer—these are items shoppers rush in to purchase when the weather changes. Trendy accessories—think of the newest style of purse in the season's hottest color—are also candidates for ground floor store space. Frequently replenished items such as hosiery may be found on ground floor locations, as are frequently misplaced items such as umbrellas. There may also be kiosks holding a variety of different kinds of items: candles, potpourri, trinkets, and jewelry boxes in which to put them. These items may be purchased by the store for resale at ever-decreasing sale prices. These may be "loss leader" items, those the store drastically reduces to entice their purchase and of other more expensive items.

Space in stores, its "real estate," as it is sometimes referred, is expensive to maintain. Utilities, taxes, and other store expenses must be paid. It must, therefore, be profitably used. Recall the "stock turn" concept; it comes into play with not just what items are purchased for stores, but also where they are placed in the store once obtained. Goods placed in ground floor locations have to "turn" frequently, or be moved to different areas, even eliminated from stock.

Ties are generally sold on the ground floors of department stores.
(© Maria Dryfhout/Shutterstock)

The retailer, or "merchant," as they are referred, is giving these items premium, highly visible, highly convenient positions in the store. They must sell well to justify that decision. Retailers often use such measures as "sales per square foot" to determine how profitably productive, or not, store areas are. The different kinds of products available and their assortment both in entire stores and in their individual departments are referred to as a "merchandise mix." That combination is often varied by determinations such as square footage of sales results.

Physical location of stores is important. Not only is it possible to determine potential customer base, it is also possible to get some idea of what those shoppers might want and where to place it based on its geography. A downtown flagship store may offer men's wear, particularly tailored suits and men's furnishings such as ties, on its ground floor. These would be items that would be likely to draw men to the store, seeking them quickly, conveniently during working hours. Cosmetics and replacement items such as hosiery would likely draw working women for the same reasons. Suburban retail stores might move men's wear to an upper floor and place seasonal women's sportswear such as T-shirt tops, shorts, or trendy track suits on the ground floor. Male shoppers, when not working, might have more time to go to upstairs men's wear areas. Women might have more time to linger, peruse, "see what's new," after making replacement purchases of cosmetics or just when passing by the store in their cars. "Know your customer!" By doing so, retailers gain insights into what items to stock, when to have them on hand, how many to provide, and where to place them in their stores.

DESIGN ELEMENTS DEFINE STORES' APPEARANCES

Take a look around the store one more time. Not only is location of stores important, so too is store appearance. You will encounter more about the visual presentation of fashion in subsequent sections. Those will describe merchandising practices such as the visual and practical presentation of items offered for sale. Store design, however, is this focus. Ask yourself about what might be the creative ways stores are planned. How do such elements as colors, interior details, lighting, music, and any number of other factors make stores unique from each other and special to shoppers?

Activities related to store design resolve issues such as those. Usually, teams of different professionals work together to plan stores' visual appearances. These include architects, interior architects, interior designers, engineers, construction contractors, and specialists such as lighting designers, sound technicians, safety, code compliance, and accessibility consultants. Those focusing on store design often work with marketing experts as well to develop exciting concepts consistent with brand image, whether department or specialty stores. Thanks to the efforts of store design specialists and those with whom they work, shopping at "Anthropologie" is a unique, accessible experience—one that is intentionally different from shopping at a store such as "American Apparel." As you will see, visual merchandising contributes to overall store design.

Practicality figures into store design as well. Think of why physical layouts of stores vary so considerably. Certainly, architecture has a lot to do with such decisions. New York City's "Bergdorf Goodman," in an unprecedented move, rechristened that store's entire basement area its "Beauty Level." There, the store allocated considerable space to its assortment of luxury cosmetics brands. Store managers made that decision, because there was no way to expand the existing size of its Fifth Avenue ground floor. As it was, they felt there was inadequate room to showcase appropriately its many brands of high-end cosmetics, jewelry, and accessories. Retailers often have to find creative ways to carve out space for merchandise in basements, nooks, and other unusual and underused areas within stores' existing physical perimeters when there is no other option but to do so.

STORES WITHIN STORES: LEASE DEPARTMENTS

Before taking the escalator upstairs, you might come across several additional areas of note. You might pass both the jewelry and the women's shoe departments. You might see the ground floor entrance to a spa or beauty salon. It might surprise you to know these are operated by companies other than the store.

Many retailers act as landlords, or "lessees," of spaces within their stores, known as "**lease departments**." "Lessors" of these areas provide such goods and amenities as jewelry, watches, shoes, furs, and beauty services. Just as you may pay rent on an apartment, lessors pay rent for occupying store space. Typically, such lessors pay monthly a percentage of sales their areas

Visual merchandising practices impact the impressions consumers have of stores. (© Erik Isakson/Alamy)

achieved. This percentage may vary, increasing or decreasing depending on sales volume. Merchandise found in these areas is not purchased by the store wholesale for subsequent resale to retail consumers. Rather, it is owned by the lessor company. Beauty shop lessors arrange for their own hairstylists, manicure and pedicure specialists, and estheticians.

These companies function almost entirely independently of the stores where they are found. At most, they may engage in cooperative advertising arrangements. In these, both store and lessor pay portions of print promotion costs, featuring both, as you might suspect. Leased departments, as part of their agreements to be in stores, follow operational policies of those retailers. This is almost always the case with respect to keeping the same opening and closing times and following the same credit and return policies. Lease agreements may provide such departments an "opt out," or decline to participate in some store promotional events. Deep "percentage off" discounts offered by stores often clearly exclude leased departments. As you might suspect, leases are another set of rules related to the "be legal" tenet of the fashion game paradigm.

HIGH FASHION HEART OF THE STORE: THE SECOND FLOOR

From the hurly-burly of the ground floor, the ride up the escalator to the second seems to take you to another world entirely. There is more of a hushed atmosphere about this floor. Perhaps the lighting is a bit different, more subdued. The music playing sounds as if it might have been intended for a fashion show. Displays presenting clothes and accessories of the current fashion season enable you to see them better—see how they are made and with what they may be paired. Here, in contrast to the mix of men's and women's fashion items you found as you entered the store are to be found the store's best women's apparel.

As you look around, especially in luxury department stores, you see "big," well-known fashion brand names on signs. This is the area where "Designer Collections" may be found in stores considered fashion forward. You also see those companies' merchandise hanging on racks, sometimes in special niches, even in "mini-stores" devoted just to one brand. Often called "couture," which more correctly refers to handmade, often one-of-a-kind garments, this is the realm of prestigious, "designer" ready-to-wear. Featured brands on this floor might include Akris, Balmain, Blumarine, Calvin Klein, Carven, Chanel, Christian Dior, Chloe, Dolce-Gabbana, Donna Karan, Escada, Eskandar, Fendi, Giorgio Armani, Givenchy, Gucci, Jil Sander, Karl Lagerfeld, Marc Jacobs, Marni, Oscar de la Renta, Pucci, Roberto Cavalli, St. John, Valentino, Yves St. Laurent. Lingerie, especially from luxury makers such as Eres (a division of Chanel) and La Perla, may be found on this floor as well.

Garments from some of these makers will be hanging on store racks throughout the floor. Others, such as those from Chanel and Oscar de la Renta, are tucked into special areas that look like small boutiques. Often, as a condition of carrying lines such as these, the parent company will require stores to "build out" (construct), at store expense, such places and offer only garments, accessories, and perhaps perfumes of that one brand. Each area has the "look" and "feel" of a freestanding boutique; all brand elements—colors, logos—are present. Usually, one sales associate is responsible for coordinating the merchandise in these "stores within stores," for which they receive compensation from the retailer. In fact, most sales associates earn **sales commissions**, that is they are compensated on how much they sell, earning a percentage from every sale made with 8 or 9 percent being examples.

The second floor of mid-market stores might feature less-expensive brands such as Albert Nipon, Ann Klein, Antonio Melani, and their own better-quality private brands. Fur salons, typically licensed departments of the kinds already described, are often found here. Bridal departments might be as well, especially in older stores. One recent trend is to move the bridal department to higher floor locations; typically, brides-to-be bring family and friends when looking at gowns. That requires space to accommodate them.

The second floor, too, is often where retailers host runway fashion shows to promote the store, or a vendor and their products, or to raise money for local charities. Retail purveyors using their stores for the benefit of charities are following another fashion game tenet: "be fair." As you will see later in this section, store restaurants and other hospitality areas are used for this purpose as well. By assisting communities where they are located, a store's attractive restaurant can become the (big) fashion heart of the store.

THE MORE AFFORDABLE THIRD FLOOR

None of this is to say that the third floor will lack fashion sense. Rather, the next floor will often feature secondary lines of established brands such as Marc by Marc Jacobs, See by Chloe, Escada Sport, and St. John Sport, to name a few. These are sometimes called "bridge" lines, meaning that they link consumers to those maker's premium "big name" lines by offering clothing stylistically similar to them but priced more affordably. Usually, there are more such **bridge— or "diffusion,"** to use another name for them—garments produced than signature collection ones. Trina Turk and Tory Burch are two lines that focus on producing trend-focused apparel for this market.

More reasonably priced accessories than those found on the second floor may be placed here. In general, there are fewer standalone boutiques as well. However, in keeping with the fashion game paradigm of building "big brands," signage for bridge lines now almost always includes use of actual logos and emblems rather than store-made "generic" signs. Trendy gifts might be placed here as well as departments featuring yoga and other actual sportswear, such as Nike, Under Armour, or Puma branded apparel.

Each of the many departments you are encountering have at least one and most likely a team of buyers responsible for stocking them. This practice is referred to as, not surprisingly, "department buying." In chain stores, by ways of contrast, buyers focus on "product line buying," or procuring one kind of merchandise only, such as denim jeans.

Third and fourth floors can and do vary in merchandise stocked on them. In general, however, "bridge" lines are often placed near the fashion center of stores; as here, only one floor away. Other classes of apparel such as "real" sportswear, "misses," "juniors" (intended for women in their early twenties), "teen" (for girls around high school age), and "tween" (junior high and late elementary) apparel may be found on either floor.

Men's wear, if not found on the ground floor, may be found on third-floor sites. This is followed in practice by placement on lower store levels such as in basements. Men's apparel is highly unlikely to be found on the second floor. In those stores where it is, it is usually expensive, fashion-forward lines of equal caliber as women's.

Housewares, gift, and wedding registry departments are usually reserved for upper floors. With branding growing ever more important, fashion designers such as Ralph Lauren, Marc Jacobs, Monique Lhuillier, and Kate Spade are extending their fashion brands to include china, pottery, glass, crystal, silverware, and linens. These products require more space for their imaginative display and stocking the many items comprising such lines.

Seasonal decorations such as for holidays are often set out for purchase on upper floors. Registry services also require space for shoppers and store associates to confer and choose products. Depending on the store, only upper floors have available space for such products and activities. Too, departments found in these areas often have fewer stock turns from less sales volume than is experienced in other store areas.

Third and fourth floors may be sites of children's wear, with areas reserved as much for play as for shopping! Space for shoppers to enjoy merchandise of this kind and not feel that they and their families are crowded may only be found on a store's upper levels. Gift wrap, credit services, and administrative offices are often found near these floors.

Usually, on about the third or fourth floor shoppers may find a store restaurant, bistro, or bar. These, too, require great amounts of space for them to be functional and comfortable. They are longstanding features of stores, as early department stores offered hospitality features on site. These function not only to satisfy shoppers, but also to keep them in stores for as long as possible. Retailers such as Nordstrom and Neiman Marcus are known for high-quality food and drink. Their restaurants and bars are, therefore, destinations in their own right for some and sources of catered food and drink for store events.

Store events are noteworthy not only for how they reinforce the brand image of the store and help establish stores as "big brands," but also for other aspects of the fashion game idea as well. Certainly, well-fed shoppers may purchase more, assisting stores to "be profitable." However, there is even more. Recall the fashion game rule: "Be Fair!" Often, stores make hospitality spaces like restaurants available to local charities or groups. Events these organizations sponsor frequently focus on raising awareness and financial support for causes they represent. Hospitals, symphonies, children's issues, health concerns such as "Fight for the Cure" sponsored by the Susan G. Komen Foundation, and many others, hold fundraising lunches and parties in these spaces. Thus, stores help others "be fair," further ethical and sustainable practices, by permitting use of their facilities for such purposes.

In very large, often older stores, furniture may be found on fourth, fifth, and even higher floors. As these items require more space to display, such placement makes sense. These floors often have among the lowest rates of stock turns in the store. As a result, goods found there must command higher prices to make up for their lack of sales volume.

As you ride the escalator down to the ground floor, it is easy to see that department stores are fascinating mixes of merchandise and geography. This mélange varies but some insight into why stores are organized as they are may be found through the fashion game paradigm.

OTHER RETAIL FORMATS

Small stores, specialty stores, and department stores have the longest stories in retail history. Yet, there are other, important retail formats, some of much more modern origin, to consider. Today, there are a great many more consumers, products, and makers than earlier imaginable. Fashion game players have devised innovative venues to address the needs of each:

Boutiques: These are the special of the specialty stores! Usually, these retail establishments feature products of one maker, or highly edited (now called "curated" as with museums or art galleries) selections of a "tastemaker" owner. Louis Vuitton boutiques are an example of the former kind of boutique. In every city, there are examples of the latter, one store to which shoppers are attracted by the creative vision of the owner in selecting the unique fashion or gift, or both kinds of items they sell.

Boutiques can feature expensive, luxurious brands, such as Vuitton, Hermes, or others. On the other hand, they may be approachable, fun venues, offering more affordable

Boutiques sell specialty items, or items devoted to one demographic group. (© Anna Baburkina/Shutterstock)

items. Cost of merchandise offered does not alone denote whether a store might be considered a boutique. Rather, its narrow range of products and sense of personality as well as the feelings invoked by its atmosphere are elements defining boutiques.

An exciting new retailing trend has been for "pop-up" stores. These are small stores, similar to boutiques, often operated by large-scale retailers such as Target. These seem to magically appear in unexpected locales for seemingly indeterminate times and then disappear. Their purpose is to create excitement—keep people talking—and buying! Pop-ups are distinguished from boutiques by such sense of timeliness, not timelessness. In theory, boutiques might exist for as long as possible. Pop-ups are planned to exist for short durations; guessing where and when the next one might spring up—and who will get there first—is part of the excitement.

Catalog stores: About the time early department stores rose to prominence, sellers such as Montgomery Ward and Sears also appeared. These retailers were known for the large catalogs that detailed the products they sold. Their success was due to the wide array of products they sold, most of which were unavailable to mostly rural customers. Importantly, though, for their success were liberal return policies. These effectively reduced the risks inherent in purchasing goods sight unseen. Advancing mail services, especially Rural Free Delivery (RFD), enabled these sellers to get their goods quickly to waiting consumers. Catalogs today have become as specialized in the products they offer as freestanding stores. From luxury retailers to discounters, catalogs are another retail channel fashion game players use to build their brands and gain profitability.

Chain stores: You see them all the time. What do you think distinguishes chain stores? These retailers have two defining characteristics. Think of Walmart, for example. Each of its stores operates under that brand name and is part of a larger, centralized management scheme. These gigantic retail organizations can function as "price makers." They can direct manufacturers to sell merchandise to them at significantly lower wholesale prices, thus lowering the costs to acquire such goods. This practice enables the store to sell items less expensively and still earn profits. Such activities are not without issue. Consumers benefit by paying less for goods under this approach. However, competing retailers, such as local, much smaller stores, are effectively driven out of business. They are unable to offer goods at the same price and remain operative. Likely, it is consumers in particular areas who decide whether they prefer chain store prices and practices or would rather patronize locally owned and operated businesses.

Direct sales: Today, Avon, Mary Kay, Amway, Doncaster, and Worth (no relation to the fashion pioneer, Charles Frederick Worth) are major forces in direct selling. This approach is characterized by its major difference from "ordinary" retail: its sales force is made up of independent agents not hired by stores or even the parent companies. Agents may purchase company products that they then resell (at a profit).

Alternatively, they present "**trunk shows**" of sample garments in their homes. They receive commission compensation on items clients order and purchase. Why do you think this form of selling—now centuries old—is so popular?

Direct selling offers a sense of community, of bringing together those with similar interests. Often, selling agents have extensive lists of contacts, family, and friends who desire to purchase products from someone whom they know and who knows them and their needs. Such personalized ways of selling enables agents to work in culturally aware, sensitive ways. This has helped to spread direct sales businesses throughout much of the world. Most direct sales programs offer agents the ability to earn income not only from their own sales, but also from the sales of agents whom they recruit to the company. This, too, is a defining and unique aspect of direct sales. While requiring sales agents to put up and carry almost all costs and expenses associated with their participation, direct sales offers motivated, well-connected representatives the opportunity to earn substantial incomes.

Reduced-price vendors: Who doesn't love a bargain! Because of that, reduced-price vendors have thrived for over a century. These retailers take many forms and offer many different kinds of products. They share the following characteristics:

Lower prices: These retailers offer fashion goods at prices less than "usual," or less than the manufacturer's suggested retail price (MSRP). Consumers who patronize these stores are likely more cost-conscious than those shopping in full-price stores.

Older products: Prior to every fashion season, makers and stores spend millions of dollars preparing merchandise they hope will sell at or near retail prices. Much of that merchandise makes its way successfully to stores and consumers. Sometimes, though, raw materials from providers arrive late, pushing production times back well into the fashion season. Thus, producers are making goods when they should have already shipped them. Additionally, goods coming from overseas remain in transit ("on the water") or take longer than anticipated to clear customs. These, too, become "late delivered" goods. Reduced-price vendors offer producers and purveyors of fashion items ways to handle quickly dated stock without incurring as deep financial losses as might otherwise result. Being separate businesses, selling to reduced-price vendors protects retailers' brand images while still offering the possibility of earning some degree of profit.

Recall the fashion cycle described in earlier sections. Where items may be considered in that sequence distinguish the following kinds of stores:

"Off-price" stores: These retailers offer goods that are still "in fashion"; that is, they may not appear as dated as those found in regular discounters. Thus, these retailers offer garments, accessories, even cosmetics and fragrances that are just about at peak in the fashion cycle. Shoppers at these stores want styles and items others have adopted and are still seen wearing and are cost-conscious in their purchasing habits.

Discount stores: Fashions that have peaked, even considered to be declining in style currency, are often found in discounters. Usually, consumers of these stores are focused on price, less on following fashion trends. Whereas "off-price" stores may receive current season (but late delivered) fashion goods, discounters may receive items that are one or more fashion seasons old. These are the goods that hung on "regular" store racks for their entire season, gone through successive markdowns, even appeared in store "warehouse," "last call," or "consolidation" sales. While usually shopworn, there are tales of legendary finds of still-wearable garments once costing thousands of dollars selling for only a few at discounters.

Factory outlet stores: From outback to on your back, among the very first factory outlet stores was that of rugged lifestyle retailer L.L. Bean—these stores and their products have grown in popularity over the past twenty or so years. Whereas other reduced-price vendors are separate business entities that purchase goods from other retailers, factory outlet stores are the retail division of a single fashion producer, such as Nike. They may also be the outlet segment of a "full-price" retailer, such as Saks Fifth Avenue. Only goods from that one maker or retailer are featured in these stores. What usually happens is this "branch" of the manufacturing company purchases at some percentage less than wholesale goods made by that one producer or remaining with the parent retail company. They then sell those goods at a price less than their usual retail prices. This means that the "store" pays less for merchandise at wholesale, consumers pay less for it than at retail, but margins remain large. Factory outlet stores are the last step for merchandise in vertically integrated companies. Private brands provide an example. Often retailers such as Saks will plan and produce garments for sale under any of their own store brands. That merchandise will appear first in its full-price stores. Excess items (overstocks), store returns, and those items remaining at the end of the fashion season then are sold to outlets.

Franchise stores: As noted, fashion is a financially risky business. Fashion companies have a great deal at stake just from making products. Their risks increase when they decide to sell their products in their own stores or boutiques. They are then in both the fashion and the real estate businesses! One way fashion companies mitigate risks of engaging in both kinds of enterprise is to permit others to exclusively sell their merchandise. Franchise stores offer opportunities for both fashion companies and astute retailers to benefit by sharing these risks. An entrepreneur (one who is willing and able to assume obligations associated with running businesses) and a fashion company agree that the former will open a store bearing the name of the fashion company and sell its products exclusively. The business person agrees to pay a fee for the right to represent the company. The entrepreneur further agrees to pay a percentage ("royalty") fee to the fashion company for every item sold. The fashion company provides its goods, brand-related media, and other assistance to the entrepreneur. Polo/Ralph Lauren stores were among the first to be operated in this way, beginning in 1971 with its Beverly Hills, California, store. The United Colors of Benetton is another recognized leader in the use of the franchise method with stores carrying its colorful merchandise located throughout the world.

"Big box" and "category killer" stores: Big box stores may be discounters such as Walmart, or even a specialty store. What is of importance is that the physical size of the store is large, often over 200,000 square feet. These stores have been popular, yet that popularity may be waning. Consumer trends indicate that shoppers are seeking stores now with more amenities and fewer confusing masses of products. Category killers, such as many sports apparel stores, offer a great deal of merchandise of one product class in one location. At these, consumers will find entire lines of, say, sportswear made by different producers. Big box, in brief, is a selling format; category "killing" is a merchandising practice. Thus, it is possible for a category killer retailer to operate out of big box stores. "Bed, Bath and Beyond" is one example of a retailer operating in that way.

Television retailers: HSN and QVC, all on the TV! Not to mention other retailers such as Shop at Home and Value Vision Media (ShopNBC)! Home Shopping Network, QVC, and the others are sellers in the sense that they offer goods for sale that they either purchased to mark up or are private-label items made under their aegis, which, too, are sold at retail prices. Each of these vendors airs special "shows" featuring merchandise of one kind, such as casual wear or cosmetics. These are touted by on-air "personalities," television or film performers, or fashion designers. Actress Susan Lucci and designers Koos Van Den Akker and Bob Mackie have promoted their various products and fashions through this media. QVC recently celebrated its twenty-fifth anniversary, confirming it as a popular means of shopping!

Internet retailers: In about a decade, the Internet has come to define the technology-driven and technology-dependent world in which we live. Around 2000, there was much excitement about how this new application of technology would change the rules of commerce. Entrepreneurs began Internet businesses, only to see them "burn through" tremendous amounts of money without earning much, if any, profits. Successful Internet ventures were often sold to larger businesses, sometimes for tremendous sums, seeking entry into the new "e-channel." Whether a failure or a success, these activities served to define, at least initially, how the Internet could operate as an effective channel for business activities. The chief characteristic of everything related to the Internet is constant change. Each year, new technologies appear—new "apps," or (technological) applications—that continue to expand integration of this medium into the lives of consumers. Buying is now a tap or two away for most people with cell phones. "Omni-channel retailing" is a term used to describe the new universe of retail—a place where consumers may gain information, shop, pay bills, enjoy a fashion show video, see visual merchandising displays—the list could go on. Omni-channel retailing includes many different media-driven ways combined with "old world" ways to engage in fashion.

The Internet has made shopping for just about anything at any time highly convenient. Now, it is possible to seek, find, purchase, and receive items within a short time without having to leave home. This is especially true of those sellers that have well-designed selling processes and product distribution facilities. Thus, successful Internet selling requires more than attractive products and websites. A host of fulfillment services, order taking, processing, payment, order filling, shipping, handling returns, not to mention customer service, are required to make the physical experience of buying attractive to consumers. Obtaining these is expensive for new Internet sellers. In addition, they need specialized marketing and placement on portals where consumers will find the "store." Thus, as a medium, the Internet is maturing quickly in terms of what is expected and required for it to function effectively.

There are several implications arising from the Internet. The first, which will be explored in subsequent sections, revolves around consumer privacy. For the Internet to "work" as a selling channel, consumers must leave a great deal of personal information with sellers. That information, from credit card numbers to personal preferences of colors, can be used in ways that protect consumer privacy or in ways that enhance retailers' knowledge of them. Data mining, or statistically reviewing this information, may be done without consumer knowledge. In short, shoppers may not know where or how their personal information goes or is used.

Perhaps the greatest success of the Internet is that it has incorporated social media functions into the shopping/fashion experience. Consumers are now able to contribute thoughts and suggestions to retail and brand professionals and create communities of information and commerce.

Social media has changed how we shop and communicate about products. (© Ivelin Radkov/Shutterstock)

THE MODERN MULTICHANNEL RETAIL WORLD

So far, you have discovered many different kinds of retail formats and explored their operation. From your own experiences as a consumer, you know stores and Internet sellers do not exist independently of each other. In fact, it is likely you enjoy, even expect, to "visit" any retailer now in person, online, or through as many other ways as possible. In short, you are a consumer in the modern multichannel retail world! Multichannel is a term that has recently come about in reference to retail. How might it be defined and its importance underscored?

Multichannel retailing is a way of doing business, a business model, in which retail sellers offer consumers the ability to purchase, learn about, and gain experience of products and services through any combination of the following means: brick-and-mortar stores, Internet sites, direct marketing and selling, or technological/social media. Incorporation of any two of these means logically would define a "multichannel" retailer.

The importance of operating as a "multichannel" retailer may be described in terms of the fashion game theory. Notably, using several different ways to reach and serve consumers is one acknowledged way to "build a big brand" for retailers. It provides retailers with the means of selling to consumers and keeping brands and brand elements in front of them. Part of building brands in this universe is to provide channels and utilize vehicles to reach consumers. Channels permit sales whereas vehicles are promotional techniques. Thus, a brand-building strategy for a retailer considering a multichannel approach might be to have both a freestanding store and an Internet site (channels) for patrons to visit while carrying out direct mail initiatives (vehicles) to inform and interest them in goods and services.

Although multichannel operation is expensive, if successfully organized, it can contribute to great profitability for the retailer. Part of any successful implementation of multichannel retailing would include following applicable laws, operating fairly with respect to consumers' privacy, and sustainably using available resources. Involving traditional and recently innovated selling practices, "multichannel" is a shorthand way of describing the modern world of retailing.

summary
Section Finale

Markets, marts, merchandise, and what goes on related to them summarize this section. This section also explored the vast world of retail stores—what enabled them to come about and thrive, what they were like in earlier times, what they are today, and how the fashion game relates to them.

Review Questions: What Did You Discover?

1. Where does wholesaling fit into the process of bringing fashion items to consumers?

2. Distinguish "markets" and "marts."

3. Where are merchandise marts located and what are some of their specialties?

4. Describe New York fashion week and its purpose.

5. What are "trade shows" and what do they accomplish?

6. What is the purpose of retail buyers and how has technology modified their role in the fashion distribution process?

7. Describe the activities of "sales reps" and where they might be found.

8. What is corporate selling, notably what are its differences with "traditional" wholesaling?

9. Describe the "open-to-buy" concept and note how it can be affected by retail sales.

10. Explain the order negotiation process that occurs between retail buyers and wholesalers.

11. Briefly describe factors giving rise to modern retailing.

12. What are department stores and how do they differ from other kinds of selling venues?

13. Specialty stores offer what kinds of merchandise and provide what kinds of services? Provide examples to support what you note.

14. Describe several issues that can cause specialty stores to fail.

15. What two concepts enable department and other kinds of stores to flourish as profitable businesses?

16. Differentiate between "flagship" and "anchor" department stores by explaining the role of each.

17. What factors contributed to the consolidation of many retail establishments, such as department stores, in the 1980s? Name examples of particular stores and describe what caused them to close.

18. Select a floor or an area of a "typical" department store and analyze what might be found there and give reasons for your answer.

19. Differentiation of stores is now common: there are many types of stores, meeting many consumer needs. Note several and the functions they fulfill.

20. What are "direct sale" merchants and how do they differ from others?

21. Note several media-related ways of selling and describe how they came about and differ.

22. Rules of the fashion game, notably, "Be a Big Brand!" influence retail practices. Note the ways in which rule applies to contemporary retailing. How do the other rules come into play within the context of retail?

Terms to Know

Markets
Marts
Tradeshows
Corporate selling
Sales representatives
Automatic replenishment programs
Open-to-buy
Retail formats
Goodwill
Boutiques
Mom-and-pop stores
Curated merchandise selections
Chain stores
Specialty stores
Branch stores
Catalog stores
Department stores

Mergers and acquisitions
Reduced-price vendors
Margin
Retail consolidation
Trunk shows
Stock turns
Destination brands
Factory outlet stores
Flagship stores
Sales "doors"
Franchise stores
Anchor stores
Lease departments
Category killer stores
Direct sales
Selling commissions
Big box stores

Target marketing
Bridge/diffusion lines
Television retailers
Internet retailers
Narrow/deep/wide assortments
Wholesalers
Retailers
Manufacturer
Vendor
Fashion retailers
Intermediaries
Exclusive corporate showrooms
Multiline showrooms
Internal selling
Full-line department stores
Limited-line department stores

Presenting Market Day Products or Services
Presentations

Purpose: This part of the Market Day Simulation Project asks you to explain **WHO** in your group will be responsible for preparing which aspects of the product/service presentation you described in detail in the previous section. In this project, you will also note **HOW** they will go about their tasks. Are there any items required?

Step One: Now that you know what your project will be about, it is time to determine who will be responsible for what tasks.

Group Member	Tasks

Step Two:
What items might you need to complete your project? Are there any special ones required? Note these: _____

_____

_____

Step Three:
Plan a schedule for completing you market day presentation. You will have a total of four work days.

Day 1	
Day 2	
Day 3	
Day 4	

Section 6: Designing and Manufacturing Fashion (Optional Project)

Styles vs. Types: Know Your Garments, Know Your Fashion!

Purpose: There are many different styles of garments . . . but are there really that many unique *types* of garments? * With this project, you will consider that question as you go about researching fashion's most fundamental aspect: how humans developed the types of garments they did in order to meet their physical, practical, and societal needs. Fashion designers know these . . . do you?

Method: Go through your closet and maybe that of a friend. How are the items you find, different? similar? How are such things as jeans different from skirts, or sweatshirts? Look at images of these items from other countries. Do they wear different types of garments than you?

Garment Type #1

Description

How worn

Garment Type #2

Description

How worn

Garment Type #3

Description

How worn

Conclusion: How many different prototypical garments did you identify? (Hint: there are at least three. How many did you find?)
Adapted from Payne, Winakor, Ferrell-Beck, 1992.

PROMOTERS: MAKING FASHION EXCITING

FAST FORWARD

Editors, bloggers, public relations gurus, visual merchandisers—they and a host of others were in attendance at the first section's fashion show. They are promoters, professionals responsible for supporting the fashion game. They make known to consumers and other professionals what is going on in fashion and fashion retail. Sometimes referred to as fashion's "auxiliary services," these fashion game players generate interest, excitement, and, to be hoped, sales through their varied and many efforts.

WHAT YOU SHOULD KNOW ABOUT THIS SECTION:

- It describes why right now is fashion's "media age."
- It overviews promotional activities—media-based and traditional—so you will know about them.
- It underscores why and how promotional activities are part of the fashion game and follow its rules.

7

Today Is Fashion's Media Age

Ever since development of moveable type and the printing press, some form of media has made known fashion's "latest," "best," and, sometimes, its "worse" developments. Yet, there is something that makes fashion communication different now. Forces in our present times uniquely drive fashion promotion, even how we think of fashion and what is "fashionable." Thanks to technology and the ways that it has advanced and been focused on enhancing interpersonal communication, promotion currently seeks not only to tell and tout, but also to involve, interact with, and build communities of users.

Every recent decade in fashion's development has a unique characteristic. Previously, this text has touched on aspects of these overarching "happenings"—collections of events and occurrences that defined, informed, and ultimately changed fashion's development:

Sideline:

Today, however, something is changing that paradigm. As never before, consumers are influencing fashion promotion, the work of promoters, even fashion itself. Can you think how? Illusion—it still offers much in the way of pleasure when it comes to fashion, yet consumers are becoming ever more empowered by technology and social media to determine what fashion will be for them.

- In the 1970s, the popularity of "designer" products led to greater emphasis being placed on brands, as they became recognized as important business assets to be built and managed carefully into the "big" brands of today.
- The 1980s brought fashion, music, and entertainment together as never before. As a result, many consumers' interest, knowledge, and impressions of fashion are now based on which performer wears what styles and brands.
- Highly specific target marketing by the 1990s became even more necessary to reach defined consumer groups. Value-focused consumers were one group sought after, as were "luxury" and ethnically identified consumers.
- "E-commerce" joined traditional communication channels by the turn of the twenty-first century, making the Internet—and then cell phones—ways consumers could obtain, share, and enjoy fashion, products, and information.

Many people shop online, which is just one way that has expanded how fashion reaches the masses.
(© Brian A Jackson/Shutterstock)

Based on these and your own ideas, how would you characterize what's happening now, what mood prevails related to fashion for these times? The answer is probably close at hand!

Think of your cell phone and how much you use the Internet. Recall how you use these and especially the ever-newer technological capabilities that may be used through them. Today, then:

Communicative "platforms" and services empower consumers with ways to shape fashion knowledge, products, services, and experiences through sharing photos, enabling multiple-party dialogues, establishing virtual communities, and using other technology-enabled means.

Because of the ways in which social media has expanded Internet capabilities and physical means of communication have advanced via cell phones, now is fashion's "media age." These developments have come to define what for many consumers "is" fashion. What do you think?

Based on your experiences, isn't part of your enjoyment of fashion how you acquire it, ways you are informed of its changes, and, particularly, how you may contribute and participate because of it? Do, for example, stores "tweet" you when new things come in, when certain items go on sale, or about special events? Do you then share that information with others? As part of letting others know about the latest fashion news, do you use social media resources such as Myspace or Facebook? With these, you can show—not just a few nearby friends, but the whole world—your purchases and how you have styled and accessorized yourself wearing them. Think how much fashion means to you, is a part of your life, not just because of what you have purchased (likely, that will always be what fashion is about), but because of these capabilities.

These are just a few examples of ways you and other consumers experience fashion through media today. Similarly, retailers, designers, all fashion game players you have encountered, use media. For one, they use it in business-to-business transactions. Internet and social media allow easier and timelier exchanges among them. From your own experiences, you know that these professionals use media to attract, engage, and keep consumers like you. Developing sustained media presence—Internet, e-commerce, social media, and "m," or mobile, commerce—targeted to specific consumers, their needs and desires—all this is now part of building, being, fashion brands. These are now what consumers expect of fashion and those who make it, sell it, and, certainly, promote it. Now, do you have a better idea of what is meant by calling this fashion's media age?

Means to Message: The Essence of Fashion Promotion

Media is the means, the ways in which promoters communicate what they have to say. To say, then, this is fashion's "media age" refers to the fact that now those methods can take on even greater significance at times than what is being said. How much more exciting is it, for example, to follow a fashion designer, personality, brand, store, or event on Facebook, rather than read about any of these in a newspaper? But for all the excitement generated by "how" promoters communicate, "what" they say—their message—is important. How might you classify into broad categories the kinds of messages promoters in the fashion game send, especially to consumers?

Kinds of Promotional Messages

No matter how enticing the language and images used, or through whatever latest technological means, there are three basic kinds of promotional messages:

Vintage fashion advertisement. (© Jeff Morgan/Alamy)

Advertising—Intended to sell a fashion product or service, this form of promotional message is paid for by advertisers. Advertising may promote an individual and the services he or she offers. As well, it may promote businesses and what they stand for. As usually occurs, advertisers allocate monies (sometimes percentages of sales or predetermined sums) to purchase either time, as with radio announcements, or space, as in newspapers and magazines. They may purchase both time and space, as with recurring ads or series of ads. In the Internet age, advertisers may purchase a form of space called "placement" on sites. Most consumers are familiar with what is termed "**promotional advertising**." This form seeks to sell specific fashion-related products or services, such as the latest spring fashions now in stores or cosmetic facial procedures. This contrasts with "**institutional advertising**," which performs such tasks as promoting an organization or event, or just generating good feelings, "goodwill," about an organization. TOMS shoes, for example, frequently runs ads noting its efforts to provide footwear to underprivileged children.

As you can imagine, ads in such publications as *Vogue* are incredibly expensive; several hundreds of thousands of dollars is common for just appearing once and that's in addition to production costs of that ad! As a result, "cooperative" advertisements are those in which at least two or more fashion game players join together to pay for advertisements. A common example of this arrangement occurs when fashion manufacturers and retailers carrying their products share placements costs. Typically, store logos are featured in the ad in such instances. No matter where or how often they appear, advertisements are there for a reason: they were paid to be where they are.

How do great, enticing, even provocative and shocking advertisements come into being? Usually, fashion firms hire agencies to develop the creative concepts that ultimately appear as print and other kinds of ads. This process includes creating images and copy, or written descriptions, that consumers will—hopefully—come to associate with the company or brand. Ad agencies are organized into teams with one or more art directors responsible for the "creative" work. Art directors plan and coordinate the activities of photographers, film editors for television work, illustrators, and copywriters to carry out the work and words used in advertisements. Agencies also "place" ads, whether print, television, or radio, in the media through "media buys," where they purchase (on behalf of clients) space in newspapers, magazines, the Internet, billboards, and, if indicated, television and radio. Media are carefully selected to be those forms most likely experienced by target consumers. Further, where ads appear geographically is another important concern. They have to appear in the specific areas where target-market consumers are located. Ads may "run" any number of times, a detail determined at the purchase of their media space.

Publicity—"Free" is not something anyone hears much of in fashion, but publicity is just that: free. Better yet, it is "freely given," that is, it is voluntary on behalf of media sources that choose to make known information provided to them by others.

Publicity usually starts with a "press release," a written communication, noted "For Immediate Release," or stating a later date for release. Store openings and fashion shows, for example, are highly time sensitive. What good would press releases about either be after such events had occurred? "Press kits," either printed or conveyed through e-mail attachments, are assorted documents detailing such things as biographical or background information, images, and statements, all intended to notify media sources about a person or business. These are sent out by a fashion business, such as a store, to broadcast media where the store is located, nationally, or even internationally. The content of the message may then be transmitted to the viewers or listeners of news reporting agencies, depending on how "newsworthy" it is determined to be. One drawback to publicity is the lack of control persons or businesses have once releases have been sent to media sources. Ultimately, they have no control over how, when, where, or even if information it contains is used.

An example underscores not just publicity but the essence of the fashion game itself and centers on Texas-based Neiman Marcus stores. If you were a retailer far from the fashion capitals of New York and Paris, how might you in previous decades interest others in your store and at the same time build the brand now known as "Neiman Marcus"? Publicity! Using press releases, Stanley Marcus, in charge of the stores for decades, made sure all important mainstream media outlets (and smaller, regional ones, as well), knew about, even anticipated, the arrival of the Neiman Marcus annual Christmas Book. Whether astronomically expensive jewelry, furs, "His and Hers" gifts, or unique inexpensive items, there were many items for the media to report on. One catalog item was a real fashion game: a chocolate Monopoly board!

In the process of garnering publicity, Marcus built what he referred to as the store's "mystique," or what would, today, be called the "DNA" of the Neiman Marcus brand. Even now, news agencies follow the store and continue to recount the store's luxurious merchandise. As occurs with publicity, sometimes these stories are editorialized, or commented upon, to reinforce "Rich Texan" stereotypes, but usually they remain humorous in tone.

Publicity is not limited to how expensive or out of the ordinary something is. Many retailers contribute to, sponsor teams, and otherwise participate in the Susan G. Komen Race for the Cure that occurs annually. Media sources are informed of these worthy efforts

Stores use many tools to generate publicity. (© Pressmaster/Shutterstock)

and mention them, and in doing so, build those stores' own brand image. In fashion's "media age," right now, thanks to Myspace, Facebook, YouTube, Instagram, and Pinterest individuals and groups issue their own publicity via posts to their sites using these social media platforms. By doing so, they may maintain control over content and placement of the publicity message.

Public relations—Sometimes referred to as "PR," this kind of promotional "message" may be just one message or a programmed series of messages, statements, or activities; in other words, public relations is a process. At its core, public relations is about image—building it, explaining it, and, when issues occur, preserving or repairing it. It might be an individual's image (as with a fashion designer), or that of a retailer, manufacturer, or consumer group. In short, PR efforts may be linked to how any fashion game player is represented. Like promotion, it is "free" in the sense that those sending PR messages do not (ordinarily) pay for placement in the media. Rather, they issue written press releases, have spokespeople make oral statements, or both. They may also "run" ads or stage or sponsor events. These may be reported on or transmitted by news agencies and other media sources. Like publicity, control is an issue with public relations efforts. No matter how timely, or well-intentioned, public relations efforts may be modified, even ignored by media and its messages remain unknown.

Advertising, promotion, and public relations form the "kinds" of messages fashion game promoters make. How do they get those messages across? What is in their professional "toolbox"? As you will discover, often they use many different means to carry out advertising, promotional, and PR-focused activities. Building multidimensional, "multichannel" programs is essential to reach targeted consumer and other groups.

Media Resources of Fashion Game Promoters

Previous portions of this section have described now as being fashion's "media age." Furthermore, you have explored the three most basic functions of promotion. Essentially, these have given the backstory of fashion promotion in our times and stated the "whys" of those activities. Now, how do fashion promoters carry out advertising, promotion, and public relations tasks? What is it about the means available to them and the prevalence of their use that has resulted in media being the prevalent force that it is in fashion? Getting an idea of those means and how much consumers have come to rely on them should give further insights.

New Media Define New Times

The Internet and the many resources it offers are now so much a part of our lives that it seems impossible there ever was a time when they were not present. An entire generation of people, perhaps you among them, has never known a world without it! Whereas previously, promoters might think of print advertisements in newspapers and fashion magazines as the primary means of carrying out their activities, now placement on Internet sites is usually their top-of-mind, starting point.

Yet, the Internet is just a first step. Thanks to cellular phones that bring the capabilities of high-powered computers right to hand and the software (information processing programs) that can now be loaded onto them, promoters and consumers are able to keep in constant touch with each other, among themselves, among interested others throughout the world. It seems impossible that fashion aficionados once had to wait to receive a monthly or quarterly magazine before they knew of fashion's latest happenings!

Getting the Message across to a New Generation

In the exciting world of "new" media, basic "platforms" are starting points for most fashion promotional activities; they are the means you are probably most familiar with.

Internet—At present, fashion game players, along with just about everyone, or more precisely, almost two billion people, with something to say, to sell, or wishing to make their presence known, seek an Internet presence. "Sites" are places in cyberspace where they may be reached or reach out to others. As such, they are the Internet's most basic platform for any activity. To be accessed, many people seek placement on search engines such as Google, where those with only a bit of information may still find particular sites. E-mail remains a popular way to obtain and share fashion information for some. Others prefer to "text" or "microblog" and to receive information that way, believing that it is faster and easier than e-mailing.

"Blogs" are forms of Internet sites, often sponsored and maintained by one or several people on any topic. Many retailers feature bloggers. Usually, they have a moderator overseeing comments made by others. "Guest," or featured, bloggers provide additional insight about trends, what's in store, and other topics. Stores gain feedback through e-mails, "tweets," and other new ways of communicating from consumers. What works on fashion blogs? The here-and-now, in-the-moment commentary about what works—and what doesn't work—that's what blogs are about!

There are so many ways in which the Internet is used in fashion . . . where to begin? Besides, within a day, an hour, or even sooner, all might all change! One important aspect of note are "virtual flagships," or online retail stores. Like their brick-and-mortar counterparts, these are the venues where consumers begin their search for products offered by a particular retailer or fashion brand. These usually contain information about the company. By scrolling around, using tabs found on the pages, or entering information in "search boxes," visitors can browse offerings from their computers or phones. From there, however, anything goes with what features Internet sites may contain! From online chat with company representatives to videos of fashion shows to using programs that permit visitors to see on screen how they might look in particular garments and accessories to building entire "wish list" wardrobes, almost anything made possible by technology finds its way onto Internet sites. And when viewers leave? "Cookies" stored by Internet sites on individuals' personal computers record user visits, what they looked at, and what they bought. With that information, stores and other hosts are able to predict future consumer interests and actions based on prior, stored activities when they return.

Are e-commerce sites (as Internet sites based on selling are referred) advertising in nature, promotional (in the sense they provide information), or serving as good PR for how individuals or companies seek to be represented to the world at large? Whatever your answer, Internet and social media provide fashion game players with a means of finding out, quickly and sometimes brutally honestly, what consumers think about their products, brands, and ways of doing business. As such, investments in technology can also be investments in consumer research.

"Social media"—If not a full-fledged Internet site, then would you prefer a "page" on **Myspace** or **Facebook**? Why choose just one? Many use both or even all three! These platforms, too, enable promoters, consumers, and just about everyone visiting these sites to communicate through such features as posting images, "liking" particular items or brands, and offering feedback. **Social commerce** is a growing, but still young trend. It began around 2009 with "f-commerce," or offering goods and services for sale on Facebook. New features on that site will effectively allow users to form "digital scrapbooks," showing others their favorite items, brands, stores, whatever they want.

It remains to be seen, as of 2012, whether Facebook will become another selling venue. However, it seems likely that it and all other social media platforms will remain a source of information and for gauging consumer interest and responding to their concerns—all important considerations for fashion promoters. So much so, promoters now monitor social media discussions to determine what consumers are thinking and saying!

Other social media sources include **Twitter**, which allows for comments to post in real time, creating a conversation-like means of communication through technical means such as cell phones. Using hashtags, (#), users may look for and respond to particular topics. **YouTube**, an online source for music and videos, is also a popular way to share fashion-related events such as shows and cosmetic "how-to" demonstrations. "Streaming videos," in which those events can appear on cell phones and computers, are also popular. These features often appear on Internet sites as icons, with the Facebook blue-blocked, lower-case "f" and the Twitter bird being common. Increasingly, the red-blocked "P," for **Pinterest** appears, as well. This feature allows users to create their own assortment of images—pinboard style—and post them for others to see and "re-pin" on their own boards. **Instagram** with its distinct camera icon now appearing on sites and its "square" image style is another photo-sharing and social media platform with an estimated one hundred million registered users. Owned by Facebook, it allows users to build and share their content. Other social media services at present include **TOUT, Google+**, and **Tumblr**. These and many more appear on sites and have their own.

The world of "apps"—It stands for "application," but, in truth, "app" stands for an important trend for future fashion promotion. "Apps" are software programs users may download to cell phones and computers. From there, they can obtain information, read entire catalogs, and in short, open an entire world of content right in front of them! Like so much technology, "apps" change frequently. Tomorrow, there may be something newer, more exciting, yet more useful. For now, several "apps" are popular enough to mention: RSS feeds, BUMP, and QR codes. From *Women's Wear Daily* comes perhaps the best definition of RSS feeds:

WHAT ARE RSS FEEDS?

RSS stands for "Really Simple Syndication." RSS feeds are a popular method of gathering news and information from a variety of Web sites and presenting them in a single, convenient location, such as a Web browser or a stand-alone application known as a news reader. The daily headlines from WWD.com are now available as RSS news feeds.

HOW DO I USE RSS?

To view RSS feeds, you need an RSS news reader. The reader allows you to collect and display RSS feeds. There are many readers available and most are free. Some popular readers include Google Reader, Feedreader, FeedDemon and My Yahoo!.

Follow the instructions for your particular news reader and paste the URL you selected in the location for the feed to which you wish to subscribe.

The benefits of RSS feeds to users have been described as making "viewing a large number of sites at one time possible." With respect to those offering RSS feeds, its benefits have been described as permitting "new content distributions (to users)."

One up-and-coming "app" is known as BUMP. Two or more users with BUMP technology can do just that with their phones—tap them together and share content such as photos and text. Promoters of fashion and retail brands might note that BUMP (along with so many apps) offers the means by which their messages can go out and reach many, maybe unexpected, people. Fashion promotion today is both exciting and challenging—not just in its messages of new styles, new trends, new brands, and new products, but also in the ways that those developments are communicated. They are trends in their own right!

Consumers today can be described as content aware, information driven, fashion knowledgeable, and seeking maximum convenience. Thanks to social media, what once took consumers hours of looking through different sources can all be done within minutes from one source. For those consumers, of course, this means that they can gain information they seek quickly and easily. For fashion game promoters, it means that they are able to get their messages—advertising, promotion, or public relations focused—across just as easily.

Sometimes near the size and shape of a postage stamp, the series of bar codes and dots provides information with just a snap of a camera. How? Using a smartphone with a camera and a downloaded QR phone "app," consumers can take a picture of any **QR code** and—presto—they are directly connected to online content. Content might include fashion images and information in rich, colorful detail such as entire catalogs. After downloading content, users can save it to these devices. By doing so, they are able to keep fashion information with them and accessible.

Considerations about Fashion and Technology

Fashion is about change. It is about anticipating what is to come, while enjoying the present, exciting ways in which fashion is manifested. In that sense, fashion and technology are ideal companions; both are about, even defined, by change. Yet, both revel in and depend on the here and now for relevance. Otherwise, consumers and fashion game players would feel little desire for new clothing, accessories, cell phones, or downloadable "apps." There is always something new about to come out, ready to make others seem so "five minutes ago."

Fashion magazines are full of advertisements promoting different products. (© picturelibrary/Alamy)

Media-based communication builds a symbiosis, a dual relationship permitting fashion and technology to benefit from each other.

But can we keep up with such fast-paced, large-scale change? For all the excitement that media and fashion generate, they also pose important and perhaps unforeseen issues. Who "owns" content floating around in cyberspace? How much information do consumers really give up about themselves as part of participating in this exciting world? Is it really protection enough to simply ignore unwanted communication? How will cloud technology, which could essentially turn the entire world into one big Wi-Fi zone, affect access by others to someone else's private, personal information?

Effective fashion promotion in the future will require players who know how to use technology in exciting, engaging ways, while also being cognizant of protecting the privacy of the very consumers they seek to reach. Right now, what might be a strategy for incorporating technology into fashion promotion? Following are six considerations for incorporating technology:

1. Use "rich" interactions that are engaging, provide engrossing online content, and allow easy navigation.
2. Use "cookies" for predictive shopping, because such information adds to the consumer shopping experience and scope of services retailers and others are able to provide them.
3. Provide user contribution options; allow consumers to feel that they have a voice in the process.
4. Always pay attention to young people, especially now as they are able to influence others through not only what they purchase, but also their social media abilities.
5. Use media in multifaceted ways that provide optimal, engaging ways for consumers to both learn about fashion, brands, retailers, and companies and also purchase from them.
6. Always maintain security and functionality, as consumers consider these "givens" characteristics without which they will not trust sites enough to return.

Old Media in New Times

New media is fascinating, yet it is not the only media. Traditionally used means of promotion, such as magazines, still remain important generators of fashion interest and sources of information. More and more, "old" and new media are used to form dynamic fashion promotional campaigns.

Magazines—Glossy and great looking, magazines such as *Vogue*, *Harper's Bazaar*, *W*, *Gentleman's Quarterly* (*GQ*), and many others are ones consumers turn to—to turn out well! With these, known as consumer publications, women and men glean fashion's latest trends and how to wear them, incorporate them into their own lives, in their own ways.

Among the most forward of these, for women, is *Paris Vogue*. From France, it unabashedly questions traditionally held ideas of what defines "fashion," gender, and sexual identity while presenting the most extreme style trends. Few other fashion magazines, for example, would put male fashion stylist and party promoter Andre J. on its cover, complete in high heels, full makeup, and beard!

Its U.S. counterpart, *American Vogue,* is less controversial in tone. It presents more wearable fashions as well as showcases aspects of contemporary culture and interesting personalities. *W* maintains a celebrity focus in presenting fashion information; it is the "little sister" to professional's *Women's Wear Daily (WWD)*. These magazines are part of the Condé Nast publishing empire. *Harper's Bazaar* is a Hearst Publications that brings fashion information to American consumers as well. It has long been known for high-quality fashion photography. Many iconic images of fashion, whether from advertisements or editorial features, appeared first in these publications. *Esquire* and *Gentleman's Quarterly (GQ)* seek to make men more fashion aware, better groomed, and savvy to ways of living well. Formerly appearing four times a year, it is now a monthly magazine. It often uses male sports and entertainment celebrities shown dressed in the latest styles to get its fashion messages across.

The list of fashion-focused magazines could go on and on. Fashion game promoters use these publications in two main ways. First, of course, they use them to run advertisements depicting the latest offerings of designers, stores, or others. In addition, promoters make merchandise available to these publications. Often, they loan magazine editors or stylists garments and accessories for use in photo stories or editorial "shoots." These are thematically consistent series of images depicting fashion trends, often shot in exotic locales or just on Manhattan streets. Yet, what good is providing many thousands of dollars of merchandise without acknowledgement? "Editorial credits" for items used in shoots appear below individual photos or at the end of the feature. Is it any surprise that items used in shoots are often the same ones, or made by the same companies, as those appearing in magazines' paid-for advertisements? Advertisements and editorial product placements in magazines build consumer interest in fashion. Although ads are extremely expensive and product loans challenging, magazines are able to reach international, national, or statewide audiences with their fashion messages.

Another kind of magazine is "trade" or professional publications. *Women's Wear Daily (WWD)* is the ultimate fashion "insider" publication. Trend followers may not be so interested in the prices of textile fibers and the latest management shake-ups in fashion firms, but such information forms much of *WWD*'s content. It also extensively covers such issues as retail operational practices, technological developments, and business practices. It cannot resist some gossip, however, and its "Eye" feature includes write-ups describing celebrities and popular culture. These are popular with both readers in the "biz" and general consumers. Fashion game promoters often purchase space in *WWD* as part of "business" or institutional public relations campaigns, such as congratulating other professionals for their achievements or announcing key personnel changes in companies.

Newspapers—This media stalwart is still used by such fashion game players as purveyors—retailers—to announce store openings, closings, and sales. Discounters may run coupons on selected items in newspapers as another example of newspaper use. As with magazines, promoters pay to use this media source with prices varying depending on how wide an audience the paper has (small communities compared with large; metropolitan cities charge less typically), what is considered "preferred" positions within the journal (first section areas that many see and read may be considered such), and how many times the advertisement or promotional message is to run. Newspapers such as the *New York Times* run many fashion-related ads as do those in other large cities. The messages may not last long and even may have to run for days or weeks at a time in order to generate consumer awareness; however, newspapers can reach readers in specific geographic areas fairly quickly. Thus, they comprise one "tool" promoters may use less expensively and often more quickly than magazines. Further, they require less technical infrastructure and maintenance than Internet and other forms of communication. They are still an important means of getting a fashion message across.

Radio and television—Come holiday time, how many advertisements do you encounter on radio and television informing you of sales and special promotions? Cosmetics and fragrance companies often prepare advertisements for national use in both media announcing holiday "gift with purchase" promotions, for example. These are followed by a voiced over announcement at their conclusion informing listeners and viewers the name of the local store where such products may be found. These stores paid for portions of the ad and for running it. When fashion game promoters need to reach a great many consumers in a specific geographic area, quickly, such "spots" can work well. These media forms, like newspapers, are among the available tools fashion game promoters have. How well (or not) they determine that any one means is effective, both in terms of financial cost and scope and the kind of consumers reached, are considerations given when planning multichannel communication programs.

Mailing lists—Printed catalogs, flyers, invitations to special events, credit card applications, and incentive "rewards" cards all depend on mailing lists for their success. Lists are collections of the names and addresses of credit card holders, consumers who left their names at the store while visiting or purchasing, those who attended events in the past, residents living in certain areas, and target consumers meeting sought-after criteria (often as determined from data mining). Success of any of these depends on how well stores, manufacturers, fashion brands, and promotional professionals collect, keep, maintain, and use mailing lists. Careful use of consumer information can result in catalogs and mailers specifically focused on recipient needs. For example, catalogs can be customized for individual consumers based on previous purchases. Retailers may offer through mailers items they would not usually carry in their stores, but they believe would be of interest to consumers nonetheless. These could be specially purchased items, such as loss leaders, inexpensive items that might incentivize consumers to purchase other (suggested) things. They may also be products the store bought in great quantities or bought "exclusively" and found nowhere else. Thus, consumers get bargain or unique items and the store maintains its image, thanks to mailing lists used in conjunction with printed media. Again, all such means of getting a fashion message across to consumers form the tool box available to fashion game promoters.

Sales are the best type of fashion promotion! (© Netfalls - Remy Musser/Shutterstock)

Experiential Forms of Fashion Promotion

Fashion—it's about new trends, feelings, points of view! Social media, print media, and other forms discussed can bring many of these to life—almost! Other kinds of promotion bring fashion to you, inviting and encouraging personal observation, participation, and enjoyment at particular times, in specific physical locations. These are experiential or experience-based promotional tactics. These, too, are among the tools fashion game promoters have at their disposal.

Visual Merchandising

Store windows and presentations of merchandise inside retail establishments are among the first ways many experience fashion. They and others get to see and touch garments and accessories to see what they are really like. Visual merchandisers are those promoters responsible for this fascinating aspect of fashion. **Visual merchandising seeks to promote fashion interest through the skillful, practical ways in which goods are offered for sale to consumers.** This form of fashion promotion is centuries old, one with a colorful, storied past. Rose Bertin, among fashion's first acknowledged tastemakers, presented window displays that appealed to French aristocratic women around the late eighteenth century. Hers were tantalizing displays, showing profusions of silken ribbons, exotic plumes, exquisite little shoes, and other sybaritic appointments with which to entice shoppers into her Paris store. Inside, they found themselves in a gilded, mirrored sanctuary, seemingly not a store, but a world singular, distant from any actual place that might actually exist. Visual merchandising then and now includes establishing an emotional "mood," a tone that defines stores, brands, and products within an appropriate physical setting.

Even after two hundred years, such illusion-based methods of promotion sound familiar and remain attractive. Vintage-inspired Tory Birch clothing and accessories may be found in stores that are designed to place shoppers right in the middle of a chic 1970s lounge with their décor and exciting use of visual merchandising. "Hollister," for that matter, could not be less like Bertin's or Birch's stores! Yet, they attract shoppers into them by suggesting beaches and summer fun with a veranda façade, complete with wicker chairs. Once inside, shoppers are seemingly transported from suburban malls to a far-away beach house, complete with ocean. Thanks to a "window" that projects webcam images of an actual California beach, in real time, shoppers see actual surfing conditions and who's riding the waves. No matter how dissimilar in time,

What type of illusion based promotion is this store promoting? (© liza1979/Shutterstock)

place, or type of merchandise exhibited, the historically significant Bertin and the present-day Birch and Hollister stores captivate through merchandising and harness its powers of excitement and encouragement.

Practically speaking, what is visual merchandising about? What does it include? It involves mounting large displays such as those found in store windows. It also includes planning layouts of store areas and arranging garments and accessories attractively and conveniently on fixtures. Visual merchandising has always been about making goods look good! *The Show Window* was a late nineteenth-century "how-to" magazine devoted to informing merchants how to imaginatively and attractively present goods for sale within the confines of window and small space displays. Published by *The Wizard of Oz* author, L. Frank Baum, its editor-owner until 1902, success of this periodical underscored its necessity. Merchants of the time were on their own in determining how, when, or even why to present merchandise displays. True, many large companies of packaged consumer goods (such as National Biscuit Company, Nabisco, and many others) provided at that time traveling teams to "trim" store windows with their products. For most fashion merchants, however, there were no comparable resources. Whatever merchandise magic they could conjure up on their own out of a spare bolt of cloth and any available props were usually the extent of stores' visual merchandising activities.

The course of "display" into the twentieth century fared slowly for decades. Store owners with small stores continued to work out designs for window and other displays by themselves. Larger department stores employed one or several individuals responsible for their displays. Some stores might be quite creative, while others less so in their displays. Much depended on the talents of those responsible and how many (or how few) resources particular stores allocated to display. One merchandising element almost all stores agreed on in these early days was the importance of holiday-themed window displays, especially Christmas ones. Seasonal presentations such as those became popular, anticipated events in their communities. Christmas windows at Macy's in New York City, for example, still draw crowds to what is, by now, a centuries' old tradition. From these general descriptions of early visual merchandising practices, what do you think remains important today?

Image was in mind with early merchandisers as they went about their work. Some of the earliest pictures of actual store windows depict mounds of merchandise, cascades of fur pelts, and hundreds of men's shirts all in one visual space. The implication: the store had so much stock on hand it could put as much of it as it wished on display and still customers would not walk away empty handed. Over time, that approach became more refined. Stores with a high-fashion image developed a more artistic, "less-is-more" approach to presenting merchandise. One such store was Tiffany & Company. Windows of its Fifth Avenue, New York, store, under design direction of the late Gene Moore, were representative of cool sophistication. Moore is considered by many to have been one of the leading window dressers of the twentieth century, for good reason. Sometimes using only a few props—a broken glass or a bent fork, and breathtaking jewelry—Moore reinforced that store's image of understated elegance for decades in his window designs.

As product-branding practices became more understood and appreciated, visual merchandising became another tool fashion brand promoters had available to them. The window displays of Simon Doonan, for example, did much to further the brand image of Barneys New York as an of-the-moment, trend-focused retailer, one emphasizing humor and style. Visual merchandising became for that store and for so many others, the outward expression of their brand image. In addition, visual merchandising became as well as a budgeted-for, highly planned, coordinated process, one in which merchandisers work with brand managers and others. The days were over of lone "window trimmers" working with little direction and few resources.

The result of these practices was consistent presentation of seasonal and fashion style themes. At any time, the displays of "fast fashion" H&M are virtually identical, whether the store is in New York, Dallas, San Francisco, or anywhere else. Similarly, those of "high-fashion" Salvatore Ferragamo are also identical throughout all stores at the same time. Not only is presentation of merchandise in store windows so thoroughly planned, so, too, are ways it is exhibited in stores.

Merchandising in Stores

Every few weeks, visit an Old Navy or GAP store, especially at some "off" time, such as on an early weekday, and you may see associates pouring over colorfully printed worksheets and pondering how and where to follow the directions these contain. Known as planograms, these are drawings or sometimes actual photographs showing ways in which new merchandise is intended to be presented in stores, every store at the same time. Considered to have originally been developed by Kmart, these instruments ensure the consistency of presentation while, of course, encouraging purchases.

Schematics of this kind direct the placement of clothing and accessories on store fixtures. There is no end to the creative uses furniture and other items have been employed to display merchandise for showing and storage purposes. Chairs, suitcases, wheelbarrows, you name it, it has probably been used. These are special-use fixtures, ones usually employed for some time, then retired as seasons or visual schemes change. "Anthropologie" stores are examples of retail venues making use of unique items as fixtures, such as antique-looking bathtubs and farmhouse-style tables. Racks, rounders, "four-ways," and gondolas are the stalwart, go-to fixtures most commonly used in retail establishments. Some like racks may be freestanding or built into walls. Rounders are racks, but in circular form. Both are capable of holding a great many items. "Four-ways" are fixtures with "arms" extending in as many different directions. These and rounders are not likely to be built into walls and other store structures as racks can be. "Built-ins" are just that: cubicles and boxes that are permanently set into walls. Usually these are intended for folded garments or accessories, but may have removable racks and closing glass doors. Gondolas are evocatively named freestanding shelf and bin units that "float" in store areas where shoppers may walk around them.

From these general descriptions of merchandising fixtures and their various shapes and uses, you can get some idea of the challenges of placing any number of them in physical spaces. Thus, store or department organization and their overall design are other critical aspects of visual merchandising. Store design, like all visual merchandising activities, is keyed to promoting store or brand image. Mass merchants offer jumbles of merchandise, crowded onto racks, set up parallel to each other. Use of signs (sometimes referred to as "signage"), or descriptive, informative cards is minimal; usually noting general merchandise categories as "Women's Active Tops," or "Children's." Boutiques and specialty stores with highly exclusive brand images usually have fewer items displayed for sale (sometimes garments are "in the back," to be bought out on request). However, come sale time, even such specialty retailers as New York's Bergdorf Goodman and Henri Bendel can resemble clothing warehouses with racks everywhere. Whether they are working for exclusive stores or off-price venues such as Ross Dress for Less, visual merchandisers in retail establishments seek to maintain attractive "sight lines" with placement of racks and other fixtures.

What do shoppers see when they scan the length and breadth of a store? Can they find their way to specific sections of interest? Do they see attractive displays or just an exit sign? These are sight-line, or field-of-vision, issues that merchandisers seek to address as they place fixtures and organize the physical layout of stores and departments within them. The actual interior design of stores is planned by licensed or registered commercial interior designers. They have gained sufficient education and experience to be legally permitted to plan interior environments. They must design such spaces not only to be attractive and consistent with store or brand image, but also to comply with a variety of different laws relating to safety and accessibility standards. Senior-level visual merchandisers and professional "contract" interior designers (as they are sometimes referred) work together to establish creative concepts and plan ways to use brand elements such as colors and signage to plan inviting, safe, and profitable store interiors.

Keeping watch over other fixtures and the merchandise they contain as well as of the store itself are mannequins. These are forms—sometimes realistic, other times highly stylized—on which representative merchandise is shown, usually styled with accessories. Mannequins can resemble women, men, and children, and be based on physical measurements and features of actual models. They may also be more abstract, even, as with mannequins for children's wear, almost cartoon-like in proportion and colorization. Again, selection of mannequins relates to store or brand image. Stores projecting a high-fashion image often display merchandise on mannequins that appear to be right off of fashion show runways. Mannequins for such stores as Abercrombie & Fitch are based on highly fit physiques of young men and women. Now lightweight and easily carried by hand, modern mannequins are a far cry from their heavy cast iron predecessors of years ago. They symbolize how far former, less well-organized "display" work has been transformed into professional, planned visual merchandising activities.

Store Openings and Fashion Community Events

Promoters seeking to get consumers into actual stores to experience the atmosphere, get to know the brand, and purchase products have two means to accomplish those goals. **Store openings are, essentially, parties celebrating new selling venues.** These events seek to get store sales off well and build their community and brand images. Many openings feature live musical performances in some way consistent with the brand itself. Billy Reid store openings, for example, usually showcase the work of musicians based in southern states of America, where that fashion brand originates.

Openings can bring many participants into stores, perhaps even converting them into long-standing patrons. They are another tool promoters have available to "get the word" out to consumers. Free publicity from media outlets, as occurred when the Dallas Morning News featured the opening of that city's H&M (Hennes & Mauritz) store (complete with Dallas Cowboy cheerleaders), doesn't hurt either!

Fashion community events involve the coordinated efforts of multiple retailers and other fashion-related businesses for some purpose. Usually benefiting a school,

Editorial stylists ensure photo shoots capture the imagination and sell the clothes. (© JLSC Fashion/Alamy)

charity, or other cause, these events are organized to boost the profiles of the promoter's client stores or other participants. Music, drink, special merchandise, and even discounted prices are lures to get people interested and into the stores involved with the event. As with all such promotional activities, organizers should consider whether the costs and efforts would be justified through realistic numbers of sales. Furthermore, thought should be given as to whether participation furthers the store and brand image. Examples of popular and successful events of this kind include Fashion's Night Out, which occurs throughout the world!

Among the hottest news in fashion promotion in recent times has been the "Fashion's Night Out" community event. The event is, essentially, an "open house" for those retailers that choose to participate to showcase their wares and provide venues for socializing. Usually happening in early September, this event occurs at the beginning of New York Fashion Week.

Personal appearances—These are public receptions of designers, product experts such as makeup artists, style-conscious personalities, and others of interest in fashion. Famous fashion designers such as Oscar de la Renta often make personal appearances in conjunction with their seasonal fashion and "trunk" shows. Rising new designers, too, use this form of experiential promotion to get exposure to potential clients. As well, representatives of famous cosmetics brand tout the latest makeup trends, skin care products, and "pro" techniques in stores carrying those lines of products. Socialites and other personalities are also known to make personal appearances in conjunction with launches of books or products with which they are associated or events sponsored by charities they support.

No matter whom or for what reason, personal appearances bring important people in fashion in contact with consumers. From these events, they gain feedback and perspective. Consumers see personalities "up close," hear them talk about their work, and gain an autograph or two. Often, stores and designers or companies agree to certain numbers of appearances contractually as part of carrying product lines. PR professionals consider using this form of promotion when doing so furthers a designer's or company's brand

Education offers many opportunities to share knowledge and experience about fashion. (© Juice Images254/Alamy)

image. Some designers or others involved with fashion are naturals at meeting the public, getting to know consumers individually, and in the process, selling their products! The late cosmetics entrepreneur Estee Lauder and fashion designer Bill Blass were experts at this form of promotion. Lauder personally performed "makeovers" and Blass fitted gowns on attendees during their personal appearances. Today, those of Stella McCartney and Karl Lagerfeld are likely to become mob scenes, as both are so popular. Other considerations include whether the fashion "star" has the time, energy, and interest in making an appearance as well as whether the event would generate enough in interest or sales to be worth the trouble to mount.

Product launches—Events intended to generate awareness of and excitement over new fashion, cosmetic, fragrance, accessory, and other items fall into this kind of promotion. New fragrances commonly make their presence known through lavish product launches. Usually beginning with an announcement event followed by several press conferences, promoters prepare printed press kits and set up electronic ones to disseminate information as quickly as possible. Enticing free publicity from other media sources and generating word-of-mouth discussion about the launch is highly desirable.

The actual launch may be several events: a series of celebrity-filled parties and "after" parties. Throughout the entire process, the product has its own Internet site featuring streaming party videos. Many of P. Diddy's fragrances were introduced through launches orchestrated by the music fashion mogul himself and featured soundtracks consumers could download. Launches of other fragrances offered consumers opportunities to participate. "Danielle," a fragrance launched by Elizabeth Arden Cosmetics for romance writer Danielle Steel, featured a short story contest with prizes. Music and writing-based features are consistent with images consumers associated with fashion personalities and their brands.

To that end, PR executives considering this form of promotion usually believe that these events further images of excitement, exclusivity, brand characteristics, and other positive associations in consumers' minds. All those while putting on a good party and attracting attention enough to generate sales worthy of the incredible expense necessary to bring them about. As with personal appearances, the success of these events can be furthered by designers and others who are able to promote effectively while appearing to enjoy a good party! Their public persona is also an added consideration. What do people think about the fashion personality involved? Do they even know them? Do they understand the need for the product itself? These are the kinds of questions promoters ask. Some celebrities, for example, are well associated in the minds of consumers with fashion. P. Diddy is one example, and so, too, is Jennifer Lopez, with nineteen fragrances to date associated with her. These great and grand productions are expensive forms of promotion. As a result, it is necessary to have a fashion retailer or business willing and able to pay for appropriate venues, services, and other costs these extravaganzas entail.

Fashion shows—Charles Frederick Worth, an Englishman working as a designer in Paris in the latter days of the nineteenth century, was the first to mount fashion shows. Today, no one would consider bustle skirts (among his signature styles) of great interest, yet in their day, they were fashion news! Long story, short: Worth, as far back as the 1880s, brought about seasonal shows on live models. No matter their history, fashion shows—lavish productions in large public venues or sedate ones occurring in boutiques—remain a promotional staple. Organized shows contrast with **informal modeling** in which models unhurriedly waft around selling departments, even entire stores, showing off garments and accessories to passersby.

Fashion show presentations usually correspond with the arrival of new fashion seasons. In Worth's day, there were two fashion seasons: fall and winter. Today, at last count, there were between four and five, sometimes as many as eight counting "pre-season," fall (usually the "biggest," most profitable fashion season of the year), holiday, resort (or "cruise"), or spring. Promoters use these shows to spark consumers' interest in fashion. It is their chance to see, up close, what designers and other producers will offer. As you experienced already, some shows are big enough, important enough, and exciting enough to bring together fashion game players as well as consumers all at one time.

If you were to design a promotional strategy for a fashion company, what might you use as guidelines for determining success? The following four ideas from a noted fashion promoter serve as such criteria:

1. Impart excitement and urgency to everything you do, whether issuing a press release or hosting an event.
2. Continuously celebrate the company, brand, product, or service involved. Always keep them positively up front in consumers' minds.
3. Link a face to a fashion company, brand, product, or service. People like to feel that they relate to them personally.
4. Always analyze what you are promoting from every angle with the goal of keeping companies, brands, products, or services "fresh"; find something new to tout.

Promotion and the Fashion Game

As you know by now, the first rule of the fashion game is: Be a Big Brand! As you have experienced throughout this section, brand building, whether that of a fashion brand or of a store, informs virtually all aspects of fashion promotion. It is about getting the word out, but in the right, brand-consistent way, and to the right, or target-market consumer. When done correctly, this can be profitable for fashion companies, as it entices and excites consumers enough to get them to purchase fashion goods and services.

As media changes, the concepts of privacy and ownership in fashion promotion give rise to legal and ethical concerns. How might fashion game promoters "be fair" and "be legal"? This section has suggested various issues and their resolutions, which other sections will explore in more detail.

Media-driven means of communication have changed the fashion promotional paradigm. Consumers may now interact easily and quickly with promoters (and with most other fashion game players). They may converse and share with other consumers equally well. This has resulted in fashion promotion becoming a source for dialogue, not just a means to sell products and services.

Section Finale

The rules of the fashion game provide insight into how promoters convey fashion information in these exciting times. This section has covered many details of how they do so. What might be said in conclusion? "New" media has not completely supplanted "old" media. Rather, all are used in varying degrees by promoters. To existing forms of media, such as newspapers, magazines, television, radio, and direct mail, the Internet and social media have added new channels of communication. With it, consumers could do what they always did, "shop around." Not only that, but they could send and receive information to others, becoming fashion promoters themselves.

Review Questions: What Did You Discover?

1. Describe what is meant by "fashion's media age." How did it come about and what does it now involve?

2. Note the various kinds of promotional messages that are used today.

3. What are some of the results of fashion's media age? How have consumers' expectations changed because of it?

4. What are virtual "flagships"? What services do they offer to consumers?

5. What are QR codes and how do they help promote fashion goods and services?

6. What are editorial credits and why are they important to fashion game players?

7. Distinguish between "trade" and "consumer" fashion publications.

8. What is visual merchandising? What does it involve and how does it further promotional messages?

9. What are Plan-o-Grams and how do they assist in visual merchandising?

10. Describe in basic terms how promotional activities further the activities of fashion game players and note the increasing role consumers play in the process.

Terms to Know

Be sure you know the following terms from this section and can give examples:

Advertising
Promotional advertising
Institutional advertising
Publicity
Public relations
Internet
Social media
Myspace
Facebook
Social commerce

Twitter
YouTube
Pinterest
Instagram
TOUT
Google+
Tumblr
Apps
QR code
Magazines

Newspapers
Radio and television
Mailing lists
Visual merchandising
Store openings
Fashion community events
Personal appearances
Product launches
Fashion shows
Informal modeling

Market Day Simulation Project Worksheet
Building Excitement for Your Market Day Project

Project Purpose: Fashion promotion comes to life with this project! How will you attract attention to your presentation? What schedule will you follow? Here, you will plan the media campaign and launch it in Section 9.

Type of Promotion | Week #1 of Campaign (image or example) | Why Used and Goals Sought

Type of Promotion | Week #2 of Campaign (image or example) | Why Used and Goals Sought

Type of Promotion | Week #3 of Campaign (image or example) | Why Used and Goals Sought

Type of Promotion | Week #4 of Campaign (image or example) | Why Used and Goals Sought

Type of Promotion | Week #5 of Campaign (image or example) | Why Used and Goals Sought

Type of Promotion | Week #6 of Campaign (image or example) | Why Used and Goals Sought

Type of Promotion | Market Day (image or example) | Why Used and Goals Sought

Type of Promotion | Afterward Media Follow up (image or example) | Why Used and Goals Sought

What Would You Do as a Fashion Promoter?

Focus: How would you apply what you have learned in this section? How would you promote a fashion product/service if you were hired to do so? In this project, you will explain your process and state reasons for what you would do.

Step 1: Select "generic" fashion products, such as T-shirts or sneakers. What did you choose: _____

Procedures: Describe how you would promote this basic product in ways that will impart its unique characteristics and make it stand out in the marketplace, attract consumers, and make them choose yours over the many others also available.

Who is your target-market consumer you seek for your brand and its products?_____

_____

What is your product's brand you have devised for it?_____

_____

What is the image you seek to be associated with your brand?_____

_____

What brand elements have you chosen to build your brand and its image?_____

_____

What kind of special event or activity do you believe will further both? Describe._____

_____

Where will your branded product be available? (i.e., in what category of retailer will you sell)_____

_____

How will selling through such channel(s) further your brand and its image?_____

_____

If there was one thing you would like your brand to be known for, what would it be?_____

_____

_____

_____

SOLVING FASHION GAME ISSUES

FASHION COMES AT A PRICE.

You know one such "price" is monetary. But are there others? This part of the text explores four challenging concerns, two each section. These are fashion-related issues facing fashion and retail industries, consumers, and even the world itself. Sections in this part of the text note there are no clear answers to the issues raised here. However, perhaps there are concessions fashion game players and consumers might make now, small "gives" that ultimately give back more over time. As for such roles fashion game players might play, it seems likely they will need to find new applications of the four rules detailed throughout this text. Perhaps you might become part of resolving these perplexing issues as the new generation of fashion game player.

SECTION 8: PRODUCTS . . . PRACTICES . . . PROBLEMS

What are some of the "prices" of fashion?

Speaking of the price of fashion, what about the price paid by legitimate companies due to proliferation of **counterfeit**, "fake," fashion products? This section explores the world of counterfeit fashion products and implications arising from their seemingly unstoppable proliferation. As well, what about garment workers who toil in **sweatshops**, under inhumane conditions? Sometimes the price they pay for doing so is their lives. Why have sweatshops continued, now over several centuries? Should consumers now ask about workers and working conditions related to their fashion purchases? This section describes one of fashion's most persistent production issues.

SECTION 9: CONSUMER AND INDUSTRY CONCERNS

What are prices paid by consumers and even by the world because of fashion?

Like to email, text, Tweet, and Facebook what you do and don't like about fashion? Such information may be a boon for fashion game promoters, now able to tailor offerings to just your sense of style, but what price might you and perhaps all of us as consumers pay should the concept of personal **privacy** become meaningless? Do you want *everything* known about you? Why wouldn't such a powerful industry as fashion continue to exist? Put another way: is **fashion sustainable**? With increasing amounts of consumption, what price does the world's environment pay so consumers may have as many of the fashion goods they want, just the way they want them, and when they want them?

How might you go about working to resolve the kinds of issues raised here? You have to be a fashion game player! The next text part describes the world in which you will enter and will give practical steps towards becoming a fashion force.

PRODUCTS, PRACTICES, AND PROBLEMS

FAST FORWARD

The fashion game, as you are discovering, is a fascinating interaction between its players and consumers. Like any other complicated series of processes, issues arise from the very activities that make the fashion game so exciting. This section explores the ready availability of counterfeit, or fake, fashion products. "Big" brands have come about and remain available because consumers continue to accept them. With that acceptance, however, have come incentives for others to exploit reputable sources and consumers alike by making unauthorized products.

Even the simplest garment and accessory items pass through many different workstations to be cut, sewn, and finished. Some workers responsible for performing these tasks enjoy fairly comfortable conditions and environments. Others, however, toil in fear in unsafe confines. This circumstance is not new. Rather, the history of fashion contains countless examples of what are commonly called sweatshops. As well, there are well-known tragedies related to them.

- It establishes the context that gave rise to the problem of counterfeit products.
- It introduces the many terms and phrases used to describe certain kinds of products.
- It suggests how fashion game rules might be used to address problems related to counterfeits.
- It establishes a context for discussing sweatshops and their persistence.
- It employs the familiar fashion game rules to raise awareness of sweatshops and suggest potential solutions.

Fake Fashions: Fault or Circumstance?

This section has a provocative title—one suggesting that someone may be to blame for the great many "fake," or counterfeit, fashion products available today. **Counterfeit products are those bearing legally registered logos, insignias, names, or other identifying characteristics without authorization to do so.** The brand name Nike, for example, is registered with the U.S. government (among others) as a trademark. While permissible for Nike to use that name, or anyone of its own origin, others may not without permission. **Design piracy** is the general term used for such unauthorized uses. The presence, indeed, proliferation, of counterfeit fashion products is one issue acing the fashion game and its players. All are elusive and lack simple resolutions. This section explores this problem and looks to rules of the fashion game for possible answers.

With respect to counterfeit apparel, accessories, cosmetics, and other merchandise, how big is the issue? In 2012, the International Chamber of Commerce estimated that internationally the total value of counterfeit and pirated products goods is around $600 billion dollars. The group, according to one source, estimates that figure to double by 2015! It also reported that seizures of such goods by U.S. law enforcement agencies have increased over twentyfold from a decade ago. There is no question that unauthorized copying is problematic and unacceptable. Yet, to establish context, the practice of legitimate copying has long played a role in fashion's history and its development.

Nineteenth-century dressmakers sought out the newest fashion information from published "gazettes" and "ladies books." Using them, seamstresses and housewives copied the latest styles as closely as they were able so as to produce garments that made them look as though they were dressed by Charles Frederick Worth even though they were far from Paris. In the post–World War II era, before the availability of "designer ready-to-wear," retailers paid for the right to copy French fashion designs. This was the era of seasonally changing skirt lengths and silhouettes from designers such as Christian Dior. Styles were soon outdated and stores had to compete with each other to have current merchandise. Stores would pay a "caution" to fashion houses, a fee guaranteeing return of their handmade couture samples. Once obtained, these models were studied and U.S. domestic manufacturers planned to produce copies at many different price and quality levels. Copying, as in these examples, was benignly intended and (largely) legitimate. Today, some forms of copying remain fairly well accepted, as noted later in this section.

"Good" copies . . . "bad" copies—why are such distinctions important? To the point of this section, what is it about present times that give rise to such huge quantities of unauthorized copies of fashion goods and what may fashion game players do? Is someone at fault for the continued presence of counterfeits, or are they just the unfair results of modern circumstance?

If you can identify this bag's brand name, you can see why counterfeits are likely to continue to exist.
(© olegpetrunchak/Fotolia)

The Context for Counterfeits

Contemporary fashion is about brands. Read any fashion publication, walk through any store, and it's easy to reach that conclusion. Advertisements and in-store boutiques promote brands by their presence and underscore their importance to both fashion and in today's life. This text emphasizes brands and stresses the importance of building "big" ones as necessary for success in the fashion and fashion retail industries.

From Adidas to Zegna and every brand in between, they transform products into shorthand messages, statements proclaiming consumers' real or aspired lifestyles. Advertisements for the Michael Kors brand, for one, depict its ready-to-wear for men and women with "jet-set," celebrity worthy sophistication. Polo/Ralph Lauren "stands for" elegant, casual sportswear. A&F "means" body-conscious (and baring) basics such as jeans. Louis Vuitton is "totally" about recognizable French sophistication as Gucci is "edgy classic." Who wouldn't want to be part of and have a part of these lifestyles? From near-constant exposure and emphasis, is it any wonder consumers avidly desire branded products?

Prices and availability of products are issues fashion professionals address as part of the brand-building process. Brands such as Coach, for example, offer goods at a wide range of prices and make them accessible and available for purchase through their own stores or at many different retailers. Ultra-luxurious leather goods brands such as Valextra offer only a few high-priced products at select vendors. Thus, price and availability become other elements building the image of brands and contributing to their visual statements. Image, price, and availability are all factors making brands appealing to consumers. These elements, however, provide incentives for counterfeits.

Because of perceived desirability, lack of attainability due to astronomical product prices, or limited inventories, or maybe consumers' desires for bargains, branded products are candidates for counterfeiters. These "entrepreneurs" are responsible for making items that appear to be something they are not: legitimate examples of products produced by the recognized companies with which they are associated. Counterfeiters may both make and sell phony, illegitimate items to consumers, or they may sell them through a system of shadowy middlemen. Counterfeit products may be of a quality high enough to fool all but the highly knowledgeable. On the other hand, there are numerous examples of "Channel," "Adidas," or other counterfeited products where quality was of little concern.

Designer clothing can make someone appear more sophisticated. (© Wrangler/Fotolia)

Distinct from counterfeits are **"cabbage"** products. To all appearances, **these seem legitimate, except they are often sold through nonauthorized outlets such as street vendors, on non-brand-sponsored Internet sites, in unexpected shops, or through personal contacts**. Such products may be "real," that is, they come from the same factories, even off the same production lines as those found in authorized retail outlets. However, they were taken out of the chain of production or distribution at some point by people unauthorized to do so. They then clandestinely sell this waylaid merchandise. Outside contractors may make items in numbers greater than ordered by design houses and sell them on their own. This is another way "cabbage" makes its way into the market.

Other product distinctions related to copying are important. When are products "inspired by" **adaptations** of others and when are they "**knockoffs**" of them? Generally speaking, **adaptations are products that are, or appear to be, highly similar to others but have noticeable differences**. Perhaps a trim feature or button styles, for example, are not the same as that on an original. Another example would be when a short-sleeve dress is made with long sleeves. These are but a few of the ways in which fashion adaptations appear. Adaptations may come from the original garment maker as part of developing that brand's product line. They may also come from other makers. These producers may want to take advantage of popular fashion styles by manufacturing them, but with simple changes that might make them more appealing to consumers in their target market. Extreme styles, of the kind first shown in high-fashion couture shows, may be adapted much less expensively for mass appeal, as well.

Knockoffs are near exact copies of fashions or accessories designed, made, or both by others. These are made to appear as exactly like the originals from which they are modeled as possible. Perhaps less-expensive fabric, leather, or leather-like component is used in their construction. The intent was to produce them as much like the real thing as possible. Extremely popular styles of swimwear and underwear, for example, originally offered by such brands as Calvin Klein (CK) are often targets for knockoffs. When made to resemble original CK products, but carry labels identifying it as that of another maker, it more than likely may be considered a knockoff. If those same look-a-like articles are labeled "CK," but are from another maker, they may be considered counterfeit.

Adaptations and knockoffs are commonly occurring activities in the legitimate fashion industry. At present, protection of fashion designs is being considered by the U.S. Senate.

Designer handbags are one of the most popular knockoffs. (© David Grossman/Alamy)

That topic and governmental registration of elements related to fashion and fashion brands in the form of patents, trademarks, and copyrights are current ways of protecting against their wrongful use.

Popularity of Counterfeits

Garments and accessories are not the only products that may be counterfeited. Cosmetics and fragrances as well are subject to imposter products. Which kinds of these do you think would be the most "popular" targets for counterfeits?

According to agency statistics about counterfeit seizures and as reported in *Women's Wear Daily*: "Counterfeit 'Sex and the City' perfume topped the list of seizures by U.S. Customs & Border Protection, which hit $51 million in fiscal 2011. . . . The perfume associated with the popular HBO movie and TV series was the most 'frequently intercepted' (in 2011)." That was the last year for which seizure statistics were available.

Women's Wear Daily further reported: "officials (with U.S. Customs & Border Protection, or CBP) also worked with the (perfume's) right holder to help crack down on illegal imports." Going further, the article stated: "CBP's Intellectual Property Rights 'National Targeting and Analysis Group' in Los Angeles focused on 138 commercial shipments of perfume for possible trademark infringement and 52 of the shipments were seized for infringing on the 'Sex and the City' trademark. The combined seized shipments contained more than 1 million bogus perfume items and were valued domestically at $8 million . . . authentic items selling at retail would have been more than $45 million. Counterfeit perfumes are a form of theft from the brand owner, and protecting American intellectual property is a priority for CBP (according to agency statements). In addition to economic harm, counterfeit perfumes are also often contaminated with unknown chemicals that can cause serious injury."

Protection of Fashion

In Europe, the original designs of fashion items such as clothing and separates garner some legal protection. The European Union, for example, provides protection to them under unregistered design copyright statutes they promulgate. This affords European designers and brands ways to seek redress when their designs are used by others without permission.

Protection of fashion in the United States may occur in several ways. Suppose, for example, you or your company developed a technologically advanced textile for which there was no other kind. Maybe you found a better way of making a cosmetic or skin care product though a process like nothing else available. A way to protect yours or your business's invention would be to obtain a patent for it. Patents are issued by the U.S. Patent and Trademark Office. **Patents** protect what is referred to as intellectual property: the know-how that enabled development of, as here, the textile or way of making the cosmetic. This form of protection, when properly applied for and with receipt of governmental approval in the form of a registered patent number, allows exclusive use of the technology making those products possible. As part of that protection, patents give their owners the right to prohibit others from using the same technology for a period of twenty years. When others use patents without authorization, known as infringement, holders may sue to enjoin, or prevent, them from further use and obtain monetary damages.

Another form of intellectual property includes, to modify legal phraseology, those words, phrases, symbols, or designs, or a combination of them that identify and distinguish one person's or company's products from those of others. To the U.S. Patent and Trademark Office, these are **trademarks**. You know them as brand names, or logos. They may be registered with the U.S. government. When they are, they are further recognized by use of ®. On the other hand, individuals or businesses may simply use™. When registered, however, they receive protection for a period of ten years, renewable thereafter for as long as the trademark remains in use. **Service marks** (SM) identify services and may be registered as well.

The **Lanham (Trademark) Act of 1946** established both registration and protection of goods and services from unauthorized use by others. As with patents, such use is referred to as infringement, either trademark or service mark infringement. The **Trademark Counterfeiting Act of 1984** goes further and provides criminal penalties against those who knowingly make or sell counterfeit goods, those bearing registered trade or service marks without authorization.

Protections described here relate mostly to names and services. What about protection of designs? **Copyrights** protect works of art (drawings and designs), words, images, music, literary works, films, television shows, and even performances. The **Copyright Act of 1976** established such protections, and subsequent amendments to that act over the years have expanded its scope. Unauthorized use of the things noted above may be considered copyright infringement for which injunctive relief is available to the copyright holder. For individuals, copyright protection lasts for seventy years; for businesses, ninety. The **fair use doctrine** allows use of what would otherwise be copyrighted materials for educational and other noncommercial purposes.

Is it possible to protect a fashion design? Currently, the **Innovative Design Protection and Piracy Prevention Act** is making its way through Congress. If passed in the form out of which it passed the U.S. Senate, the act provides: "a copy of a design would have infringed if it was found to be 'substantially identical' to the original work with little or no changes to set the design apart." Penalties for false representation would range from one to ten thousand dollars. In addition to fashion designs, the bill proposes to protect the design of clothing and accessories and eyeglass frames. At present, the status of this legislation remains unclear; however, its introduction by New York Senator Chuck Schumer and progress from committee to full Senate hearing and vote and passage to the U.S. House of Representatives for consideration signals progress toward protection of fashion designs.

Regardless of the outcome, **trade dress protection** may be possible. Currently, the entire appearance of some fashion products, or its packaging, or both may receive protection from infringing, unauthorized use by others. This is, however, limited in scope and claimants have a difficult standard: They must prove that consumers would be substantially confused by the allegedly infringing item, its packaging, or both to prevail. Legal protections of these kinds are available to fashion products as resource for perceived unauthorized use. What might consumers and fashion game players do to preserve brands?

"Real" or "Just Really Good"?

Not all consumers are just looking for bargains by purchasing counterfeits. A great many would like to purchase "real." But think of all the purchasing choices they have! Shoppers can go to stores of all kinds and sizes to find merchandise assortments as well as go on the Internet and visit resale and vintage shops. As careful as some may be, they nevertheless end up with items that are "just really good" copies. From consumers' perspectives, how might they have avoided being duped? Is there anything fashion game players can learn and apply in their practices to help consumers?

When it comes to quality, counterfeit products run the gamut from visibly fake to near-perfect replicas of their authentic counterpart. Counterfeiters, like legitimate producers, avail themselves of technological advances and high-quality components. Knowledge helps consumers discern designer from dreck merchandise, but only a few fashion fanatics have time and energy to devote to getting to know the many details of authentic products. According to a *Wall*

Street Journal article (Holmes, Elizabeth. The Finer Art of Faking It. *Wall Street Journal*, June 30, 2011), there are five things consumers can do so they "Don't Get Fooled":

1. Buy directly from the brand, in their stores and boutiques.
2. Find a company-authorized retailer selling the brand.
3. Check authenticity policies when buying secondhand. Does the seller guarantee (i.e., take back) should the item prove to be counterfeit?
4. Be wary of discounts. Top luxury brands don't discount heavily, if at all.
5. Take a good look at websites when purchasing online. Do they seem valid? It is estimated that 60 percent of counterfeit goods seized in 2010, for example, were from China. That percentage was up 18 percent according to government statistics because of increased use of mail to fulfill Internet sales orders. Chinese sites found selling counterfeit goods have had spelling, grammatical, and incorrect language-use and syntactical errors, indications that they are not sources for authentic brands.

From these points, it seems that brands have (another) big job: finding ways to educate consumers about their products and to ascertain whether they have obtained them. Other measures include adding serial numbers, holographic identification tags, and hidden means of authentication. Each of these is currently used to denote authentic products. As noted in previous sections, Blackglama brand furs have security numbers in their labels, visible only when exposed to certain wavelengths of light—from lamps found only at authorized retailers! Sales associates at brand-sponsored stores, as well, have been trained, or have learned, to assist consumers in telling authentic from ersatz products. Rules of the fashion game offer other insights about counterfeits and how their impacts may be minimized.

Finding Solutions Using Fashion Game Rules

This section's discussion about counterfeits should have brought to mind the four rules of the fashion game. The inherent dishonest nature of counterfeiting, for example, should have triggered thoughts about ways in which its tenet "Be Fair!" applies to and is circumvented by its practice. How might the interplay of fashion game rules and the issue of counterfeiting be more clearly delineated? Excerpts from federal sources related to cases that the government successfully intercepted spells out how counterfeiting is one of the dark issues contemplated by rules of the fashion game. Addressing the counterfeit issue, attempting to find solutions to its practice and presence, will likely require fashion game players to incorporate ever-more sophisticated business practices and consumer communication programs within the framework of these rules.

BE PROFITABLE!

Establishing and operating businesses requires incredible financial expenditures. Protecting going concerns is costly, too. Developing a profitable business model, one capable of generating dependable revenues and delivering discernible profits, includes finding ways to protect patents, trademarks, and brand identities. These are in addition to putting into place facility and personnel safeguards.

Essentially, the practice of counterfeiting (as with other fashion game issues addressed in this part of the text), requires fashion game players to act defensively, to plan for piracy and find ways to protect investments in intellectual property. Auditing outside manufacturing contractors, maintaining transparent supply and distribution chains through oversight and evaluation, monitoring retail practices at points of sales, and maintaining vigilant watch for any kind of suspicious, unexpected activities are all suggested bases for defensive plans. Such plans require budgeted

This load of counterfeit products is a serious problem for the legitimate fashion industry. (© Moreno Soppelsa/Shutterstock)

expenditures of company assets. Whether ultimately successful or not, costly protective measures nonetheless affect profitability.

BE A (BIG) BRAND!

Establishing big brands is important. Companies do, indeed, "go to great lengths" to do so. This text and this section have stressed that brands are able to become "big" because of consumers. It is they who accept or reject brands as they do changes in fashion styles. Considering the power of brands and the power of consumers, might the two work together to combat counterfeiting? Could, for example, brands stress in advertisements and through social media that consumers be on the lookout for counterfeits of their products and, when found, alert brand managers? Consumers might be incentivized to do so with "rewards" of branded products. Consumers clearly want to participate with brands they like. They desire, even demand, input into the development process of branded items. They follow favorite brands on social media as entertainment. Is consumer involvement the only solution? Probably not. Many brands are simply too huge to fully implement such a plan. There will always be consumers who value bargains over brands as well and have no problem purchasing unauthorized products. However, gaining consumer participation may be but one of many ways brands use for their protection.

Do consumers really need to be told that counterfeits are "bad"? Might they figure that out for themselves and feel differently for not having purchased the real thing? All but near-perfect counterfeits, or products "cabbaged" from authorized makers, have quality issues. Certainly cheaply made, low-end goods may not last through a fashion season before disintegrating. High-end ones resembling products of luxury brands may fair better, but ultimately do not last as well as originals. Over the time it takes for these issues to arise and as their cheapness becomes obvious to owner and observer alike, other feelings set in. The euphoria of having obtained a bargain is replaced, some commentators have suggested, by feelings of guilt and remorse. Those same sources have noted that these feelings soon take the form of even greater desire for authentic branded products. Do counterfeits actually help sell the real brands? It remains to be seen. There can be no denying that purchases of counterfeit goods do deprive holders of rights to them of financial return. Also true: consumers are likely getting inferior products but not necessarily at inferior prices. Would ever-more vigilance on the part of brand managers to spot counterfeits and greater reliance on legal means to protect them be one course of action? Might those steps be coupled with introduction of ever-newer, even more exotic looking, obviously more expensive products, always dangled in front of consumers to keep them wanting only the authentic ones? Brands (and their production and promotions budgets) will have to find answers to the counterfeit problem within parameters such as these. As a future fashion game player, could you?

BE FAIR!

This tenet reiterates the inherent unfairness caused by counterfeits: consumer confusion, loss of profits, even lack of safety to name just a few issues. Again, might consumers themselves be called on to "be fair" as part of the brand-building plan? In this instance, They can be asked to be "fair" to the brands they purport to like so much and to themselves, as their choices may affect them and their possible safety when they do not purchase authorized, branded products. To be sure, communicating such messages to consumers poses challenges to brand managers. However, brands have proven that they can be powerful platforms for social justice and for environmental change. These are the kinds of fairness concerns that brands have raised awareness about, ask consumers to address, and contribute financially to support their resolution. They have motivated consumers to action. Maybe brands can next turn attention on simply making consumers more aware of problems—and dangers—caused by counterfeits.

BE LEGAL!

To be legal means to be aware of which laws affect businesses and how they do so. Obvious examples of this have been explored in this text. Laws related to the formation of business enterprises and conducting commercial transactions are two such examples. With respect to "being legal" when it comes to counterfeits, how could anyone—other than a legal professional—know all the many federal and state statutes related to protecting intellectual property, including brands? Fashion game players are not legal professionals to be sure. They can, however, know which law enforcement agencies are charged with protecting national and international brands and the assets of companies that own them. The above passage notes how many agencies are involved and how they interact with each other and the court system to bring about enforcement. Fashion is about keeping current. Fashion game players are well-versed in popular style trends and their sources. Using similar ways of thinking, they may be increasingly called on to be knowledgeable about current law enforcement techniques (such as where to notify about possible violations). As well, they are asked to understand which agencies are responsible for enforcement of possible violations and assist them in their actions.

Persistence of Sweatshops

Discussions of sweatshops and the oppressive working conditions they represent often begin with mention of the Triangle Shirtwaist Factory fire of 1911. It is thought that 146 workers, most of them young women, died when fire swept through the locked factory in which they worked. However, conversations could just as easily start with recounts of the November 2012 Bangladesh factory fire. In it, 112 to 115 people were killed under circumstances highly similar to those at the Triangle factory. As this text goes to press, news reports indicate that floor after floor of an

Fashion industries must be aware of the laws that affect business. (© Kuzma/Shutterstock)

Humanizing repetitive labor of the kind found in factories remains a challenge for fashion game players. (© CROSS DESIGN/Fotolia)

overcrowded Bangladeshi garment factory collapsed onto each other, killing at least three hundred people. Both are examples of current sweatshop disasters tragically repeating history.

Most descriptions of sweatshops also include the 1996 scandal involving television announcer Kathie Lee Gifford. In that incident, the **Institute for Global Labour and Human Rights** disclosed that garments she endorsed for retail giant Walmart were produced in Central American sweatshops. However, sweatshops' seeming persistence in garment production could just as easily implicate the Kardashian sisters: Khloe, Kim, Kourtney, as well as their mother Kris Jenner. In 2012, approximately seventeen years later, that same labor group disclosed that fashion items made for the K-Dash and Kris Jenner Kollection brands were produced in Chinese sweatshops.

Representing over one hundred years of fashion trends from Gibson Girl garb, as shirtwaists once were, to vinyl motorcycle jackets for those "keeping up with" styles offered by television's famous family, from New York City's Garment District to anonymous factories in countries far away, the presence of sweatshops remains a stubborn fashion game issue. Rules of the fashion game provide insights into what is being done to address them. How might you, as a student or future fashion game player, work with those rules in mind to end sweatshops?

What Are Sweatshops?

Your efforts might begin by understanding what constitutes sweatshops. For that, there are several perspectives to consider. The International Labor Rights Fund describes **sweatshops** as "work environments that include some of the following characteristics: pay is less than a living wage; excessively long hours of work are required often without overtime pay; work is done in unsafe or inhumane conditions; and workers are systematically abused by the employer or suffer from sexual harassment, and/or workers have no ability to organize to negotiate better terms of work." From a domestic viewpoint, sweatshops have been defined by the General Accounting Office, a U.S. governmental agency, to be "an employer that violates two or more federal or state labor, occupational safety and health, workers' compensation, or other laws regulating an industry." Together, these two descriptions make clear that sweatshops are places of hardship and oppression for their workers.

Adding to Sweatshop Definitions

These descriptions do not convey the hidden nature of sweatshops. For all the definitions defining them, duplicity hides them. Were it possible to see the Triangle factory, open and obvious in New York City as it was, its appearance might give pause when viewed from today's perspectives. However, modern sweatshops are usually not as apparent, or as public. Typically, they exist in places such as Bangladesh, Mexico, Central and South America, and many parts of Asia, far from consumers in the predominately Western nations who wear their products. They are becoming even more difficult to find, as their locations can change frequently from one hidden spot to another. It is not uncommon for unpaid foreign workers to arrive at what they thought were legitimate garment factories only to find the entire facility—equipment, work-in-progress, everything—moved in the night, leaving them penniless.

Sweatshops are still present in the United States. They continue to be found in or near port cities, for example. Easy transport in of raw materials and convenient access to transportation for finished goods makes ports such as New York and Los Angeles amenable to sweatshops. Availability of labor is another factor. Domestic sweatshops have been found to include unassimilated, marginally literate, economically disadvantaged, and legally compromised workers; those with little knowledge, means, or abilities to realistically pursue recourse when exploited.

Like foreign sweatshops, domestic ones are not readily apparent. Infamous U.S. sweatshops in modern times, such as those discovered in the 1990s in and near Los Angeles, California, were hidden, "disguised" as such innocuous places as apartment buildings. The furtive nature of sweatshops makes them difficult to locate wherever located. Their continuing and clandestine nature gives rise to a question: How did sweatshops come about? What is it about their beginnings that contribute to their places of modern-day oppression?

Rise of Sweatshops

Earlier text sections detailed contemporary fashion production processes. The issue of sweatshops (and, as previously noted, design piracy) arose as production's earlier, highly sequential, and mostly U.S. domestic nature transformed into a series of international sourcing steps. While coordinated for efficiency, flaws exist when production or portions of it are contracted out to others outside the company. Such fragmented supply chains, it has been noted, furthered the advent of counterfeit goods. As well, the mosaic of different contractors and subcontractors involved in garment construction under the sourcing system makes it possible for sweatshops to take hold.

For decades, the U.S. textile and fashion manufacturing industries were preeminent in the world. As late as the 1970s, raw materials and finished garments produced domestically were plentiful, usually of high quality and economically feasible to make and sell. European and Asian countries produced not only specialty fibers such as silk and cashmere, but also well-made fashion items. These, however, were usually available in small quantities and at high prices. Scottish cashmere sweaters of the 1950s, such as the decade's famous "twin set," were true luxury items. On the other hand, Carolina textile mills and New York "dress houses" located on Seventh Avenue, to say nothing of regional makers, filled stores with volumes of merchandise of many different varieties and plentiful assortments. Consumers could have domestic fashion goods at whatever quality and price level they were willing to tolerate and pay.

To be sure, conditions were not perfect for workers in domestic textile mills, dress manufacturers, and some retail stores. The 1979 film *Norma Rae* dramatized actual events related to unionization of the J.P. Stevens textile mills in North Carolina. Conditions depicted in the movie mirrored longstanding true-to-life ones. Those included loud, hot manufacturing plants, long hours, lack of medical care, and any real ability on the part of workers to unionize.

Mills and plants were known to forcefully resist workers' efforts to form groups for the purpose of bargaining for better working conditions, wages, and benefits. Unions gave their worker members "voice," the ability to negotiate with mill and plant owners and managers over such issues. Working conditions and wages were concerns causing garment workers to unionize around 1900. By 1976, individual textile and garment unions joined forces to form the Amalgamated Clothing and Textile Workers Union. As of 1995, that union joined with the International Ladies' Garment Workers Union to form the present-day **Union of Needletrades, Industrial and Textile Employees** (UNITE).

Finally, sales associates in Woolworth's and a great many community department stores were often poorly paid for their work. These factors are important, as together they describe conditions that workers faced. It would be conditions that mills' and factories' fashion game providers and producers faced, however, that would change the nature of domestic textile and fashion production and would aid in the development of sweatshops.

By the end of the 1970s, imports were prevalent in the U.S. marketplace. Cars, furniture, and, of course, textile and clothing items more often than not were imported from foreign countries. These gained traction with cost-conscious consumers. That decade was a time of high inflation; prices rose frequently and dramatically. U.S. makers across all industries felt the pinch to produce goods more and more cheaply to compete with low-cost goods from abroad. Yet, many could not survive in this cost-driven, overall more competitive, ultimately cheaper price driven environment. Overhead swelled for U.S. businesses in other ways as well: payment of higher wages, the offer of better (or any) health care, plus coping with rising production costs made U.S. goods less affordable. Taxes and legal expenses further added to costs. No longer could any of these be added to retail prices consumers would consider paying. Consumers more and more purchased cheaper foreign-made goods to save money.

This spiral of growing costs and dwindling markets led domestic manufacturers to sell off physical factories, lay off workers, and "outsource" work, piece-by-piece, to foreign, cheaper producers. Thus, by the 1980s, fashion production had morphed into a series of independent processes with individual producers completing single aspects of garment and accessory making (say cutting fabric or sewing in zippers). These were coordinated by sourcing and supply chain managers. This roundabout method was usually less expensive than domestic "in-house" production formerly was. That was true even when transportation and other expenses were figured in. Those mills and producers able to keep costs and corresponding retail prices lower and lower remained in business. Arguably, by the late twentieth century, competition and resulting economies of scale had become the true drivers of fashion. The low costs they seemed to bring with them definitely influenced consumers.

With competition came sweatshops. By the mid-1990s and the "Kathie Lee" debacle, sweatshops and their oppressive labor conditions were well established. Why? Consumers wanted fashion goods as cheaply as possible. Producers and purveyor-retailers sought ways to attract and keep consumers with lower and lower prices. This, in the light of production costs that continued to mount. Together, these caused makers to look to all kinds of labor sources.

Oppression needs opportunity to operate. Cost pressures of the 1980s and 1990s provided just such openings. To gain lucrative production contracts, faraway sources turned to child, forced (imprisoned) labor, workers who could be paid virtually nothing. This reduced overhead costs for manufacturers to whom goods were sourced. Cost concerns brought about the need for great volume as well. Production times in sourcing facilities were greatly accelerated. Laborers were coerced and abused in order to produce many more thousands of cut and sewn garments. Foreign contractors sought profits as ardently as the fashion brands they served. Lack of real oversight from fashion companies sourcing production overseas allowed sweatshop conditions such as these to take hold and proliferate.

In fairness, domestic sourcing professionals were often in the dark about the working conditions found in their contractors' shops. Prior to written vendor/producer guidelines and unannounced worksite visits, common now, they were not shown the "true" circumstances behind the manufacture of garments that would ultimately bear their labels. Revelations of sweatshops—especially those involving "big" brands such as Gap and Nike, implicating celebrity endorsers and designers—and outright tragedies did have an effect. They incentivized consumers, fashion game players, and governmental agencies to act. Their goals were and remain ending currently oppressive sweatshop labor practices and preventing new occurrences of them. Many means have been used to accomplish these ends. Rules of the fashion game with which you are familiar enable you to recall and use them.

Efforts to End Sweatshop Labor as Defined by Fashion Game Rules

From the perspective of the fashion game and its rules, where do they apply?

Several popular brands of athletic shoes have been associated with sweatshops. (© Kitch Bain/Shutterstock)

BE A (BIG) BRAND . . . AND BE FAIR!

Lines of protesters, boycotted products remaining unsold, and consumer "watchdog" groups demanding answers and petitioning for abolishment are just a few of the realities fashion and retail companies face when sweatshop issues arise. University student groups, it should be noted, have been especially active in raising awareness about sweatshops and campaigning for shuttering them. Founded in the late 1990s, **United Students Against Sweatshops** (USAS) is one such organization dedicated to this cause. Why are student groups particularly interested in this issue?

One reason may be the popularity of college, university, and sports team licensed merchandise. Educational institutions permit, or license, vendor-producers to make any number of clothing items using their trademarked or copyrighted identifiers. Do you have a T-shirt, sweatshirt, or cap displaying your school's name, emblem, or mascot? Many thousands of students do! Concerns about origins of these colorful products gave rise to educational institutions establishing codes of conduct for their makers. Some institutions have even gone so far as to join together in groups such as the **Worker Rights Consortium** (WRC) to ensure that makers of school licensed merchandise follow these organizations' conduct codes. As well, numerous "grassroots" groups found at colleges remain dedicated to informally raising awareness about sweatshops and bettering workers' lives. To be sure, universities and colleges are big brands, but what about "big" brands such as the Gap? What are they doing that both helps that brand's image and, more importantly, is fair to the workers who make the items found in almost every shopping mall? In other words, what are they doing about the sweatshop issue?

"Social responsibility" has become a brand element in its own right for contemporary fashion companies and retailers. As with any other means of identifying and describing brands, it, too, is multifaceted. Just a click at the bottom of Internet sites takes viewers to written mission, or "vision," statements, code language, and lists of steps companies now take to ensure fair labor standards and practices. These are aspects of the social responsibility element:

Mission statements—Sometimes referred to as vision statements, or "Our Vision," these set out the basic goals of companies' social responsibility policies and areas of focus. Gap, Inc.'s mission statement, for example, makes clear the company's priorities such as protecting the "environment," "employees," and continuing "community investment" are similar to the fashion game issues explored in this part of the text.

Vendor codes of conduct—As noted in this section, sweatshops came about because of economic conditions and lack of both standards to follow and any real oversight. The purpose of vendor codes of conduct is to establish guidelines previously left undefined.

Consumers should become involved in helping to end poor labor conditions through legislation and other means. (© Orhan Cam/ Shutterstock)

Oversight and audits—Rules, codes, and guidelines are important, but so is enforcement of their provisions. Certainly for those strictures to have any clout with third-party vendors, some means of oversight is necessary. This may take the form of unannounced inspections of facilities, auditing of records, and worker interviews.

Not only do companies oversee production, as items work their way through the supply chain of third-party contractors, so, too, may consumers. Patagonia sportswear, for example, offers its "Footprint Chronicles." With that feature, interested consumers may see where contractors are located and the products they make.

Consumer involvement and company participation have worked to twin aims. Both have actively worked to end or at least mitigate foreign and domestic sweatshops and the poor labor conditions they represent. Social responsibility efforts, moreover, have provided brands, whether of "big" or any other size, with another basic way to define and distinguish their identities. What other efforts might be done toward ending sweatshops?

BE LEGAL!

Federal and state actions have also worked to address sweatshops. Two examples include the formation in 1996 of the **Apparel Industry Partnership** (AIP). Begun by President Bill Clinton, this taskforce, in which membership by apparel and accessory producers is voluntary, brought forth in its first year of establishment an initial vendor conduct code. These makers worked with human rights activists and unions to do so.

States such as California have been active in anti-sweatshop efforts as well. In 2010, that state passed the **Transparency in Supply Chains Act**. With passage, companies doing business in California must disclose their efforts to address "slavery" of the kind found in sweatshops where workers are paid poorly if at all and held under inhumane conditions. As well, they must address efforts related to "**human trafficking**" (as occurs when workers are brought into this country then held in "debt bondage," that is until they "work off" fees their transporter/captors believe they owe for passage). Luxury brand Gucci has thoroughly documented its efforts under terms of this act in its corporate disclosure. Of note is mention of company compliance with standards set forth by **Social Accountability International**, based in New York City, and whose "mission is to advance the human rights of workers around the world."

Although lengthy, the Gucci corporate disclosure is informative. For one, it applies to a great many kinds of goods, both fashion and fashion-related. As well, it states what internal efforts the company takes to educate its employees. Were you to work for this organization, you might be responsible for training others, developing further policies in compliance with state law and standards of workers' rights groups, or perhaps even auditing the practices of contractors.

BE PROFITABLE!

At the heart of profitability requirements on the part of fashion businesses is **globalization**. As this section discussed, domestic garment makers turned to foreign sources when it became unprofitable for them to continue operations in the United States. They were willing to pay businesses in other countries to perform tasks such as textile processing, cut, sew, and garment assembly work. These outsourcing activities are the kinds of exchanges of "trade and transactions" contemplated by the International Monetary Fund's definition of globalism.

Proponents of globalization and its practice note, among other things, that it raises the living standards throughout the world. Going further, they believe it creates opportunities for advancement that people otherwise would never have had. On the other hand, some view globalization as inherently exploitive in nature: once corporations have benefited from plentiful, cheap labor, they move on to newer venues when production costs become too high or other conditions make staying unprofitable. Further, they argue that globalization robs countries of natural resources and strips away at their cultural heritages, producing one homogeneous world.

Proponents on both sides of the globalism debate are vocal and powerful. Often public demonstrations and protests related to this issue are heated, requiring police intervention. This is but a brief summary of what are complicated concepts—ones that economists, political policy makers and analysts, sociologists, demographers, statisticians, and professionals of many other disciplines follow and weigh in about with their theories and findings. What about those in fashion and retail industries? How might they navigate between these two highly opposite philosophies—and still remain in business?

Costs and consumers are two factors likely to affect the actions of fashion game players. Global sourcing and the problems it engendered (such as sweatshops) as well as expensive efforts to rectify them, such as social responsibility management (SRM), came about because U.S. production pushed the prices of goods higher than most consumers were willing to pay. If U.S. consumers were willing to pay for domestically made fashion merchandise, even if doing so meant paying more, might globalism issues subside? At least, might abuses such as sweatshop labor be easier to identify and rectify if they happened in the United States and not in faraway countries?

Those questions remain unanswered. After all, the Triangle disaster occurred in this country, even if over one hundred years ago. Unobserved, uncorrected abuses might occur again, only this time in secret facilities. Before that issue becomes relevant, however, the initial question remains: Will U.S. consumers be willing to pay and pay "extra" for merchandise made in their own country? One commentator has suggested:

> (Americans) are more likely to pay for "Made in America" if there is a value proposition tied to it. . . . The Italians have done that, and in that kind of trade-up, people are willing to pay extra money for something. You can market to the economic recovery, the need for more American jobs and social responsibility, but it takes on greater meaning if it's coupled with emphasis on quality, as some of the premium denim brands have seen. (Barbara Kahn, as quoted in: Karr, Arnold. "USA: Consumers Say They Will Pay." *Women's World Daily*, September 5, 2012; retrieved November 28, 2012.)

SRM practices have become among the elements now building fashion brands. They not only address fashion game issues, but also establish the ideas and ideals that brands represent. At present, these practices seek to correct problems brought on by globalism, such as sweatshops. Perhaps they should imply something more? Might nuance become part of social responsibility policies and practices?

The hue and cry surrounding disclosure that Ralph Lauren's 2012 U.S. Olympic and Paralympic uniforms, symbolic representations of the United States, were, in fact, foreign made (although not in sweatshop) is notable. It reiterates the idea that consumers want to feel good about their brand choices and product purchases. So much so, they become upset when negative associations come to light. Alternately, consumers seek out brands engendering good feelings, emotionally affirming emotions. Brands such as Eileen Fisher and others that embrace social and environmental responsibility enjoy great consumer goodwill.

Putting all the pieces together, could it be possible for "Made in America" to come to mean "Not Made in Sweatshops" in the minds of consumers? Doing so might make consumers feel as though they have made responsible, positive choices. Incorporating these ideas and the feelings that go with them into fashion brand identities may ultimately prove profitable. Yet, any success financial or otherwise will only come if consumers recognize and appreciate such efforts and are willing to pay for them.

Section Finale

summary

The presence, even continued desirability, of counterfeit products is one issue arising in the fashion game. "Being" a brand of any size requires building desirability into products; consumers have to want them. One implication of building desirability is creation of incentives to cheat companies and consumers though counterfeiting. This section has explored why and how counterfeits exist. As well, it has defined important terms related to intellectual property, ones on which legal protections are based. These include patents and trademarks, notably. Although admittedly only partial solutions, this section has suggested how the rules of the fashion game and implications of their use might be used to at least ameliorate persistent design piracy problems.

Counterfeit products are but one problem. This section has explored another, that related to unfair labor practices often found in "sweatshops." The presence of forced, low paying, even highly dangerous labor has long plagued the fashion industry. In modern times, the fashion industry has responded by initiating greater oversight of garment and accessory production processes. Federal and state legislation, too, has been responsive to this problem though passage of stricter laws governing workplace conditions and imposing greater accountability on fashion companies. Yet, despite these considerable efforts, many consumers appear more concerned with acquiring fashions at the lowest financial cost, no matter human costs. Perhaps insights derived from the Fashion Game paradigm, notably that of being a "big brand" could satisfy both acquisitive consumers and bring about better workplace conditions.

Review Questions: What Did You Discover?

1. What are counterfeit products? How might they be recognized?
2. What kinds of other non-legitimate fashion products are there and how do they come about?
3. Describe some of the legal protections in place to address counterfeit products, prevent their occurrence, provide protection to consumers, and redress companies whose product "ideas" are wrongfully used.
4. Describe the concept of "design piracy." Can you find reports of its occurrence in the fashion press? What do these articles indicate about the presence of this issue and how the fashion industry and others are attempting to address it?
5. What is at least one definition of a "sweatshop"?
6. Describe how sweatshops are often able to elude detection. What ideas have been put forward to prevent these occurrences?
7. How has globalization both directly or indirectly influenced the continuation of sweatshops?
8. What is "human trafficking" and how does it relate to the presence of sweatshops?
9. What roles do oversight agencies play in preventing the spread of sweatshops?
10. How might consumers become involved in fighting the continuation of sweatshops?

Terms to Know

Be sure you know the following terms from this section and can give examples:

Counterfeit products	Copyrights	United Students Against Sweatshops
Design piracy	Copyright Act of 1976	Worker Rights Consortium
Cabbage	Fair use doctrine	Mission statements
Adaptations	Innovative Design Protection and Piracy	Vendor codes of conduct
Knockoffs	Prevention Act	Oversight and audits
Patents	Trade dress protection	Apparel Industry Partnership
Trademarks	Institute for Global Labour and Human Rights	Transparency in Supply Chains Act
Service marks	Sweatshops	Human trafficking
Lanham (Trademark) Act of 1946	Union of Needletrades, Industrial and	Social Accountability International
Trademark Counterfeiting Act of 1984	Textile Employees	Globalization

Tracking Market Day Preparation Progress, Part Three

Project Purpose: This is the next to last workday! Fill us in at its completion as to what has been done and what remains . . . take "before and after" images for this one. Your presentation should be taking shape.

Step One: **Take pictures of how you are coming along as you begin.**

Step Two:
What has been accomplished? _____

_____

What remains to do? _____

_____

Step Three:
Additional questions: Have you made sample products, or other visual aids? Do you have "take aways" for visitors? What will make your presentation standout . . . and . . . outstanding?

_____

_____

_____

_____

Include drawings or images of these:

Section 8: "Behind the Seams" of Fashion Production (Optional Project)

Project Focus: You have seen how important workers are to the production of fashion items. So, from your perspective, what is missing? What should be done to protect workers . . . realistically?

Step One: Identify what you think fashion game players are NOT doing that they should! In other words, what NEEDS to be done!
(Hint: You might note that many do not even know what goes on in factories, since they are far away.)

Step Two: If you were working as a fashion professional, how might you address this need?

Step Three: What could the fashion industry . . . the other Fashion Game Players. . . . do to address the problems you identified? How might they do so and remain operative as well?

Step Four: What could consumers do to help? If they are so important to fashion (and they are), shouldn't they lead the way toward more ethical means of fashion production?

CONSUMERS AND SUSTAINABILITY CONCERNS

FAST FORWARD

Fashion's "media age" is now! These are times when social media offers consumers information, entertainment, and convenience as close as their cell phones. Yet these attributes give rise to a larger, more concerning issue: privacy. Daily, often freely, consumers give information away to those whom they know and those they do not. Should consumers value privacy? How might fashion and retail professionals respect consumer privacy? This section introduces this complex issue facing fashion game players and consumers.

Privacy concerns address *how* participation in fashion occurs. But what if there were fewer options related to fashion for them to engage? Meaning? *Whether* fashion can continue as consumers expect depends on how well they, the players, act now. Fashion's raw materials face growing worldwide competition, greater and greater natural resources face depletion, and environmental conditions grow more uncertain. This section explores as well *why* it behooves fashion game players to seek the use of resources more sustainably.

(Opposite page) Source: © gabe9000c/Fotolia

WHAT YOU SHOULD KNOW ABOUT THIS SECTION:

- It explores basic concepts surrounding privacy, how information is obtained from consumers, and applies rules of the fashion game as a means of resolving such issues.
- It defines sustainability and examines ways in which its principles and practices may be incorporated into the production of fashion products.

Privacy Issues in a Multichannel World

Privacy—what does it mean to you? Even if you are comfortable sharing personal information with others, as a fashion game player you will be working with consumers, each of whom may not be so forthright or understand what privacy is all about. Consumers, it has been noted, control fashion's direction. Yet, when that power is coupled with the unknowns of technology, a force that changes almost daily, it can be difficult to focus privacy issues, much less resolve them. This section identifies issues related to privacy, ones that you will face and be asked to address.

Fashion can ask consumers to make uncomfortable choices. Skirt lengths for women: modestly near the ground or scandalously high above the knee was a 1970s-era fashion dilemma. Breathtakingly skin-tight "designer" jeans or those with comfortable "breathing room": the style conscious man of the 1980s had to decide. Today, however, fashion poses a question more challenging than just style choice, one whose answer remains unknown, even unknowable. Participation or privacy?

Privacy is generally thought of as the protection of personal information. For example, health and financial records of individuals are two kinds of intimate information accorded legal protections. You have explored why contemporary times may be thought fashion's media age. Social media, for example, is used by brands and consumers alike to tout fashion's latest trend, newest products, and most happening happenings. The world is now watching, noticing, commenting on the actions of everyone through technology-driven media. As the Boston Marathon bombing incident of 2013 showed, these activities are recorded, kept, and reviewed. Perpetrators of that tragedy were identified after study of high-resolution security tapes the police obtained from the Lord & Taylor department store.

You have also gotten to know the multichannel nature of contemporary retailing, a world that has come about because of technological advances. Now, physical stores, the Internet, direct selling, and social media platforms (among others) are all part of making shopping a convenient, richly interactive experience for consumers. That is possible because of the information retailers, search engines, and media such as Facebook gather, analyze, and then use to bring them about. Data, by the way, most consumers give away unknowingly with just one Internet site visit, search query, "tweet," or post.

Considered together, these focus fashion's modern-day, uncomfortable choice: consumers now have to decide whether full participation in all that fashion has to offer, its convenience and excitement, is more important than their own personal privacy. **Privacy** has many different interpretations. Most understandings of it include **the ability to exclude others from actual physical presence, or to gain access to information about individuals or groups. Going further, the concept of privacy means that both have the ability to select what others know about them.**

If ever there were a difficult landscape for fashion game players to navigate, it would be that in which privacy, legality, fairness, profitability, and brand management issues are located. Are game players the guides through this difficult area or are consumers? The latter control much of fashion's direction in terms of styles that make it to the streets or remain on store racks. Although fashion game rules cannot provide answers to how to resolve the participation/privacy problem, they provide some means of exploring options available for how players may work with the challenges it presents.

Be a (Big) Brand! and Be Profitable!

So what about those "personalized picks" that appear when you return to an Internet site? Those occur thanks to "**cookies**" or **text files sent from an Internet site to users' computers**. Once inserted on computers, the host site is **able to identify and store information about whatever users look at**. Even simpler, consumers voluntarily allow online retailers to store personal and business information, such as shoe sizes and credit card numbers. These are stored for use in "My Account" features designed to make future shopping quicker and easier.

These and so many other features do, indeed, make shopping convenient and mostly pleasurable. Just perusing sites can be entertainment. But even with advanced security settings and encryption in place, at this time, consumers have questionable control over what happens to their information once they enter a site, hit "buy," or "send" buttons, or "search" online. But as the "picks" example shows, consumers aren't the only ones potentially benefiting from technology. Information, whether gotten by cookies or given by consumers, is used by businesses. How it is used is an issue within the larger one of privacy.

Privacy is especially highlighted by use of **search engines, or software programs able to seek out and transmit to users terms, phrases, and images posted on the Internet**. At present, it is not clear whether consumers are willing to pay for some kinds of content. The ability to search and to find information appears to be services for which they are not. Thus, Internet search engines are faced with having to obtain revenue from somewhere. Advertising revenues from other businesses are probably the only realistic alternatives, lacking revenues from consumer fees. Ads need information for relevance and appeal to consumers. The information obtained through searches is the kind of data on which advertisements thrive. It is that information gathered from unknowing searchers that is then sold to advertisers. **Data mining is the process by which such data is isolated and organized for application**, usually in the retail industries for use in advertisement and marketing programs. Technological advances provide ever-newer ways of obtaining consumer and product information. Many search engines and sites note information obtained from them is not made available to third parties like advertisers. However, as the Gucci example described below indicates, there are ways in which data can and is shared for marketing purposes even with such statements.

So, the participation/privacy issue facing consumers is mirrored by another one with which businesses have to deal: potential profitability or almost certain oblivion due to lack of revenues from any source? Personal information can be used to build brands. If used in ways consumers do not know about, understand, or to which they consent, brands will suffer. Knowing the extent to which to use information is a difficult challenge.

Be Legal!

If you were a fashion game player, how might you "Be Legal!" when it comes to the Internet, privacy, and consumers? To be sure, laws and their requirements are complicated. Not only do laws differ by countries, but they change from state to state within the United States. At present, federal privacy laws in this country relate to such issues as credit reporting and health care services. It is at the state level, notably in California, that laws have stepped in to protect consumers. In brief, under the **California Online Privacy Protection Act (OPPA) of 2003**, businesses gathering consumer data from that state's residents must clearly post an online privacy policy and adhere to its terms.

A typical privacy policy statement includes language that sets a template, a methodology for companies to follow. To be clear, any individual or business obtaining personal information identifiable with any California resident is required to have such a policy. Think of how many companies that might include! True, this law and its provisions are narrow in scope; it is intended to protect California residents. It is included here because of its thorough tracking of that state's laws on the issue. Furthermore, requirements of this legislation might be adopted by other states and used to form new laws with which fashion game players must comply. What may now be California's law may become federal law. In that vein, its implications are worth considering for all consumers.

In such statements, you will note that it explains what that company will do with data gathered as a result of online sales and from personal information obtained in stores. Usually, sales associates ask if customers would like "to register" their name, address, preferences, physical size, and sometimes credit card information. By furnishing this, consumers are consenting to the retailer's use of that information. The company states it may use that information to market to that person through specialized mailings. However, this is of note: Although a retailer states that it will not sell, or otherwise make available to third parties, the personal information it obtains, it will share that information within that retailer's group of stores that it owns or controls. For example, Gucci Group, at present, is part of the Pinault-Printemps-Redoute group of luxury brands (now formally know as Kering). Thus, registering with Gucci means registering with as many as thirteen other fashion brands! Facts such as that and the implications they give rise to are not mentioned. Is this, then, really a full disclosure?

Whether consumers are able to determine the "whole story" about disclosure of their information (even with laws in place to protect them) is an issue within the larger issue of Internet privacy. Another sub-issue concerns the responsibility consumers have to protect themselves. In the excitement of an in-store Gucci purchase, or the convenience-seeking online buy of less exotic things, who stops to think? The attention of most consumers is focused on walking out with the brown and gold shopping bag for all to see or turning to other computer tasks. Does anyone really think about "opting out"?

Policy statements tell us that we may go away and ask Gucci or any other business or individual we do business with to stop following us. But who wants to? As a result of shopping, Gucci will send notice when those not-quite-affordable shoes go on sale. Our credit information is stored with an online seller, so that reordering is even easier. This situation is yet another challenge for fashion game players: how easy do you want it to be for paying customers, ones who know and like the brand, to be able to just go away? In other words, who do you serve as a fashion game player: the brand or the consumer? Have you done both by complying with laws such as California's and leaving it to the consumer to decide what they want to do?

Privacy policies and the statements describing them are important legal requirements. The scope of both fluctuates as online and mobile activities become more fully integrated within multichannel selling practices. Consumers are made to appear as if they have the ability to pick and choose who or what will receive their personal data. However, as the privacy policy statement for Gucci notes: "Gucci . . . is the ultimate data controller." Is that fair?

Be Fair!

Have consumers already decided this issue? Some groups of them appear to have done so. Young adults and teens, for example, those who have lived most if not all of their lives "online" see no issue, certainly not one requiring a choice. This group values transparency and sharing of information. As well, they feel in control: They can set privacy controls high on their Facebook pages, or they can use "do not track" controls on search engines, among other techniques with which they feel comfortable.

On the other hand, older consumers feel less, if at all, comfortable with the idea of voluntarily posting personal information. Perhaps grudgingly, the most reticent of them will buy online for convenience, but only from retailers they feel they know and they know have secure sites. So exists a vast body of consumers/users, each with differing degrees of acceptance and comfort with technology.

At present, what may be said about the "privacy issue" is this: Consumers can choose the information they give. To some extent, they can control its dissemination. To that end, the Gucci statement notes, they may disable Gucci "cookies," technological means that track site movement and selected preferences. Consumers are told they may call and have their names removed from mailing lists.

Thus, fashion game players are faced with how to present consumers with the option of how to be fashionable or how not to be bothered. Should it always be the consumer who has to make decisions? Might, for example, they be asked to "opt-in"; that is, as a routine practice no information is obtained from them unless consumers say so? For now, it appears as if a majority of consumers and businesses do not desire this approach. Facebook, however, has initiated its "Wisdom" feature, which allows users to choose to have their personal data made available to marketers, retailers, and others. That said, it remains the consumers who are charged with defining privacy as best as they are able given imperfect information and monolithic technological advances about how and by whom it will be used. How they might do so has been suggested by many sources:

1. **Heat cameras** that track customer traffic through a store;
2. **Wi-Fi** to track consumer cell phone use; and
3. **Radio frequency identification** tags that track how often any piece of merchandise is picked up and put back on the shelf.

> If I want to do a promotion with Facebook fans, I can use our . . . programs to reach consumers (with offers, coupons, polls, etc.). But before I begin the campaign, I can use Wisdom to create a psychographic profile that looks specifically at Facebook's users' age, educational background, income bracket, relationship status and more. With Wisdom, I can merge the **CRM (Customer Relationship Management)** . . . software programs that track and record consumer and business purchasing activities . . . and Facebook data and look at past transactions. With all this aggregated information, I can personalize the market to a specific channel. ("Getting Personal: Retailers Mine Data to Offer Consumers Tailored Experiences," Cotton Incorporated Whitepaper as reported in *Women's Wear Daily*, August 2, 2012.)

This passage exemplifies how personal information may be gathered and defined for use. The article states that this approach is the future of retail apparel selling. As well, the article states another facet explored in this section in the following way:

> Retailers have to walk a fine line when it comes to personalization, so as not to infringe on shoppers' privacy. "'This can be solved by shoppers reaching out to the retailer, rather than the other way 'round. Personalization should be based on shopper interaction with the site, as well as the retailer's Facebook, Twitter and other social network sites.'"

Do you agree? If you were a brand manager, how might you ask consumers to make these kinds of choices? Or would you at all?

The Future of Fashion

Perhaps the title of this section made you pause? Of course, you and many others might think, fashion will continue! The industries associated with the making and selling of fashion goods and accessories have been around for centuries. Why wouldn't fashion keep being the powerful commercial, economic, and social force it has been?

At issue is how fashion will maintain its presence in these areas. Such a concern becomes especially poignant when considered in the light of the incredible demands brought about exponentially by the increasing numbers of people in the population. There are more people than ever before to clothe with little indication that such a trend might cease. As well, it is becoming more and more apparent that there is a heavy environmental price to pay for fashion. In the push to satisfy demand for fashion items brought about by increasing populations, natural resources such as air and water are being used at an alarming rate. Sometimes this use is responsible, as when businesses use "clean" practices to restore them to usable conditions. However, others continue to strip the earth of its resources and pollute the environment to dangerously unsafe levels. Over time, such practices leave the planet much worse off, unable to replenish itself.

What might you need to know in order to participate in fashion in the light of these challenges? For one, what is meant by the term "sustainable"? Although there are differences in language used, one commonly cited definition is that of the United Nations, referring to **sustainability** and sustainable development as being: "development that meets the needs of the present without compromising the ability of future generations to meet their own needs." In essence, this means "do no harm" now, in order that subsequent generations may be able to function in the same way.

How might this conceptual definition be expanded on to provide further guidance as to its mandate? Sustainability with respect to fashion has come to involve two other concepts. The first of which may be inferred from the examples above: protecting the physical environment in which we live from dangerous and harmful practices arising from the production of fashion products. Another concept is one that gave rise to the fashion game rule, Be Fair! As you have discovered, that includes protection of worker safety and, more broadly, recognition of human rights. Both of these concepts contribute to current understandings of sustainability and give insight into how fashion may, indeed, survive and continue to be the force it is for later generations.

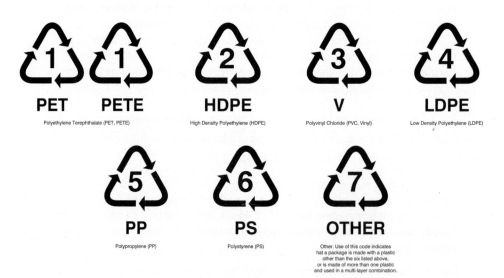

Pictograms for the recycling symbols for plastic products. (© Luka Skywalker/Shutterstock

Preparing to Work with Sustainability

What terms do you need to know when discussing sustainability? Among the most used is that of "carbon footprint." Usually, it is used to reference the impact of a practice or activity. For example, products made in one country and shipped to others for sale often are said to leave a large carbon footprint because of such distances shipped. Production processes required to manufacture the product emit gasses including carbon dioxide into the air. Coupled with emissions from ships and trucks needed to transport those products means that some fashion products such as running shoes (often made in China and India before being shipped elsewhere) cause large quantities of gaseous emissions, or have a "footprint."

The fashion production process is inherently wasteful. The many scraps of fabric that result from cutting are often lost or discarded. The idea of **zero waste** contemplates rethinking fashion production such that selvage edges that are cut away as well as trimmed edges are eliminated from the process. Fashion design then becomes an organic process of finding ways to drape and skillfully cut material into garments.

Fashion and Sustainability in Context

According to the Environmental Protection Agency, "the average American throws 54 pounds of clothes and shoes into the trash each year. That adds up to 9 million tons of wearables that are sent into the waste stream; an increase of 27% in the last eight years." At the same time, "vintage" apparel, essentially reusing the sartorial castoffs of others, is a popular trend, especially among millennial generation consumers.

Use and reuse—both practices give rise to the overall issue of sustainability. When it comes to fashion, are we consuming too much too quickly and then all too quickly throwing our former delightful purchases in the dustbin? Can this continue? Judging from the packed racks at stores and the equally full tubs of clothing simply thrown away regularly, there seems no end in sight to this process.

Fashion historians and anthropologists have noted that in the past garments were worn, worn again, and whatever of them was usable was used again, in whole or usable parts until nothing but rags remained. Ultimately, those scraps were sold to "rag and bone" collectors who resold textiles to paper mills. The expected life of clothes was much longer then. Thinking about the many clothes you have donated, given away to friends, or just thrown away over the years the question arises: Why?

Perhaps industrialization was among the reasons. By now, you and countless other consumers have gotten use to the sheer volume of fashion items available. A glance at any Internet site, a trip to any store, and the amount of goods for sale is obvious. Consumers, thus, have incredible selection and quality available to them now. Competition moreover brought ever lower and lower prices to these goods.

Availability of such inexpensive, higher quality goods had another effect. Along the way, consumers forgot how to do sewing, mending, and "turning" tasks that kept garments going until they became other useful items. Of note, such frugality was not limited by social class. In the early 1900s, Edith Wharton went so far as to describe one of her heroine's many laments as being that a favored gown was unavailable, returned to Worth in Paris for refurbishment, suggesting substantial future wear. Intended conservation coupled with learned skill and inspired creativity, if not the attentions of the venerable Worth, kept entire households reasonably well-dressed for centuries.

Why did such impulses and the skills that went with them seem to have vanished?

Recycling clothing is important to improving sustainability in this industry. (© beermedia/Fotolia)

Fashion merchandising has successfully accomplished those objectives. That's right. The very topics on which this text has been based are at issue in this section! What this means: Fashion options available to consumers today are astounding because of the successful way fashion game players over the years have profitably manipulated ways products are offered, places where they are sold, prices asked for them, and promotional means used to exhort their purchase. Merchandising has largely reduced questions of whether fashion consumers should be fashion conservators to one: Why bother?

Each season, indeed, every week or so at stores like Zara and H&M and Old Navy, there are entire new shipments of jeans, T-shirts, hoodies, just about everything to wear to fill a closet. Purchasing from these ever-newer selections, consumers can simply cast aside undesirable items without bothering to repair holes or clean stains, much less make new garments from old ones. Activities regularly carried out by great-great, great, and even grandmothers such as making garments from patterns, "cutting down" elders' jackets and pants to fit younger family members, or stitching quilts from garment scraps have largely been relegated to Martha Stewart–tutored weekend, fun craft projects. To borrow that domestic diva's language: "Is that a good thing?"

Good . . . bad . . . not sure? As with each issue discussed in this section, there are no clear answers. Certainly, there are countervailing concerns as to whether it is "good" that a conservation culture has been so thoroughly supplanted by a consumer (some would argue disposable) belief system when it comes to fashion. Assume millions of consumers, content with the current content of their closets and those of their family, stopped purchasing fashion items. Moreover, these men and women took up needle and thread and brought back remaking activities performed on garments. To mirror the Wharton example, ask whether it would be "good" if all of a sudden socialites asked Oscar, Karl, or any other designer to "just re-do" gowns and suits for a few more seasons of opera openings and symphony league luncheons and not bother with all the big shows they mount, those spectacles of conspicuous consumption costing so much. Suppose thousands of moms told their children they didn't need the newest sneaker—a polish and new laces would make them look even better. Gone would be thousands of jobs. Millions would be lost in sales revenues and taxes. Commerce depends on consumption.

Sewing and mending products is another way to improve sustainability. (© Eprom/Shutterstock)

Considering the Fashion "Process" in Terms of Sustainability

This text has explored much about fashion in a fairly "traditional" way. As with other sources and references, you first gained an understanding of forces that influence and move fashion's direction. As well, you were introduced to the basic components of fashion and the providers who make available those items. You reviewed the fashion production process and ways finished merchandise is sold at both the wholesale and retail levels. Using that basic, sequential approach and rules of the fashion game, how might the concept of sustainability add to those discussions?

Fashion Components and Sustainability

That water bottle you have could—one day—become part of a pair of jeans! Eco-Denim, introduced in 2011 from Columbia, is produced from thread made in part from plastic. With a soft texture, like that of old jeans, the resulting fabric, according to reports, is made with 32 percent recycled PET (polyethylene terephthalate) bottles. After the bottles are crushed, they are spun into thread. Woven with cotton, the finished product costs about 10 percent more to produce than denim made with all cotton fibers. This is but one example of fashion components recycled from sources that would otherwise remain unused, or, worse yet, would remain in landfills.

Eco-Denim is produced from thread made partially from plastic. (© Angel Simon/Shutterstock)

Eco-Denim is not the only component of note. Lyocell, the generic term for Tencel, is produced from wood pulp. Introduced in the early 1990s, this textile product begins as wood chips that are then dissolved in a solvent (itself recycled) and extruded through spinnerets to produce fibers. These are then treated for color, texture, and other characteristics. The resulting fibers may then be blended with others such as cotton, then woven or knitted into textile fabrics. It, like Eco-Denim, is more expensive to produce than "regular" cotton-based textiles. On the other hand, both are from recycled materials and are themselves able to be recycled.

Textiles require water for their manufacture, color, finishing, and, of course, cleaning. The amount and quality of water that results from those processes is of concern. Levi Strauss & Company conducted a study that found that the amount of water used to produce their famous 501 style jean was substantially less than that used to wash them over time. The company initiated a new label "Care Tag for the Planet" that instructed wearers to wash jeans less often.

As well as water, air is involved in fashion. Rather, the quality of air is affected by the production and transportation of clothing. Think of this: Many garments begin as cotton fibers in one country and then are transported to any number of other countries for processing and production into garments. They are then shipped, affecting natural air and water resources, to retailers throughout the world. Closer to home may mean cleaner for air. Yet, with reduced domestic textile and garment production, or as in some countries even less, air-quality conservation appears difficult.

Among the leaders of large-scale sustainable practices is Patagonia Sportswear. As part of building that brand, the company has initiated a garment recycling program that has for almost twenty years collected thirteen hundred pounds of clothing. Although their items travel great distances, according to sources, this process actually saves in energy costs and harmful emissions.

Sustaining Sustainability

This section has introduced you to basic issues surrounding the concept of sustainability as it relates to fashion. With this section in mind, you might wonder how a "real" fashion company, one with the goal of promoting and advancing sustainability, accomplishes such objectives as it produces new products each fashion season. Enter Julie Bee's, founded and operated by Julie Brown in Atlanta, Georgia. A profile in *Women's Wear Daily*, July 15, 2013, includes how she and her team work to make their business as well known for sustainable practices as for great-looking shoes. As well, she mentions the specific steps they take to do so and problems they face going forward in to second year.

What might compel a fashion entrepreneur to open a business with the expressed goal of promoting sustainability? Lack of available, acceptable options! Julie Brown noted:

> I couldn't find anything I was really drawn to . . . I didn't know what I was getting myself into, but I'm passionate about [sustainability] and what's happening in the field.

But what do you think it's really like to design and manufacture seasonal collections with sustainability as a goal? How do production practices change when that concept is figured in? Again, the article notes:

> To reduce the environmental impact [that results from shoe production], the pumps, flats, and sandals use vegetable-tanned leathers and 100 percent organic linens and cottons. The line also makes use of vintage, recycled, and deadstock fabrics and leathers . . . . All of the brand's styles are made in two factories outside Los Angeles, where [the team] can personally oversee production and avoid shipping supplies and products back and forth overseas.

From this, you can see that the brand is concerned not only about sustainability, but also with keeping production close-by, the better to ensure product quality and high-quality work-place conditions.

So where do sustainable components of the kind described here actually come from? The article includes descriptions of how the Julie Bee team works, as the founder notes:

> [We look for] vintage and recycled pieces, things that were excess runs and leftovers, and incorporate those into our designs. [Where we find them] varies. The team looks for things that will have enough for several size runs. It's all over the country. [We find] some stuff here in Atlanta, some in California and New York. You find them in fun places and you never know when they will appear.

What other issues do you think the Julie Bee's company might face and what kinds of long-term initiatives might it seek to establish? To wrap up, the article about this incredible company and its determined owner recounts the following:

> Finding the right kind of leather is one of our biggest challenges. There's so much out there, but so much of it isn't eco-friendly. But I know there are lots of people out there doing what we're wanting [to use to produce products]. One of the things I'm excited about is creating our sustainability guidelines and having them in [place] in the next few months for the general consumer. And we'll be looking at how [suppliers] are processing their leathers and where they are getting them, as well as looking for alternative energies and how they are treating the water.

Is sustainability becoming of interest to you? Perhaps if you considered the kinds of new career paths (areas where you might standout and have a positive impact) it offers, it might become even more so.

Section Finale

Who does not want to be part of the excitement of fashion today? More than clothing and accessories, fashion has come to mean experiences, "happenings," information to be enjoyed then shared. Social media and other forms of technology have brought about exciting new ways to participate in fashion in its many forms. It is possible to be both consumer and consultant through these. Yet, these forms of technology present the very real issue of privacy. Those who participate in fashion's media age do so at the cost of their own personal information. Whether voluntarily given up, or "mined" from data such as details of personal searches and purchases, consumers are asked to provide highly specific, highly personal information to many, unseen, unknown others. At present, consumers seem to have divergent views of whether this is desirable or not. While some consumers are comfortable with this reality of modern fashion, others are not. This section has defined these issues and suggested ways future fashion game players might address them. Fashion is about consumption, the use of resources. This section asks provocative questions about whether and to what extent fashion should encourage such practices and what game players might do to ameliorate the effects of consumption it has brought about. With so many new consumer markets expanding all the time, practical answers to sustainability concerns appear more necessary than ever before.

Review Questions: What Did You Discover?

1. Define privacy, both as noted in this section and for yourself. Do you notice any differences in these and how might you address them?

2. Recount some of the ways consumers give up their personal information, both intentionally and unintentionally.

3. What is "data mining" and how does it affect consumers' privacy?

4. What does it mean to "opt-out"? What are some implications for consumers when they choose such a course of action?

5. How has the fashion industry both encouraged consumers to give up their privacy and tried to protect it?

6. Define sustainability and describe its importance to the future course of fashion.

7. What are some sustainable practices noted this section. What are their benefits and implications?

8. What are some of the human costs associated with consumption and sustainability? How might these be balanced with any perceived need to conserve resources?

9. What are examples of ways fashion entrepreneurs are now attempting to address sustainability?

10. Why should consumers bother with sustainability? What would say to someone who does not perceive this issue to be of concern?

Terms to Know

Be sure you know the following terms from this section and can give examples:

Privacy	California Online Privacy Protection Act	Radio frequency identification
Cookies	(OPPA) of 2003	Customer Relationship Management
Search engines	Heat cameras	Sustainability
Data mining	Wi-Fi	Zero waste

Market Day Simulation Project Worksheet
Launching the Market Day Media Campaign

Project Purpose:	In Section 7, you (or your group) planned a media campaign. It goes "live" here with only a few sessions before Market Day. How will you attract visitors to your presentation?
Step One:	Determine what needs to be done to get your media campaign off the ground. Do you begin "Tweeting"? Put up a simple Facebook page? Draw posters? This is the session where you will devote energies to these tasks.
Step Two:	At the end of this session, describe what you have done and note links to media, or collect images—anything that let's us know better what you and your presentation will be all about!

Section 9: Privacy in Fashion's Media Age (Optional Project)
Finding Out How Important Privacy Is . . . or Isn't!

Project Focus:	Fashion is growing ever more exciting for everyone thanks to the advent of social media. Experiences are now just as important as products! But at what price? In this project you will interview several people of different ages to find out their impressions of privacy. You will then draft a short memo of your findings.
Step One:	Identify at least ten individuals of different ages interested in following fashion.

Name _____   Age _____   Name _____   Age _____

Name _____   Age _____   Name _____   Age _____

Name _____   Age _____   Name _____   Age _____

Name _____   Age _____   Name _____   Age _____

Name _____   Age _____   Name _____   Age _____

Step Two:	Interview your group to find out their impressions about privacy in fashion's media age.

1. How do you engage with technology? Do you use the Internet? Have a cell phone? Use Apps on your phone?

2. How often do your use these? What kinds of tasks do you use them for?

3. How secure do you feel about sharing personal/private information through these?

4. Do you think businesses adequately inform you of how they use your information and protect the information required for you to use technology in these ways?

5. How do you protect yourself? Do you think there is anything individuals can really do to protect themselves?

Step Three:	Write up your findings. Use the Rules of the Fashion Game as a guide. For example, how might fashion companies "Be a Big Brand" by listening to and incorporating information of the kind you discovered here? How might they "Be Legal, Nice, and Profitable" in doing so?

PART FOUR PREVIEW: THE **FASHION GAME** IN **MOTION**

NOTHING STANDS STILL.

The fashion game is in motion, making fashion products ever-more available to an ever-growing world seeking them. You are also moving, working through studies, transitioning into a meaningful career. How might you and fashion join forces? First, this part of the text takes you far away to introduce you to just a few of the issues facing fashion game players as they take their brands and business practices overseas. Specifically, it makes advanced but understandable applications of the four rules of the fashion game to suggest how they do so. Next, this part returns "home," to your very own personal efforts to find a place in the fashion game. Internationally, personally, and jointly, this part of the text keeps the fashion game in motion. Step aboard!

SECTION 10: THE FASHION GAME IN THE WORLD

Fashion has never been more international.

How does merchandise—appropriate with respect to place and culture—make its way into foreign markets? How might fashion game players know whether it is "right" for such distant consumers? Merchandising missteps may be unavoidable. Yet, most might be prevented by learning more about different people and their beliefs. International consumers may be just as fashion trend and brand aware as those in Western nations. To reach them, however, requires focusing merchandise and merchandising efforts on them, their needs, and understandings. International trade is governed by a complex set of laws and treaties. Avoiding legal missteps takes an understanding of the regulatory environment surrounding international trade. This section of the text introduces you to cultural-, trade-, and legal-related issues surrounding the quest for international consumers.

SECTION 11: ARE YOU READY FOR THE FASHION GAME?

What are your career interests?

Finding your place in the fashion game means first **identifying careers** available in fashion, retailing, merchandising, or any number of related occupations. This section builds on the very first one opening this text, now better understandable after learning more about the fashion game paradigm. You have seen those players in action and learned about their businesses. This section explains more about them, describes their education and experiences that led to them becoming those fashion game players. This section further prepares you for discovering in the final text section very practical ways of making your first career moves.

SECTION 12: MAKING YOUR FIRST FASHION GAME MOVE

What will your first move be as a fashion game player?

After you have an idea where you would like to go professionally, what kind of practical tools will you need to help you get there? This section prepares you for successful completion of fashion-industry-specific résumés, cover letters, and that all-important interview! There are openings for you as future fashion game players, places where you can make your professional career move as a fashion game player.

After your time with this final part of the text, you will have a better idea of how to put your own fashion career game in motion!

THE **FASHION GAME** IN THE **WORLD**

FAST FORWARD

The world of fashion is the world! This text has explored fashion and fashion retail industries largely from the perspective of the United States. As well, it has included activities originating and occurring in Western European nations such as France and Italy. Yet, to provide a more encompassing point of view, this section considers why and how fashion "travels" throughout the world.

Led by consumers' interests and demand for brands and products, fashion depends on cultural conditions and economic trends for its worldwide movement. Fashion game players apply rules with which you are familiar to meet the different needs and issues these present. International fashion acceptance depends on people, those who understand different societies and how to interest, even inspire, consumers found in them.

WHAT YOU SHOULD KNOW ABOUT THIS SECTION:

- It defines issues arising internationally such as differing consumer preferences and trends arising from them.
- It describes basic cultural and economic issues involved with international expansion of fashion.

10

(Opposite page) Source: © T. Tulik/Fotolia

- It applies fashion game rules in advanced ways to issues arising from different consumer cultures and ways of conducting business.
- It identifies several countries currently of interest to fashion professionals and describes issues affecting expansion in them.

Placing Yourself in the International Fashion Game

A job not only in fashion, but also international in scope might be where you find yourself. It could happen! Perhaps you will work in sourcing, a career in which you locate raw materials providers (suppliers) and producers (makers) throughout the world. Maybe you will be hired as an account executive for a fashion brand sold the world over. As a top-earning retail sales associate, you will develop a worldwide roster of clients seeking your expertise—your knowledge about them and their lifestyles. Entrepreneurs starting fashion businesses such as retail stores, especially those with Internet presences, can expect international attention as well. These are but a few ways in which fashion, retail, and professionals in each are now not just confined to one or even a few areas of the world, but connected to many.

Sideline:

Patience and partnerships may help build bridges for fashion's expansion throughout the world. As well, information found in this section will help you begin to understand how you may participate in international fashion and fashion retail businesses.

This worldly scope is not a new trend. Fashion's "passport" has been—and remains—the desire of consumers all over the world for unique things to wear, to have, and certainly to experience. From that grows appreciation for fashion. In centuries past, for example, silks imported from China were honored as precious by Europeans, used only to construct special garments. American home seamstresses of the nineteenth century eagerly sought colorful, detailed sketches from France so that they, too, might dress "a la mode," just like their Parisienne counterparts. In countless other times and in so many former ways, fashion crossed borders, led by consumers' interest. Today, fashion continues its travels to places where new markets of consumers seek it. This process, the fashion game in motion, brings with it even greater career opportunities than ever before. It's easy to see how with just one example.

Who does not have at least one pair of running shoes? Think of the many professionals responsible for this typical and decidedly international purchase you, or anyone, might make in any mall, at any store. Before you put them on to run the track or run to class, those shoes have logged many miles on their own. Thanks to the efforts of unseen fashion game players, the colorful components found in running shoes come from many places—the textile mesh upper portion may have come from a Chinese mill, the foam sole may have been made in India, and the entire shoe constructed in Mexico. Someone, maybe an entire team of people, in those areas was responsible for specifying, ordering, and purchasing each component as well as coordinating completion of each production step. Not only that, the shoe's brand may be owned and controlled by a fashion group in, say, Italy with designers and other workers there—some of whom would be responsible for organizing worldwide product distribution and retail sales. The mall operator and retailer where you purchased those shoes may well be based in the United States, somewhere like New York City. They have professionals there and in the location where you purchased your shoes.

Fashion depends on cultural conditions and economic trends for its worldwide movement. (© Jeff Metzger/Shutterstock)

Internet shopping has made fashions from around the globe accessible to everyone. (© JMiks/Shutterstock)

From this count, five countries (at least) were involved, not to mention efforts of numerous professionals in each, just to offer one person one pair of one style of one brand of shoes: you. Whether through faraway friends made via social media or in the course of your career, the world will be your world. In the light of this phenomenon, how might you step aboard the always-moving game of fashion to find your career niche? Gaining basic insights into international consumer trends as well as recognizing issues such as cultural differences are important initial steps. With insights in mind, you will better understand how to interpret the fashion game rules with which you are familiar and apply them on a global scale.

Overview: International Consumer Trends

You are familiar with the fashion game rules as identified in this text. Step back for a moment and think about where they came from. Countries such as the United States were responsible for their development, but not without contributions from Western European nations. Other highly industrialized places such as Japan were instrumental as well. Historically, these have been among the leading areas in the world for development of fashion and retail. The fashion game rules arose from practices occurring in these highly commercialized, consumer- and brand-oriented, legally, ethically, and financially complex places.

There are many world nations besides these as sophisticated, or becoming so, about fashion. Individuals in them, however, may not be experienced with fashion, or are governed in their consumption practices. In places like China, for example, few options existed until recently for consumers to obtain fashion-related products and Western-based brands. Previously, they might see images of foreign fashion styles and branded products as worn by others far away. Yet, for political and economic reasons, such things were not available for them to purchase. According to 2013 surveys, however, fashion brands such as Louis Vuitton, Chanel, Estee Lauder, and Levi Strauss are among the most highly regarded and sought after in China now!

Western shirts such as these are now sold in China. (© Shmeliova Natalia/Shutterstock)

In other countries, such as Saudi Arabia, interest in and financial means has long existed for consumers to obtain fashion goods. Religious and corresponding social norms, however, continue to govern dress now as they have done for centuries. These two examples underscore just some of the consumer- and culture-related issues affecting movement of the fashion game in the world today.

On the one hand, there are places such as China where consumers (though growing in affluence and purchasing abilities) have long been unable to fulfill any desire for fashion-conscious products. They are now anxious to do so and exhibit strong demand for them. On the other hand, as in longtime wealthy, fashion-aware Saudi Arabia, fashion consumption is highly controlled. There, too, is much demand for fashion goods, but those must be presented in culturally sensitive ways. For example, standards of modesty govern how and how much of women's body may be shown in public.

What do you think these divergent kinds of consumers—found throughout the world in other places such as Russia, India, and Brazil—mean for fashion and fashion retail professionals? What other considerations besides consumer demand might fashion game players think about as well?

Issues and Practices Affecting the Worldwide Fashion Game

Fashion game players need to understand non-Western consumers in order to satisfy their needs and wants. Recognizing various economic and political issues that will have an impact on whether and how they will reach shoppers and purchasers in those markets is another consideration. With both of these ideas in mind, they—and you—can modify game rules to better apply to other areas of the world and consumers located in them.

The United States, most European countries, and Japan are considered to have highly saturated markets for consumer goods including fashion ones. In these places, consumer needs and desires do not go unsatisfied: numerous products are available for purchase at many price and quality levels. Many such products are **imports—items made in parts of the world other than those where they are finally sold**. Usually, they are from locations where they may be made as inexpensively as possible. Previous text sections have detailed importation of fashion products and noted that the United States is among the largest importer of fashion and fashion-related items after Western Europe. Because trade of all kinds, both within the United States and externally, with other nations is so important to the country's economic well being, two federal agencies oversee it. These include the U.S. Department of Commerce and the U.S. Federal Trade Commission.

Because of the incredible availability of fashion items made possible by inexpensive imports, it is difficult for fashion game professionals in the countries noted above to expand whatever market niche they have achieved. Competitors are ever-present to fill perceived voids. To remain profitable, fashion professionals of every kind from providers of raw materials to promoters of fashion products turn to consumer markets in other parts of the world where opportunities are present for growth. They seek to do so with **exports, which are goods sent to others for sale**. The number of imports compared with exports, expressed in the United States in dollar amounts, is referred to as the "**balance of trade**." At present, in the United States, the balance of trade is considered "**at deficit levels**," meaning that the nation imports more goods than it exports. According to government statistics, the United States imports forty-three billion dollars in goods more than it exports. This is expressed as a "**negative trade balance**."

This is believed to create a spiral-like phenomenon further increasing U.S. dependency on foreign goods while at the same time sacri-

Sideline:

Whether this trend is desirable or the extent to which it should be sustained is subject to debate. Consumers faced with managing personal budgets may appreciate lower prices brought about by imports. They may have, as well, greater selections of foreign-made items from which to choose. Public policy makers, however, may doubt whether the situation is advisable economically for the United States. Over time, they contend, the country becomes more dependent on continued domestic purchasing of imported goods. When greater and greater amounts of consumer spending are devoted to going overseas as it does with trade deficits, it becomes ever more unavailable for any domestic use.

ficing our own production. This causes ever-greater reliance on imports and sending more and more to other countries. Furthermore, jobs are lost to those other countries, it is contended, as they hire more workers to meet demand for new products. These basic consumer market and economic conditions that are thought to come from trade deficits, especially lost sales revenues and domestic jobs, are broad issues currently affecting both consumers and worldwide operation of the fashion game.

Currency and its fluctuations are concerns. Specifically, the value of one country's currency against that of others' is an issue. Currency values change daily. Even in small amounts, spending power of one country's "money" varies compared with that of another's. The "strength" of a country's currency is a measure of how much it can purchase when converted into that of another country. "Strong" currencies have greater spending power when changed into other currencies. Right now, the British pound is thought relatively strong compared with the U.S. dollar. Consumers in the United Kingdom get more dollars back when they change from pounds. This situation means that U.S.-made goods are less expensive, perhaps are bargains, for pound holders. In contrast, the dollar is "weak" for U.K.-made items, as it has more limited purchasing abilities in places where that currency is honored. In 1999, members of the institutions of the European Union (a consortium of nations located throughout the European continent) adopted the "euro" as common currency recognized by, at present, seventeen "Eurozone" nations and five others. Like the British pound, it, too, is strong in spending power compared with the dollar. Fashion goods from Euro countries like France and Italy are expensive for U.S. dollar holders. This is one reason fashion game players seek out materials and producers for their products in non-European countries such as Bangladesh. Efforts expended costing-out fashion goods and planning market targeted, profitable suggested retail prices are wasted if consumers feel they cannot afford them.

With respect to currency, debate continues about whether China manipulates its renminbi (a unit of which is the commonly referenced yuan). Some believe that China may keep its currency artificially lower in value through complicated financial transactions, processes intended to offset losses caused by doing business with countries with stronger currencies. By doing so, it is thought, China keeps its exports inexpensive for foreign consumers so they will continue to purchase them. By now, it seems clear that fashion and finances are strongly related. Fashion game players should be aware of how internal and international "money matters" affect consumers' abilities to purchase goods and how they affect their own abilities to produce and market them. As long as Chinese-made goods continue to dominate the U.S. consumer market, awareness of Chinese currency policies will remain crucial.

Agreements related trade and legal constraints are two other issues of which fashion game players must be aware when considering international operations. The World Trade Organization (WTO) wields great power when it comes to **trade**, or **the physical exchange of goods from one county to another and between counties**. Begun in 1995 and based in Geneva, Switzerland, the group seeks to "[Provide] a forum for negotiating agreements aimed at reducing obstacles to international trade and ensuring a level playing field for all, thus contributing to growth for all. The WTO also provides a legal and institutional forum for the implementation and monitoring of these agreements, as well as for settling disputes arising from their interpretation and application." At present, the group oversees about eighteen agreements among its 159 (2013) member nations. WTO agreements only apply to member nations. Questions about compliance with group requirements arise nonetheless. For example, a member since 2001, China's reluctance to follow WTO provisions related to foreign oversight of its trade practices remains at issue. Of interest to fashion are WTO agreements related to textiles and clothing. In 2004, the **Multi-Fibre Agreement** expired. In existence since the 1970s, part of that pact included the **Agreement on Textiles and Clothing**. This sought to eliminate **quotas**, or **governmentally mandated import limits**, on such products. However, quotas remain. Under the U.S. quota scheme, two kinds of quotas exist: absolute quotas and tariff-based quotas. In this approach, absolute quotas are just that: "total" amounts of products that may be admitted into the country on a first-come, first-served basis. Once the allotted amount of such items enters, no further ones may come in. Under the tariff-based scheme, specified quantities of goods may enter at a lower tariff rate than they ordinarily would, but only for a specific time. After that, higher rates, or duties, are imposed.

Tariffs are charges placed by one country on items or products imported from other nations. They are taxes on items coming into countries. Countries such as the United States impose tariff amounts according to a schedule. Currently, the **Harmonized Tariff Schedule** (HTS) is used in international trade. Developed and overseen by the World Customs Organization (WCO), based in Brussels, Belgium, the HTS is used by approximately 170 of the group's member nations. They develop their own duty rate schedules, how much they will impose on imports. However, such taxing guidelines must be organized in specific, uniform ways using the six-digit coding system mandated by the HTS. This approach classifies raw materials and finished items in consistent, transparent ways. Each "contracting party," in HTS terms, is aware of the exact nature of exports sent and imports received. They can then base their tariff amounts accordingly and collect information about trade activity with other nations.

Tariffs are **protectionist** in nature, meaning that they are put into place to safeguard raw materials providers (such as cotton fiber textile products), holders of brand names, and producers of fashion items in receiving countries. Often, imports may be substantially cheaper than domestically sourced items, thus gaining competitive advantage in the market. As well, there may be such quantity of incoming raw materials and goods so as to effectively drive down prices to unprofitable levels. **Protectionism** is in contrast to **free-trade policies**. The latter seek to eliminate or significantly reduce trade barriers. As well, they aim to further enable individual countries in their efforts to provide or produce those raw materials or goods in which they are most proficient.

An increasing number of consumer items, including fashion ones, are certified as "**fair trade**." Different organizations have established standards that businesses must follow to label and market products in this way. Fairtrade International (FLO), World Fair Trade Organization, Network of European Worldshops, and European Fair Trade Association, groups collectively joined and referred to as FINE, are but some of the many groups involved. Although various definitions for "free trade" result from this situation, the presence of this certification usually means that businesses producing or making items have followed certain guidelines. These rules include payment of market-condition (i.e., not unreasonably low) prices for raw materials and wages sufficient to support the livelihood of workers. As well, child or other kinds of exploitive labor were not used to harvest raw materials and produce items. Consumer interest in fair-trade products is growing in the United States and is quite strong in other countries, such as the United Kingdom. At present, department stores such as Macy's offer African-made, free-trade products, usually decorative textile items, jewelry, and baskets to U.S. consumers. Trade-related theories and how they are carried out in practice are complicated in detail, often political in nature. Recognizing their presence, understanding their intentions, and acknowledging their impacts are necessary steps to keep the fashion game in motion internationally.

Translating Fashion Game Rules

With general awareness of international consumers and a basic understanding of global trade issues and practices, you are better prepared to "translate" the fashion game rules with which you are familiar. You are ready, in other words, for more advanced interpretations and applications of them! What follows is an overview of issues that international fashion game players face as they implement its strategic rules.

Be a (Big) Brand! and Be Fair

"Big" brands—even up and coming ones—are built on elements. These include not only tangible ones such as symbols and colors, but also intangible ones such as feelings, moods they evoke through images, words, and phrases. Consumers perceive brands, their defining elements, and express emotions about them differently. This is especially true when brands enter international markets, those far from their countries of origin. In European countries and the United States, for example, many fashion brands run ads featuring barely dressed models. These are published in those countries in print advertisements "as is." Only the most provocative or disturbing ones provoke any substantial outcry.

For example, in many Middle East nations Islamic cleric police known as Mutaween have the power to confiscate print media, shut off access to other forms of information such as the Internet, and close retail stores for running advertisements deemed offensive by religious standards.

People in other countries are influenced by "western" fashion through magazine advertisements. Even so, some native dress customs still apply. (© Manzrussali/ Shutterstock)

Other issues face those companies during international expansion. Fashion brands, as one instance, may be slow to realize the power their names have and miss opportunities to develop products suited to new market tastes, such as developing abayas (long, black, floor-length shawls) with brand-identified, but still appropriate elements. Others have noted that religious and cultural standards influence purchase decisions and merchandise should be planned accordingly, such as not stocking flashy yellow gold items for men.

From this discussion, brand building joins another fashion game rule: Be Fair. In this sense, "fairness" refers to becoming and remaining sensitive to cultural and religious standards. Examples, as these, from the Middle East underscore this. Of course, there are other examples from other parts of the world as well. Surveying countries, their peoples, and local beliefs, customs, and observances are part of developing "fair" marketing plans. As well, inputs about language use are further ways in which fashion brands may expand effectively.

Practical advice includes vetting advertisements and print items with authorities before making them public and complying with specific cultural requirements. For example, stores close or dim lights during prayer times in many Islamic nations. Gender roles and their manifestation differ throughout the world. At present, depicting women driving cars by themselves is common in countries such as the United States. In Saudi Arabia such activity is forbidden to women, and forbidden for others to show, even to suggest. This example underscores how activities assumed to be commonplace in some cultures might be out of place in other cultures.

Correct use of language, words, terms and phrases, and sounds can carry different meanings. What may come across as humorous in one language may not make sense or be considered vulgar when translated into others. Language, like images, should be checked with native speakers, even linguists, before public use to prevent malapropos. With opportunities to advance brands in the international fashion game come challenges. Creatively blending and knowledgeably, sensitively applying rules such as these are ways to address goals.

Companies such as Channel and Dolce & Gabbana are mindful of showing more conservative attire in some countries to adhere to strict social norms. (© Andrey Burmakin/Shutterstock)

In Saudi Arabia, women do not wear "fashion" in public. These burqas cover all skin, which is the accepted moral code in Saudi Arabia. (© Zurijeta/Shutterstock)

Be Legal

Fashion game players face legal issues related to how international businesses are run and organized. In many countries it is common for monetary fees to be paid to local authorities. Are such payments legal under U.S. law for U.S.-based companies to make? At issue is whether such payments are illegal bribes or the means of facilitating quicker actions from local authorities. If found to be the latter (and not otherwise prohibited by the host country), U.S. law may permit them. Bribes, kickbacks (undisclosed "refund" payments for getting work or favorable treatment), falsification of trade and legal documents, as well as shipment or receipt of "phantom" nonexistent goods are just a few examples of corruption of which international trade professionals should be aware. Walmart was found under the **U.S. Foreign Corrupt Practices Act of 1977** to have bribed construction officials in Mexico to obtain building permits in that country, for example. Provisions of this federal statute define prohibited and nonprohibited payments that arise from facts such as these. The law also imputes sanctions, usually fines, when violations of its provisions are found.

Think about this: As a fashion or retail professional, it is likely that your company will ask you to explore how that business might expand into international markets. Very possibly, you might lead or be on the team sent to any of the countries mentioned in this section or that you read about in other sources.

You and your team are on the ground in another country; with guides and interpreters, you are on the lookout for people and places to do business. Even with much preplanning for this moment, nothing can quite compare to being there for the first time, making the first physical assessments of the location, the people there, and the scope of the assignment. What do you do?

When faced with such situations, many fashion and fashion retail companies develop business relationships with local businesses or entrepreneurs to get their businesses going. They may have no other option. Foreign businesses may be prohibited under local laws from operating or owning property in those host nations. To begin working abroad, foreign businesses may join with locals in **franchises**. These contractual arrangements usually involve local business entities or entrepreneurs purchasing rights to use such names as H&M (Hennes & Mauritz), Claire's, The Body Shop, Marc Jacobs, Ralph Lauren, and many other mid-tier and luxury brands. These local fashion game players then run operations in host countries, returning a percentage (usually 50 percent) to the parent, "big name," companies. Franchises are common in the Middle East, Mexico, and South America.

Be Profitable

Profitability is critical for the success of any business. Fashion and retail companies, particularly, face further profitability pressures on entering international markets, such as the imposition and collection of value added taxes (VAT). This system of taxation is found throughout European Union nations, such as France and Italy, as well as Canada and the United Kingdom. Other VAT countries include India, China, Mexico, Australia, Sweden, Denmark, and Norway. Although there have been discussions for decades about whether to implement a federal VAT in the United States, those talks and related studies have yet to yield substantive results.

Exchange rates between companies affect profitability for companies doing business worldwide. (© Ivsanmas/Shutterstock)

The VAT system is a detailed method of gathering tax revenues, one requiring retailers and others throughout the product supply chain to account to governmental taxing authorities. There are costs associated with performing the required tasks and preparing reports, expenses that businesses must anticipate and include when determining the selling prices of goods. As well, they must devote personnel to account for it, increasing labor and costs associated with it. VAT adds to the final price paid by consumers for goods they purchase at the time and place of purchase. At present, Internet sales of goods are exempt from the imposition of VAT charges. Thus, fashion game players "building (big) brands" have further incentive to expand their fashion brands online.

Building a New Fashion World with BRICS

Paris . . . New York . . . Milan—these are fashion's most well-known places. What about Sao Paulo, Moscow, Mumbai, Beijing, Durban, and South Africa? These cities represent the growing importance and influence of Brazil, Russia, India, China, and South Africa. Referred to as "BRICS" nations, they are countries at present with the fastest-growing economies. As such, they represent incredible opportunities for fashion and fashion retail businesses and brands to expand their reach. Luxury brands and products in particular are especially desirable and desired by consumers in these places. With an expanding economy, many more are able to purchase merchandise they have long admired.

The fashion game is in motion, but in which direction? This section has explored west-to-east expansion of fashion. What about east-to-west expansion? With a gigantic workforce, one skilled in textile manufacturing, garment production, and Western retail practices, might China become an influential source for fashion in future years? Might it become the "next" Paris, Milan, or New York? What do you think?

Perhaps China's roles as a great innovator might occur as fashion game players address product development, styling seasonal fashion lines, and merchandising and managing retail stores to meet consumer needs and expectations. At present, these concerns are raised about fashion products emanating from there; they do not appear to be attuned to Western markets. Yet, the Chinese market is notable for its sheer size: The country has over one billion inhabitants who need and want clothes. Women's Wear Daily has identified several Chinese retailers and their related brands.

1. Metersbonwe: A casual wear brand with more than forty-five hundred Mainland Chinese stores, it plans to move into North American markets soon.
2. Bosideng: Known for outerwear such as coats, this chain of ten thousand domestic Chinese stores opened a London flagship in 2012.
3. Youngor: A stylish menswear line sought out for trend-aware, but appropriate business attire, this brand owns four hundred stores in China with a network of two thousand others and has a design center in Italy.
4. Erdos: A leading Chinese cashmere brand, this company has over three thousand points of sale in China alone and sells to U.S. and European stores. At present, the brand seeks to amp up design interest by hiring French and Italian designers to give it luxurious, fashionable appeal.

5. Li-Ning: A giant, but troubled, shoe brand that has over seven thousand points of sale throughout the world. Its attempts to take on Nike and Adidas have proven difficult, especially in the high-end shoe market.

6. Ochirly and Anta: Large, but troubled Chinese casual wear brands, both are fighting consumers' perceptions that imported brands are of better quality.

(Source: Farrar, Lisa. "Chinese Homegrown Brands to Watch" W.W.D., December 28, 2012.

These brands may be making only scant inroads into the U.S. domestic market—for now. It seems reasonable though that they may face issues similar to their American counterparts. Their own domestic markets may be saturated. Further company growth may need to come from finding foreign markets. Which will it be? West meets east, or east meets west with consumers? Might both "sides" of the world have something to offer all consumers? Opportunities for U.S.-educated and trained fashion game players like you will help answer these questions either when working for domestic employers or those from countries such as China.

For all the promise, growing pains are present in each of these countries. Hyper-inflated currency values continue to push prices astronomically upward in Brazil. Few can afford necessities, much less luxurious imported, branded fashion items. Corruption, political instability, and lack of intellectual property protections are issues that have been raised and that await resolution in Russia. Presence of these factors would inhibit investment by foreign-owned businesses. India's vast bureaucracy inhibits whether businesses are able to enter that market and expand when they do. Claims of currency valuation rigging continue to plague China, as does the presence of counterfeit products believed to originate there. South Africa, the newest group member as of 2010, is the least populous and its market remains economically fragmented and difficult to assess. All of these countries levy tariffs on goods coming into their ports and have VAT taxes, further contributing to prices consumers pay for imports. Gaining new consumer markets is the exciting result of international expansion for fashion companies. To accomplish that goal, extensive knowledge of economics, national and international politics, and culture are required of fashion game players.

Section Finale summary

This section has introduced you to basic aspects of international business as they apply to fashion, fashion retail, and the fashion game concept. The fashion game is in motion! How well you and others are aware of divergent ways of doing business, cultural differences, and are able to adapt to constant changes, perhaps the better you and they will function and survive in the worldwide arena.

Review Questions: What Did You Discover?

1. How do fashion game rules apply to international expansion of fashion brands and companies?

2. What are some of the ways fashion companies alter their images and messages in different countries? Why do they do so?

3. Describe the ideas of balance of trade and trade surplus? Why are they important to fashion?

4. How does the value of currency affect fashion? How do consumers react to their "buying power"?

5. What are tariffs and duties and how do they affect fashion and fashion consumers?

6. What are the BRICS nations and how might their impact of the word be described?

7. What is "protectionism" and how does it relate to "free trade"?

8. How is China posed to become an even greater fashion and retail force in the future? What are reasons for such potential?

9. What are some issues identified in this section likely to affect international businesses, including fashion ones?

10. What does V.A.T. stand for and, in general, how does it affect consumers' abilities to purchase fashion goods?

Terms to Know

Import/export
Balance of trade
Trade surplus
Trade deficit
Currency/currency valuations
Free trade
"Fair trade"
Protectionism

BRICS
Tariffs
Quotas
VAT
Franchises
Partnerships
Harmonized Tariff Schedule
Trade

Multi-Fibre Agreement
Agreement on Textiles & Clothing
Protectionist
Free trade policies
U.S. Foreign Corrupt Practices
   Act of 1977

Market Day Simulation Project Worksheet

Project Purpose:	In Section 3, you explained aspects of your brand, including a general statement about what it stands for on many social issues such as workplace ethics and sustainability. As a break from preparing your Market Day presentation, draft a "White Paper" position statement to include.
Step One:	Select from among the Fashion Game issues detailed in this part of the text and write it out in as much detail as possible.
Step Two:	Describe the issue in your own terms and what is going on that creates the concern.
Step Three:	What is being done about the issue . . . and what more should be done in your estimation?
Step Four:	How will you address this issue in the production/providing of the goods or services you propose to present at Market Day?
Step Five:	Write up your findings and proposed conclusions in a one-page report (include images, if possible) that you will include in your media campaign and make available during your Market Day presentation.

Section 10: When Is Too Much . . . Too Much? (Optional Project)

Project Focus:	By now, you are familiar with many different kinds of fashion game players. Who among them does something unique, exciting, or effective about the kinds of issues addressed in this part of the text? Describe their work, then tell whether and to what extent you might be able to do what they have toward addressing issues of ethics and sustainability.
Step One:	Select from among the many different, interesting fashion game players; identify that person, or company.
Step Two:	What kinds of social issues described in this section did they face?
Step Three:	Describe some of the challenges that player or company faced.
Step Four:	Describe how you might become involved with these issues and what you would do.

ARE YOU READY FOR THE FASHION GAME?

FAST FORWARD

FAST FORWARD

How will you participate in the fashion game? Put another way, what fashion or related careers are there? This section provides an overview of several careers, a survey that brings together all the ideas with which you are now familiar: the fashion game, consumers, game rules, and let's not forget its newest player—you!

WHAT YOU SHOULD KNOW ABOUT THIS SECTION:

- It describes potential career pathways leading to becoming a fashion game player.
- It explores career options based on the four fashion game player designations.

11

(Opposite page) Source: © Africa Studio/Fotolia

This image shows that there are many facets of the fashion industry that are all inter-related. (© iQoncept/Shutterstock)

As a reminder, consider the fashion game players you encountered in Section 1: "The Fashion Game and Its Players." Here, you will come to better understand the requirements for the kinds of careers those professionals followed. Why not you, too, in an exciting fashion or related job? After this section, you may be able to identify one or several of interest. In the final section, you will learn practical skills that will set you on your way to becoming a fashion game player.

Fashion Career Paths

Before you find yourself at work planning the next season's buy, sketching at a drawing board, sitting in on another brand management meeting, or assisting customers in a great store, you probably asked what kinds of fashion careers could get you to such places. In very broad terms, fashion careers may be described as **entrepreneurial** or **employment-based careers**. In the former, individuals work on their own behalf in businesses they form and operate. In employment-based careers, workers are involved in businesses established by others. Each approach has its share of rewards and challenges. Which basic career path might be right to follow? The answer depends on you!

Entrepreneurial Fashion Careers—and You

Many well-known fashion designers have been entrepreneurs. Countless fashion retail stores, specialty boutiques, and wholesale showrooms came about through the work of one or a few people as well. Many "big" brands related to fashion, such as those offering cosmetics, got started thanks to the efforts of entrepreneurs.

Entrepreneurs are those willing and able to assume the risks of running businesses. It is challenging and demanding work, even more so when one person is involved in the venture. Thus, entrepreneurs usually have to sacrifice great amounts of personal time and financial resources to begin and continue their businesses.

You have ideas, great ones at that, about fashion. Making them realities is your challenge as an entrepreneur! All but the most personally wealthy require financial backing from some source to bring their ideas to fruition. Fashion legend Christian Dior, quoted above, received initial backing from French textile industrialist Marcel Boussac in the 1940s. Without that, there may not have been any "new look" or Dior fashion brand today. In modern times, designers Mary McFadden, Carolina Herrera, Tory Burch, "P. Diddy" (Sean Combs), and Kanye West began fashion businesses and brands using their own considerable means. These are the dream scenarios: ideas and the wherewithal to see them through. What about "real-life" fashion entrepreneurs?

The reality for many starting out in fashion, whether as designers or retail store owners, is that money is tight! The "real" reality is that these entrepreneurs have to scrounge for funds to buy fabric or inventory in order to have sample garments made to show buyers or to hang in their stores for consumers.

Some resort to "maxing out" credits cards to bring about their business. Then, they must wait for wholesale buyers or retail consumers who will purchase enough so that there will be enough money to start production, keep stock available, or pay bills. Season to season, the challenges are enormous operating fashion-related businesses. Often, designers-owners-entrepreneurs go without personal pay to meet expenses.

None of this is meant to discourage you or dissuade you from fashion entre-preneurship. Whether you want to open your own design business or a retail store: Just be realistic! Failure rates for new fashion businesses are high. Estimates vary, but it is thought that 80 percent of new fashion businesses do not survive two years. If one business venture fails to pan out, many entrepreneurs forge on to begin others. Through any attempt, though, financial support is critical. What do you need to know about obtaining and managing such resources?

The **Small Business Administration** (SBA) is a U.S. government agency that offers many services to budding business people. These include information about how to get started and where to obtain funding. With respect to the latter, the SBA offers loans through financial institutions such as banks. These are sources of start-up funds for many new entities, including fashion businesses.

Another source of funds is from "backers" and "**venture capitalists**." These are individuals or companies providing businesses with start-up funds. Backers usually have personal relationships with the fashion entrepreneur. For example, they may have been friends or clients. On the other hand, entrepreneurs may seek out support of venture capitalists whom they do not know. No matter their name or relationship, both are **investors**, or **those seeking profits from their financial support**. This can occur when businesses they fund are sold for amounts over what investors spent. It can also happen when those entities "go public," as discussed previously. Section 12: "Making Your First Fashion Game Move" outlines business plans of the kind usually required by outside financial backers. Entrepreneur, freelancer, whatever the title, many in fashion and related careers find working for themselves works for them!

Most financial investors will require a detailed business plan. The business plan should include all of the sections detailed in this chart. (© Vaju Ariel/Shutterstock)

Working in Employment-Based Fashion Careers

Entrepreneurship is not for everyone. Most working in fashion do so in businesses established by others, working as employees. Might this career path be for you? Entrepreneurs find that they must perform many kinds of tasks whether they enjoy, or are particularly suited for them, or not. Those employed are hired for and expected to perform specific duties. Even when quite broad in scope and encompassing many tasks, these fall within the range of activities for which employees have education, experience, and, of course, interest.

Working for others can mean doing work you enjoy with people you enjoy, a steady pay-check, and benefits, such as health insurance. Or it can mean disaster: a series of disappointing jobs, each emotionally and financially unrewarding. How can you avoid that? Drive and ambition to do good work and advance as well as the ability to work well, or at least respectfully, with others are important considerations for success in a corporate career. Do you have these abilities? As you begin an internship or gain a first job, experience and sophistication are key attributes. How might you accomplish these many things with any corporate job you consider?

What does all this really mean?

Corporate career advancement requires sophistication and interpersonal know-how. It requires not only greater knowledge and expanded skillsets (i.e., can you perform an ever-wider range of job-related tasks well), but also incredible savvy in dealing with others. How might you work with a difficult member of your senior management team, even a boss, or a company chief executive officer without losing credibility or the job itself! Management and career coaches can be important resources of information for advanced employees about how to navigate through complex work relationships such as these.

Corporate Careers—and You

The exact career steps you take, from entry level to executive, vary greatly. Fashion design, production, and retailing each has requirements to be met before moving on to successively greater responsibilities and higher pay.

Fashion design careers, for example, may begin as a member of a team, working on one aspect: researching color and style trends or assisting senior designers. Jobs related to production might include working in "sourcing" positions, those responsible for locating components such as fabrics, findings, and trims used on garments and accessories. You will explore these items in the next text section. Other positions might place responsibility on you to find makers of garments and accessories that will bear the company label. As you advance in skills and contacts, you may have to travel to faraway locations and work with contractors there, sometimes for days or months, and assume even greater responsibilities for others and their work.

Whether in design, production, or other corporate capacities, you will be responsible for results others do or do not bring about! To this end, you may, as a mid-level production manager, oversee any number of workers to ensure adherence to production and shipping schedules. Likewise, managers must work with other employees to make sure that print and other media projects present timely, coordinated messages that are consistent with brand and company values.

By the time you reach the "C-suites," or "chief" offices, such as chief operations officer, chief marketing officer, or even chief executive officer, you will likely have a great many people reporting directly to you. These may be individual workers or sizable work groups. Whether entry level, mid level, or senior level, meeting tight deadlines, achieving targeted results, and working with others and their contributions (good, bad, indifferent) constitute the daily life of those in a corporation.

Sideline:

Do you, as the saying goes, "play well with others"? Much of corporate life is all about that and wielding education and industry knowledge in productive ways to further your own career.

Working well with others is a major component of success in the fashion industry. (© Mangostock/Shutterstock)

Fashion Game Players and Their Careers

With an idea of basic kinds of fashion careers and considerations about them, you next may be curious about specific careers, whether entrepreneurial or employment based. As you might suspect, there are literally thousands of possible jobs to explore. How might such a great many be narrowed down and organized into a recognizable, understandable few? The first text section introduced you to the four groups of fashion game players. As you recall, these are providers, producers, purveyors, and promoters. As you will further recall, the basic functions of each are as follows:

Providers: These are the fashion game players responsible for making available textiles and other raw materials forming the garments and accessories that we wear and use.

Producers: These might be called the "fashion makers." Working from designs, producers encompass many different fashion specialists who plan, cut, sew, and prepare fashion items for consumer use.

Purveyors: This text distinguishes two kinds of purveyors, or sellers, of fashion and related items. Whether operating a fashion wholesale showroom or an exclusive retail boutique, purveyors take fashion from off the rack to on your back!

Promoters: Editors, bloggers, visual merchandisers, educators, any number of professionals, promoters are the fashion game players responsible for getting the word out about what's new and exciting, what you should wear, where you should be, right now in fashion!

Surveying Careers Using Fashion Game Designations

Using the designations for fashion game players as set out above provides an easy way to survey just a few of the many hundreds of careers possible in fashion, fashion retail, and other related industries and professions.

There are many careers available in the fashion industry. How do you find one that meets your particular skills and interests? (© Sean De Burca/Shutterstock)

Providers

As you know by now, these are professionals responsible for developing the components from which fashion and accessories are made.

Fashion Career Notes: Textiles

Textile production (the making of "cloth" or "fabric" as referred to by most consumers) requires knowledge of chemistry, engineering, and production principles. Although many fashion design and merchandising courses of study require one or two classes devoted to textiles, actual four-year undergraduate degrees in textiles are available. Many textile engineers complete such programs. Similarly, many professional textile designers complete specialized studies in that area. At their core, both kinds of programs emphasize an understanding of textile fibers, their components and characteristics, and how production processes can impart and modify them. Conservators preserve textiles in ways that are respectful of their historical experiences. Highly technical, too, careers as conservators begin with specialized undergraduate education.

Producers

These fashion game players are responsible for designing and making fashion and accessory items.

Fashion Career Notes: Fashion Designer

The path to a fashion design career begins by obtaining an undergraduate degree. In the process of doing so, you will design and present work for review. High degrees of proficiency in sketching, draping, patternmaking, and garment construction are necessary. Would-be designers should develop and maintain a portfolio of images expressing their creative viewpoint and samples of work showing their technical expertise. Fashion design is highly competitive with many applicants seeking the relatively few jobs available at any time. However you are able to distinguish yourself—good grades from a top-notch design program or successfully completed

If you choose to work in manufacturing, you will need to have a good understanding of textile fibers and how production processes affect them. (© Max Bukovski/Shutterstock)

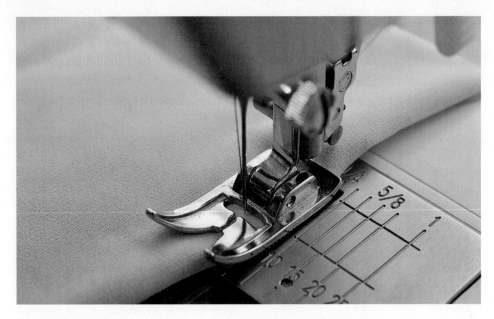

Garment construction requires extensive practice to become a professional. (© Andreja Donko/Shutterstock)

work you have been able to sell to stores on your own—will help you get your foot in the door!

Fashion Career Note: Garment Production

Patternmaking, sample garment making, and production quality control are just a few careers available for those who really enjoy the detail work of fashion. Most of these topics are covered in undergraduate fashion design courses; however, class time is usually not enough! These disciplines require extensive practice, experience, and patience in order to obtain professional-level proficiency. As with many fashion careers, beginning and maintaining a portfolio of successfully completed work is crucial, as are references of satisfied clients and employers.

Purveyors

This text recognizes two kinds of purveyors, or sellers of fashion. Wholesalers, who make fashion available to retailers, and retailers themselves, those responsible for selling clothing, accessories, and other fashion items to "end users," or consumers.

Fashion Career Notes: Fashion Showroom Representatives

Many wholesale showrooms hire individuals to assist retail buyers in knowing fashion collections, writing orders, and understanding showroom policies. Undergraduate degrees in fashion and work in these specialized selling arenas are helpful starts to a career. Fashion wholesaling is for those interested in and able to work with other professionals and their businesses. They help retailers develop and grow their own businesses by identifying and offering products, styles, and brands that they believe will be successful—that is, profitable—in retail stores. Wholesalers need interest and savvy in fashion business practices.

Fashion Career Notes: Fashion Retail

Keep doing what you are doing! The purpose of this text is to explain how the fashion and fashion retail worlds operate using the fashion game theory. Here, you will explore the many kinds of careers available and what they require. In general, undergraduate degrees in fashion merchandising and marketing or retailing is beneficial for any career in retail. Unless your desire is to operate your own store, retail careers are "corporate" careers. These require abilities to work with others under time and profit-producing pressures within defined management structures. As you study further, continue thinking what kind of work tasks would hold your interest. Industries related to fashion offer something for every background and skill set.

Many fashion game players begin fulfilling careers working in wholesale or especially retail selling venues. Because retail is such an important career entry point for many, it deserves special mention. Retail careers can take many forms. Of course, there are retail sales careers. These are commission-based jobs, meaning that the sales associate earns a percentage of each successful sale, adjusted for any merchandise returns. Not to be discounted as a career path, such positions can be quite lucrative. Some sales associates with large client followings have been known to earn as much as or even substantially more than those following salary-based merchandising and managerial retail career paths.

Sideline:

Buying careers center on obtaining salable goods for retail establishments. Retail buying is about making the right goods available to the right customers in the right quantities at the right time. That is: warm coat in winter, swimsuits in summer! Assistant buyers (who often start on the sales floor as associates) are usually responsible for tracking merchandise sales, making sure markdowns occur correctly, and keeping records of what does and does not sell.

In general, knowledge of and expertise with such programs as Microsoft Excel are required for buying careers. "Number crunching" is really what the retail world is about, especially determining store or business profitability through mathematical means. Entry-level or assistant buyers often are charged with keeping records of what sells, performing markdowns, and monitoring the availability of stock. Mid-level buyers, those on the job for a few years, might be responsible for procuring one kind of goods (such as hosiery items) or products from one particular vendor (as occurs in cosmetics and fragrance departments), all within price ranges consumers will accept without having the store resort to excessive, unprofitable markdowns. The scope of their work may encompass obtaining these items for one, several, or many stores.

Higher-level buyers oversee merchandise selection and purchasing procedures for entire departments, or areas, and determine the "merchandise mix" offered to consumers. "Mix" refers to the assortment of products offered and may refer to that array found in one or many stores. Often, buyers must mathematically determine ways to offer items for which they have to pay a great deal with those they do not and not damage their stores' fashion image and still make a profit.

One recent trend in retail buying is to include inexpensive items along with costly ones with both reflecting the store, or brand, image and conforming to profitability projections. The next time you see impulse-purchase-priced scented candles next to "splurges," such as expensive accessories, you now know why! Merchandise mixes such as these permit items to sell each other. For example, consumers who may not be able to afford an expensive item may take the less costly one, believing the allure of the prestigious product carries over to it. Likewise, affluent consumers may take both, believing that each item has appeal—is imbued with a particular brand's characteristics—and they can enjoy each in different ways. As you can see, skillful mixes help stores sell more merchandise and satisfy consumers of all budgets.

General merchandise managers (GMMs) oversee the entirety of company buying and merchandising operations. For example, they work with teams of buyers and merchandisers to plan how and when goods will be presented in stores. They, along with high-level buyers and senior visual merchandisers, are responsible for identifying the trends, the brands, and the products they believe will draw and keep consumers interested in their stores from fashion season to fashion season. That's why they were present at the fashion show opening the fashion game!

All retail careers require people skills. This is perhaps best underscored in retail management positions. Daily, managers are tasked with dealing with shoppers in various states of happiness, store employees, and outside vendors, all with their own concerns; in short, any one coming through the store, having business with it in some way, become managers' responsibilities. These busy people usually begin as department or area managers, working to ensure smooth running of their spheres of responsibility. This means accommodating shoppers as nearly as store policy allows. It also requires making sure that associates maintain set store standards and procedures. One example of such responsibilities includes making sure that "opening" and "closing" practices are followed, preparing the area for the day's selling activities, and accounting for them afterwards. More advanced retail managers have responsibility for larger and larger stores areas, over more personnel, or over specialized store functions such as operations (shipping, receiving, and security being examples).

Senior retail managers usually have responsibility for the entirety of activities related to large, highly visible, highly profitable (or all three) stores. As well, they may have responsibility for several or more stores with local store managers reporting to them. Some managers with large-scale responsibilities come first from sales, merchandising, or operations backgrounds. Stores such as Macy's offer flexible managerial career paths for those interested in gaining as many career skills as possible. In general, the quantitative skills required of buyers are less indicated for those with other responsibilities. These fashion game players must know how to organize employees and motivate their activities with the goals of keeping shoppers satisfied.

Promoters

Many different professionals promote fashion, generating excitement for it, adding to what we know about it. Many possibilities exist under this fashion game career designation.

Fashion Career Notes: Fashion Editor

Editors often have journalism backgrounds with undergraduate degrees in that subject and, by the time they are senior editors, extensive, progressively more challenging experience covering particular subject areas, such as fashion. Discovering popular, new design talent, tapping into moods of the times, and gaining profitable readership are the tasks that define successful fashion editors.

Fashion Career Notes: Stylist

Stylists may come from a variety of different backgrounds. A general education in fashion design or merchandising is helpful. Start building a portfolio of images and videos of your work. How you interpret fashion trends for others is what styling is about. Get to know sources (such as stores) to obtain clothing, accessories—everything—then find people interested in your services and see where it leads!

Fashion Career Notes: Public Relations and Special Events Planning

Backgrounds in journalism, advertising, media, and fashion can get you on your way to a career in public relations. Success in that career means getting to know people and working with them and their companies for the launch of new products and services. This involves writing releases and having extensive press and other media contacts with which you can generate excitement. Usually, successful public relations professionals work for others and "build their own book" of clients before starting their own businesses. Similarly, those interested in special events, such as mounting fashion shows and launching new products, work with other event planners to learn how to bring together the many others needed to bring about these projects before starting their own businesses. An undergraduate degree in fashion merchandising can be beneficial toward learning the fashion industry and how it operates.

Fashion Career Notes: Corporate Sponsorship

Thinking about the corporate life? Usually, large businesses such as those noted above as well as major retailers and fashion manufacturers employ communications, public relations, community outreach, and many others who oversee event sponsorships. At least, undergraduate degrees are required to get started. Those can be related to fashion, marketing, and management. Executive—key decision making—positions usually require years of successful work with sponsorship projects.

Fashion Career Notes: Blogger

With a computer click, almost anyone can start a blog. Many with a "passion for fashion" have gained notoriety after starting their own fashion blogs. They are, however, not the only ones. There are blogs for and about almost every possible subject now! If it is truly your interest and passion, then why not start one of your own, perhaps chronicling your fashion education and undoubtedly colorful work experiences. With a unique perspective, who knows what might happen! Many Internet sites now afford you the opportunity to start a blog at no cost. Could it become a career? That depends on whether you are able to receive financial support through advertisers who pay to appear on your blog or receive financial backing from individuals and companies. Good Luck!

Fashion Career Notes: Fashion Forecasting

With a degree in fashion design or merchandising, plus work experience with established fashion forecasters, you may well be able to make such a career a reality. Getting to know the fashion and retail industries and their operations are critical—repeat—critical. That means understanding, in detail, such topics how fabric and garments are produced and how fashion designers and their businesses work. Mostly, it means knowing consumers, studying them, and learning from them what their interests are and what they seek from fashion. With this knowledge, forecasters are then able to estimate what will intrigue consumers in the future.

Fashion Career Notes: Visual Merchandising

Visual merchandisers harken from undergraduate fashion merchandising programs, then work their way through the ranks of intern, staff, or assistant visual merchandiser, and then head of visual merchandise departments. Manual and artistic skills as well as knowledge of color and design principles, plus understanding brand marketing concepts, are necessary competencies. This exciting area of fashion merchandising, by the way, was pioneered by L. Frank Baum. Does that name sound familiar? He was author of *The Wizard of Oz*.

Fashion Career Note: Museum Curator

Curatorial programs offer special courses devoted to building, preserving, and presenting museum costume and fashion collections. In essence, there

Anyone can become a fashion blogger. All you need is a computer or tablet. (© James Thew/Fotolia)

are two aspects to curatorial careers: understanding the technical, science-based ways in which highly delicate items might be preserved, and knowing how to present them in ways that interest museum or gallery goers. Without their patronage, curatorial jobs, even entire departments, may be eliminated. It also means working with budgets and "politically" with others. In general, careers in this area usually begin with undergraduate degrees in curatorship, plus work in museums as interns, then as staff members.

Fashion Career Note: Fashion Education

Fashion education usually requires degrees in consumer sciences, human ecology, or a similar field with emphasis in fashion design or merchandising. For those interested in university-level careers, such as professorial ones, obtaining doctorate (PhD) degrees in such disciplines is critical. Doing so means first obtaining undergraduate and master's degrees as well as completing original research. Lecturers usually have extensive industry, or "hands-on," experience. High school and middle school fashion educators have degrees in education usually with special focus on consumer sciences.

Fashion Career Note: Careers in Other Areas with Fashion Emphasis

Perhaps you are thinking about a career in any area besides fashion! Yet, you, like many, enjoy fashion. You might be surprised to know there are many ways to incorporate your interest in it while pursuing an entirely different career:

Accountants work with fashion and retail clients to ensure that they follow sound, acceptable business practices. Financial planners devise business plans for burgeoning fashion and retail companies to help them start and grow.

Attorneys handle the contracts (binding agreements) these entities enter into among many other issues, such as assisting two or more fashion companies joining together, "merging," or offering percentage ownership in their businesses "going public." The more you know about fashion and the operation of its various industries, the better! Lawyers and accountants often engage in "due diligence" research in the process of mergers/acquisitions work or when fashion companies initially offer stock to the investing public. Conducting such research requires in-depth knowledge of how fashion businesses operate.

Demographers, psychologists, and sociologists study consumers as individuals and in groups that they form. Fashion industry professionals use that information to target trends in buying and the use of fashion products. Fashion and social sciences definitely benefit each other.

Recall the fashion game rule "Be Fair"? As you have learned, doing so includes working in ethical, sustainable ways. If these inform how you would like to work, there are several career areas to consider, ones on which integrity of the fashion industry depend:

Law enforcement and criminal justice professionals work to ensure that consumers are protected from illegitimate fashion products. They also seek to ensure that makers of "real" items, those who hold patents and trademarks for branded products, do not have their ideas and efforts effectively stolen by others. The goal of these professionals is to maintain the ethical integrity of fashion products. They do so by carrying out search warrants; confiscating questionable, possibly counterfeit, or "fake," fashion goods; and working with court prosecutors to adjudicate alleged violators.

To prevent fakes from re-entering the marketplace, these professionals also ensure that they are destroyed. Many law enforcement professionals become highly knowledgeable about branded, "designer" products and are able to spot even the most plausible imitations!

Advocates and members of special interest groups (SIGs) express their viewpoints about such issues as the use of fur products, sweatshops, and child labor. They seek to raise public awareness of their particular issues and promote changes, again with the goal of ensuring ethical, humane animal harvesting (or none) as well as fair labor practices throughout the world. Thanks to social media, advocacy groups (comprised of professional organizers and interested consumers) are influential forces such that all working in fashion careers must understand and with whom they must work to find solutions.

Fashion encompasses many different disciples. For example, those with interior design or decorating backgrounds—or those interested in applying fine arts education—may find work in the burgeoning area of home product design. Driven by color trends, holiday seasons, or both, this can be an exciting way to bring fashionable designs into homes. Knowledge of product manufacturing, sourcing, and legalities such as licensing agreements, similar to those learned though fashion merchandising, can make this a unique fashion-related career choice.

Finding Fashion Career Options

From the first section to right now, this text has suggested different careers, ways for you to participate in the fashion game. Where do you think you might turn to find actual jobs, ones that will get you on the way to a great fashion career? As well, you probably would like to know the "big" question: How much do these jobs pay?

Careers in home product design and interior design use many of the same skills used in fashion design. (© AlexRoz/Shutterstock)

Thanks to the Internet, there are resources available. Of course, don't forget to check with any employment or career services available at your school. As well, remember, fashion is an industry about networking, making connections, and putting your ideas together with the resources of others to make things happen! Looking for a job, one you can turn into a career? Think about the following ideas to get your search started:

1. **Find a place for your talents!** Is there a store you would like to work for? What kinds of jobs do they offer that you might be interested in? If possible, ask through human resources or personnel departments what kinds of qualifications they seek from employees.

2. **Find someone you admire!** Is there an individual who has the kind of job you might be interested in? Find out through your own research as much as possible about what that person actually does, how he or she got to where he or she is professionally. If possible, seek an in-face appointment or make an inquiry through a "contact" feature, noting your interest and what career development suggestions they might be willing to share with you.

3. **Carve out a niche for yourself!** Ask what it is you do well and enjoy doing well. Using the knowledge and experience you have, find ways to stand out, ways others respond to and want to seek your contributions. Many begin fashion careers as sales associates, selling "on the floor." Build your fashion knowledge by keeping track of customers, what they want, what they don't want, and what services are needed to support sales, such as more frequent deliveries of new merchandise. Share such information with buyers and merchandisers. By showing your interest and knowledge, you position yourself for consideration when other job openings become available.

4. **Have patience!** No career is easy to establish and fashion-related ones are no exception. It often takes several years of experience to obtain work with anywhere near attractive salaries and benefits. What that means for many is perseverance through what can be difficult years out of school. Perhaps an irony of fashion is that its promotion and appreciation of products, experiences, and even lifestyles require a great deal of money to obtain, yet careers in the fashion industry often do not pay enough for those who work in it to purchase such things. In short, you have to love what you do, even when it becomes a struggle to pay off student loans and meet current expenses. Doing so can be a difficult balancing act, but one you should be aware of as you consider a career as a fashion game player.

Fashion Career and Salary Information

Need a quick reference for jobs and salaries in the fashion industry? The following table summarizes several of the most commonly used references for such information. Good luck!

Career Resource	Attributes
www.stylecareers.com www.wwd.com/wwdcareers.com	These are the "go-to" sites for the industry standards for fashion career searches. Interested in particular companies? Check out their Internet sites. Many have job openings posted and allow you to register for updates.
www.salary.com www.cbsalary.com	Knowledge about compensation and benefits is critical toward determining whether you can afford to take a particular job. These resources enable you to make such determinations. Note: Build your own career file of what jobs you like and how much they pay, so that you will be prepared to negotiate for jobs.

Figuring out what you are good at is the first step in establishing a career in fashion. (© Eric Audras/Alamy)

Putting Your Interests and Abilities into Perspective

By now, you have aspirations for a fashion career and probably some fears as well. How might you take stock of yourself, now, to come to understand ways to fulfill your goals and alleviate at least some of your fears? Professionals in many disciplines often use **SWOT analysis** to review both personal and business issues. Focused on assessing competitive advantages, this method can, at times, be very complicated. For example, when fashion companies are considering whether to engage in new kinds of operations, introduce new products, purchase new facilities, or any of a number of business activities for which they will face competition from others, they often use highly sophisticated SWOT analysis methods. Using it here need not be. It can be a good way to put your interests and abilities into usable perceptive.

To begin, think about the kind of fashion career you want to follow, one that really interests you enough to dig in and find out all you can about. What do you know about the people who already have these kinds of jobs? With the answer to this question in mind, answer the following questions posed by letters making up the SWOT acronym. Both section projects focus on using SWOT analysis, one for your entry in the Fashion Game Simulation Project and one for your personal career development.

> **S—Strengths:** What do you know or do better than anyone else? Especially important is this idea: What attributes do you have that you feel give you an edge, an advantage over others in the career you are interested in pursuing?
>
> **W—Weaknesses:** What about you—in terms of your education or experience—creates disadvantages relative to others pursuing the kinds of careers you are interest in? Do you need more education, experience, or both, or something else, in order to gain the kind of job you want?

O—Opportunities: What is available to help you gain what you need more of? What resources are out there in the community, in education, and among co-workers, family, and friends to help you overcome the weaknesses you identified?

T—Threats: What stands in your way, preventing you from obtaining your goal? This is the opposite consideration of opportunity in that it involves finding out those actual issues and problems to address and overcome in order to reach your goals.

Section Finale summary

If you are truly interested in fashion, then the people who drive the industry, those who move it forward in all its many exciting directions should be of interest as well. Research those individuals and their careers as best you are able. Through doing so, you can and will come up with ways to join their ranks, maybe even surpass them. The fashion game approach should enable you to gain an overview of the kinds of "players" there are and what functions they perform, and to identify what is of interest to you. Then, through your research, your drive and tenacity, you can become one yourself! Fashion offers many career possibilities, so many that just a few are considered here. Whether on your own or working with others, there are challenges and rewards to consider.

Review Questions: What Did You Discover?

1. Describe the two basic kinds of career paths there are and give examples of each.
2. What are entrepreneurs and how have they been involved in fashion?
3. Describe the role of investors and venture capitalists as they relate to fashion businesses.
4. What is a general career pathway for those interested in a corporate retail career? How does that differ from entrepreneurial or sales-focused careers?
5. Note at least several of the kinds of careers offered by each type of fashion game player.
6. The acronym SWOT stands for what kinds of questions?
7. How might SWOT analyses be used both professionally and for personal career searches?
8. Give some ideas about how a student might identify and obtain a job in the fashion industry.
9. What are several resources to which they might turn for information about career options and salaries?
10. What are some fashion-related careers that are not directly involved in the production, manufacture, selling, or promoting of fashion?

Terms to Know

Entrepreneur
Small Business Administration
Venture capital/venture capitalist
General merchandise manager

Visual merchandising
Stylist
Fashion editor
Fashion forecasting

SWOT and SWOT analysis
Employment-based careers
Investors

Welcome to Market Day!

Project Purpose: The big day is here! This is your log of the exciting events that happened.

Step One: Attach an image and a brief written description of your presentation.

_____
_____
_____
_____
_____
_____
_____
_____
_____

Step Two: Describe the venue where the event is held. How many presentations are there? Take us to the event in your description. What is the atmosphere like?

_____
_____
_____
_____
_____
_____
_____
_____
_____
_____
_____

Step Three: Are there other presentations of interest to you? Perhaps ones related to a product or service similar to yours or your group's? Describe some of the more memorable, unique, or exciting ones.

_____
_____
_____
_____
_____
_____
_____
_____
_____
_____
_____

The Power of Promotion in Fashion in Other Countries

Project Focus:	After completing this project you will come to see how fashion promotion persuasively and effectively imbues seemingly similar fashion items with highly different characteristics and personalities.
Step One:	Select two of the same fashion item. For example, jeans by two separate makers.
Step Two:	Compare and contrast the two item in the following ways:

In what ways are your selected items similar in components? _____

What are their prices? _____

What store types are they found in? _____

What are the images of these products' brands?

_____

_____

_____

_____

How are they presented to consumers? (Are you and others able to access them easily, or must you go out of your way to find them?)

_____

_____

Find examples of promotional materials used to promote these two items. What impressions do they imprint on consumers about these items, their qualities, and characteristics?

_____

_____

Step Three:	Write up your evaluation of these two products, especially noting how marketing and merchandising practices make them distinct.

_____

_____

_____

_____

_____

_____

_____

_____

_____

_____

_____

_____

_____

_____

_____

MAKING YOUR FIRST FASHION GAME MOVE

FAST FORWARD

What remains for you to discover? Perhaps how to start your own fashion career! From designers, stylists, merchandisers, educators, and other professionals, you have previewed many different fashion and fashion-related careers. How might you choose "the one"? Recall the purpose of the fashion game: providing a framework, a way of thinking about fashion, fashion retail, and other related industries. Next topic: preparing you to become one of those fashion game players yourself. That's what this section is all about. Here you will find tools and suggestions gleaned from actual fashion game players about how to make that all-important, certainly bold, first move in the fashion game.

WHAT YOU SHOULD KNOW ABOUT THIS SECTION:

- It explores ways fashion game rules may be used to define your own fulfilling career goals.
- It notes ideas for preparing résumés and other documents for fashion and fashion-related careers.
- It suggests ways for better using social media resources to gather fashion career information.

12

Curriculum Vitae

How you market yourself, whether it be how you dress or how your resume is prepared can make a big difference in your success in finding a job in the fashion industry. (© vesna cvorovic/Shutterstock)

What Should My First Move in Fashion Be?

So much lies in store for you if you choose a career in fashion. How might you begin, indeed, make your first move? From the perspective of this text, *The Fashion Game*, there is so much to suggest. **This is important: Here's a checklist, a point of departure, to get you started:**

1. Consider how the rules of the fashion game, the four you have gotten to know and experience throughout this text, can—and do—apply to you.
2. Define an initial career path. You may change your mind or other opportunities may appear that seem more appropriate—Great! You have to have a place to start, as explored here.
3. Organize the materials you will need to begin down that career path.

Step 1: Using Fashion Game Rules in Your Career

Why not start with using the rules of the fashion game, as set out in this text to launch your career? If you are like many students, indeed, if you are like many already with jobs, you may not be sure what your long-term career interests really are. This is especially true when it comes to fashion, retail, and industries related to or involved in some way with them. After all, there are so many different options to consider—possibilities that change almost daily. What to do? How to start? Finding a first job and deciding a career direction may be confusing and a little frightening.

There is good news!

If you like to draw and are good at it, you might consider a career in fashion design and sketching.
(© illustrart/Shutterstock)

Be (Your Own) Big Brand!

You have seen how branding practices are used to differentiate products. By focusing on identified, targeted consumers and their interests, aspirations, and needs, brand professionals are able to imbue sometimes identical items with unique characteristics. In doing so, they make them appealing to consumers. They use evocative language as well as exciting images and graphics. Furthermore, they present brands and products associated with them through new media forms such as the Internet, social media, and mobile technology. Many of these same brand-building techniques are applicable to individuals.

How can you use what you know about branding to help find a job or even develop a career?

FORMING PERSONAL BRAND STRATEGIES

Branding is about highlighting and maintaining a distinct image, whether that image pertains to products or professionals. True, the two differ—people cannot be "programmed" to appear and function as similarly as products. However, individuals can and do stand out as if they were brands. How, then, might you form your own personal brand and strategies related to it to build a career in fashion?

Begin with what you know: What of your education, abilities, and experiences will make you stand out from others? What do you think you can do—and do better and be more passionate about—than anyone else? **Think what your "target career market" might be as the first step in this process.** What would interest a fashion production company, or retailer, for example? The first might be concerned with finding employees with strong technical skills. Thus, are you interested in and able to show a special talent, such as remarkable accuracy and speed draping fabric, making patterns, using CAD programs, or even cutting, sewing, or finishing garments? Can you show examples of work of those kinds?

If you are interested in being a fashion stylist or promoter, can you show published images of your accomplishments, ones that highlight a unique fashion point of view? A fashion retailer, in addition, might be seeking employees with great selling skills or quantitative abilities, even ones with a talent for visual merchandising. Again, which of these might be interesting to you and that you are able to demonstrate? In sum, what of fashion do you know about and is of interest to both a potential employer and to you? If you are interested, yes, even passionate, about something, you are likely to pursue it thoroughly.

This is important: Follow your instincts, do what you love and do well, and you are on your way toward building a brand identity that is reflective of you, personally, and helpful toward finding a career.

USING ELEMENTS TO BUILD A PERSONAL BRAND

Passion and ability are crucial. So, too, is attracting the attention of employers. What brand elements are available to help accomplish that? Fashion brands have colors, symbols, and so many other details to draw consumers to their products. **When it comes to building your own brand, the words and images you generate are the most powerful tools available.** What words describe you, your education, and your work? How might a paragraph read describing your important accomplishments? Particularly, what might you write that would convince potential employers of the value you would add to their organization?

These may be tough questions for you to ask yourself, much less answer right now. You may not yet have concluded your education. You may have limited work experience—right now. However, fashion brand professionals ask everyday how they may position their items to be ones consumers seek over others. Fashion employers, in turn, ask who of the many applicants they encounter show that they understand and are able to have a positive impact on their business. How, then, do you become the candidate they choose over all others?

LAUNCHING BRAND YOU

The Internet has transformed the world, bringing people together from all over, joining them by interests and activities. Perhaps you have your own site already. Whether you do or not, **personal Internet sites** offer a platform for showing your brand to the best advantage. There, you can present your educational qualifications, describe your work and related personal experiences, post images of work you have completed, and even invite others to post comments and questions. There are many ways to build a website now. From hiring a professional site designer to using an existing template as a model, options exist to produce a memorable platform for your brand.

Social media offers another—almost immediate—platform for you to build your professional brand, as will be explored soon. Here, just know that it provides ways through which you may show your brand to others. With Facebook, for example, you can describe yourself, your interests, and your work. Furthermore, it offers the ability to post images of your work or your insightful comments on other's work. With the advent of mobile technologies such as apps, which enable individuals to check on Facebook updates from their cell phones, it is easier than ever to show you, your brand, and your accomplishments to many others, all within seconds. Not to be overlooked either is LinkedIn. This social media outlet allows professionals to post their place of employment (if available), their credentials, and their work experience. Many employed by businesses as human resource or personnel executives routinely search for new workers through these means. Read further to discover how to use these forms of media.

The burgeoning "**blogosphere**" or the exciting world of **Internet blogs can be another brand and career builder**. Countless programs now offer you the ability to be, effectively, a published author and authority within minutes. Tavi Gevinson and BryanBoy have become influential thought leaders in the world of fashion through their blogs.

There is another platform, the importance of which cannot be overlooked in such a people-oriented business as fashion. Connections made through **personal networking** are another way for you to present yourself and your brand to others. These are made through one-on-one contacts. Are you interested in working in a particular segment of the fashion industry, for a particular fashion company, person, or designer? Look for ways to meet people in them or the individuals themselves. You do not have to be in a "fashion capital" to take advantage of this approach. Store owners, buyers, and those "in the fashion know" in your own area can provide information and, likely, direct you to other groups, businesses, or people related to your interests. Put more directly: Personal connections and informal networking (made even more available now through social media) are ways to get your name out among others in fashion.

This approach, which requires strong social skills and much personal patience, can be an effective way to build your personal career brand. Think creatively, in unexpected ways, about how best to personally present your skills to others succinctly, quickly tell others about yourself and gain their interest. In all likelihood, you were drawn to a fashion career because you are creative or appreciative of that ability in others. Use that interest to find unique, interesting ways to get to know others in the segment of the fashion or fashion retail industry that interests you.

How you dress and present yourself is an important aspect of building your career brand. (© Auremar/ Shutterstock)

Be Fair

By now, you have seen the two parts of this fashion game rule: ethics and sustainability. Fashion businesses endeavor to include such characteristics in their practices and build them into identities, those defining brands. How might you include aspects of the "be fair" rule in both your personal and career practices?

ETHICS AND YOUR FASHION CAREER

With respect to ethics, employers are increasingly expecting their workers to have such personal traits as fairness, honesty, integrity, and lack of prejudice. Serious consequences can ensue for breach of these. With the advent of social media, examples of instances when these traits are not exhibited can be made known to others quickly. John Galliano, once highly esteemed for his design direction at Christian Dior Couture and his own eponymous label, was fired and subject to French legal sanctions (including losing the prestigious Legion d'Honneur award) as a result of his highly derogatory, offensive comments, all captured on a cellphone camera and transmitted to the world via YouTube. Fashion, like all industries, offers daily opportunities to make choices, each with consequences.

Few could argue (successfully) that Galliano acted ethically. Less obvious examples are difficult to resolve. Fashion, like all businesses, presents opportunities for conflict between "should" and "is." How so? Often, little is known about the true origins of clothing. Sourcing professionals may only rely on information they are told as to who actually makes items and where production occurs. They may have no reason to suspect malfeasance. Yet, shouldn't, by now, they question whether sewing piecework was carried out by unpaid child labor in homes or by paid workers in factories? Have they acted ethically by not inquiring further? After all, they "should" ensure that fair work practices are observed throughout the entire production process. Yet, they do what "is" common: nothing. Hampered by time, logistical, and monetary constraints, they push on to new projects after they write orders or other work.

Are consumers interested in ethical issues? Like professionals, they "should" be concerned about ethical sourcing for the clothes they wear. Yet, what they seem to do is customary: seek out and be willing to pay only the lowest prices. Have shoppers acted ethically when they barely look at the "made in" label and ask nothing more than "Is this on sale?" Should something more be done by fashion and retail professionals to underscore to consumers the importance of what for many of them is an "out of sight, out of mind" issue? Think about this: Nationally prominent grocery stores, coffee shops, and restaurants routinely tout their "fair trade" (i.e., ethically sourced raw materials processed by competitively paid-for labor) coffee and tea drink offerings. Compare the number of signs, table tent cards, and posters seen in these establishments with what few there may be in fashion retail stores concerning apparel and accessory items. Are consumers more attuned, then, to this issue related to food and beverage products, but not—yet—to fashion-related ones? Certainly, there are many fashion brands built on fairness and sustainability. But their numbers are few compared to the huge number of companies that do not comply with sustainability practices.

How might you change that in your career?

These are the very questions that future fashion game players will likely be called on to answer. Shopping sites offering "feedback" or product review features often contain consumer queries about such issues as whether products are of "free trade" origins when that information is not clear. As you think about building your personal career brand, consider how you might include elements of ethics, particularly those difficult to reconcile.

SUSTAINABILITY AND YOUR FASHION CAREER

Sustainability, or careful stewardship of resources before, during, and after production of items, is a clear trend for the future of the fashion industry. You have seen examples of these concepts in such practices as recycling and "upcycling," making more useful products out of earlier ones. Too, you are familiar with attempts to reduce pollution and the "carbon footprint" left in the wake of product manufacturing and transportation. Developing expertise in sustainable practices is one way to differentiate yourself and build your brand. Fashion businesses are increasingly seeking out those who understand sustainability and how its principles may be incorporated in price-sensitive, profit-conscious ways.

It is easy to say that sustainability is important. Making sustainability a reality is less so. For one, imparting sustainable characteristics on fashion products requires extensive knowledge and abilities. To that end, it means knowing a great deal about components comprising fashion products. Textiles such as cotton fibers and finished fabrics such as washed denims require tremendous resources for their production. In particular, extensive quantities of electricity and water are necessary. Finding ways to reduce those amounts used in the production of raw materials is one step toward bringing about sustainability.

Bringing about sustainable practices also entails thoroughly understanding the fashion production process. During production of even simple garments, much fabric is "cut away," leaving scraps that are difficult to use. For sustainability to take hold as a pervasive industry practice, much re-engineering of the entire fashion process—from making component raw materials to handling its by-products to finding ways to reuse unwanted garments—is required. Recently, "zero-waste" philosophies are informing fashion design and production in order to meet some of those challenges.

To note, again, the "zero-waste" idea: It is based on ways of finding methods that utilize every part of available. Doing so would result in reducing the amount of waste and odd textile piece goods that remain. To accomplish this, the entire "traditional" production process, beginning with initial garment or product design, would be more thoughtfully considered. What might you contribute to the "zero-waste" dialogue? Could you find a way to use raw materials thoughtfully in the production of fashion? Or, as a merchandiser, could you find and promote the new generation of fashion producers who are incorporating such practices? Rethinking traditional ways of garment production is at the heart of "zero-waste" design.

What happens when the "zip" goes out of that Zara, when the excitement of "H&M" becomes "ho-hum"? Something else will be required to advance sustainability; something more challenging: rethinking! At its core, fashion is about consumption, not conservation. Generations of consumers have been programmed to look for the trendiest, newest exciting products, and then discard them once they do not satisfy such standards.

Reusing raw materials used in fashion construction contributes to the "zero-waste" movement. (© Africa Studio/Shutterstock)

"Fast fashion," as with Zara and H&M, with their quick production turnaround times and endless stream of new items, is one result. This means that it is now possible to have entirely new, up-to-the-minute wardrobes every few weeks. But think about the following idea. After trends pass, clothing worn and seen, exclaimed over by others—what becomes of them? Will—should—anything of further use become of them? Repurpose not refuse? How might you build a fashion brand and a business around that concept?

Clothing is highly unlikely to be repurposed today by consumers. In fairness, who of us is skilled enough to entirely remake clothing, to "turn" them, as did our ancestors? Why should we bother for that matter? What would you do to convince consumers otherwise? How might you incentivize clothing reuse? One example would be offering price discounts or other incentives on purchases of new items when consumers bring in a previously worn item. Items thus obtained might be donated to charities or, after preparation, made into new products. What do you think?

If sustainability is to take hold, it will likely turn the traditional fashion production process on its head. If your passions lie in rethinking fashion and its processes, then, an entire career based on finding solutions to issues defined under "be fair" might be yours! When you think about successful fashion careers, those of prominent designers, retailers, any of the fashion game players you have encountered, ask how they became so, how they became thought of as style leaders. Often, they became so because they brought out products, provided services, or offered both that others were unable or unwilling to. How might you become an industry leader, sought after for your knowledge and expertise? Resolving issues related to ethical sourcing and "zero-waste" practices might be one way.

Be Legal

Laws define numerous kinds of relationships, including those involving business dealings. You have seen how laws are used to form and operate fashion businesses. Additionally, you have explored laws protecting fashion creativity. There are endless examples of how law and fashion interact. How, then, might you use this rule—be legal—of the fashion game to personally build a brand identity for yourself and your career? One idea is to take a good look at what you want to do, then look again, and again! Use, in other words, a 360-degree approach to discover in what ways laws might affect you, your work in fashion, and others. To get you started, understand that store policies have legal implications.

Many begin their careers in fashion via retail management. How might you use this 360-degree approach successfully in such an arena? Suppose, for example, you are responsible for a department in a large store. Image, then, that you are at the center of a circle. What legal interests might be important for you to consider when working in that capacity?

IDENTIFY INTERESTS OF STAKEHOLDERS

First, of course, would be those interests of employees such as yourself and other workers. You and they are **stakeholders, individuals with personal interests ("stakes") in results**. Ask whether the store's employment practices, for example, the processes through which they hire and, yes, terminate staff are legally permissible. If you are not sure, learn more about your concerns from other managers and from legal resources. Keep up to date with these requirements from human resources or other personnel managers.

Next, consider the interests of the store. Are their practices with respect to other stores and businesses in line with what you think is legally permissible? Again, if you have questions, describe what is of concern to you and then seek answers. Related to that are the interests of those with whom the store does business, such as outside, third-party vendors and contractors. These might be wholesalers and other purveyors of goods and services. Do those individuals and businesses work with the store, even with you, within what you believe are established legal parameters? For example, do both they and the store deal fairly with each other? Does each honor obligations such as those established by written agreements, such as contracts? Seek answers to your concerns from credible sources.

Of course, store shoppers have interests to consider as part of this analysis. Are, for example, products offered and sold by the store possibly "bad," that is, unsafe for them to use? Is the store for that matter, safe for them? Does it comply with laws about access? Again, if you, as a

Determining safe manufacturing practices is another career option in the fashion industry. (© sspopov/ Shutterstock)

manager, are unsure whether some condition or practice of the store raises legal concerns, seeking answers to such issues is critical. Understanding consumers' needs and how they may be legally protected is important for managers. If you find that you are particularly interested in consumer safety and legal protection issues, a full-blown career as a product safety or legal professional may form the basis of your career brand. How well you recognize potential legal interests and seek their resolution may be another characteristic that defines you as a fashion professional.

FINDING LEGAL ANSWERS

"Being legal" in your career endeavors does not mean that you have to know or will know how to resolve legal issues. As you have seen, being able to identify interests and issues of those involved is the important first step. Identifying and working with others and their interests are necessary for career success. The next step involves knowing where to turn for legal answers. Higher-level managers, human resource directors, and legal professionals are all sources of knowledge about how to legally protect various interests. Fashion professionals are expected to know the legal environment impacting their industries and the specific work they do. Accomplishing this takes time; education and experience are necessary to gain a more complete understanding. Using the steps of identifying interests and seeking timely, legal resolution of issues those concerns raise are effective ways to incorporate this fashion game rule into your career brand.

Be Profitable

This rule might better be reclassified as a requirement of the modern fashion game! No matter your career interests and how you position your personal career brand, employers seek those who can—and do—earn profits for their organizations. Costs of running businesses coupled with lack of earnings are the one-two punches that have knocked some highly heralded fashion houses out of existence. Fashion lore contains legions of examples of designers and businesses that have been unprofitable and ultimately failed, despite the creativity they exhibited or excitement they generated.

French designer Christian Lacroix is an example. Known for using bold, Spanish-inspired prints and colors in his designs as well as much-heralded pouf-style skirts (and immortalized by name on the British television program "Absolutely Fabulous") Lacroix has—absolutely—disappeared. Lacroix's parent company, Louis Vuitton/Moet-Hennessey, sold off the brand after years of ownership. It was estimated that in the company's twenty-plus year existence, it **never earned** a profit! It did, however, generate much media attention for LVMH and the French couture industry. Now, except for a few product licenses, such as men's neckties, little remains of a brand that was once the darling of the fashion press and trendsetters.

Fashion is expensive to make, to sell, to promote, and, of course, to purchase. It is easy to justify spending on all of these on the basis of "it takes money to make money." A cycle of spending and overspending to produce minimal results can ensue. Yet, recall the goal of the fashion game: consumers. Profitability follows when they have reasons to buy or continue to buy what you or your business offers them: they are the "**profit centers**"of the business. Also required is that production (and other) costs have been kept as low as possible: these are the "**cost centers**" of the business. **Reconciling these while maintaining the integrity and image of the fashion brands with which products and stores are associated is part of "playing," working in, the fashion game.** Working within the context of these may be another way to build a personal career brand based on rules of the fashion game.

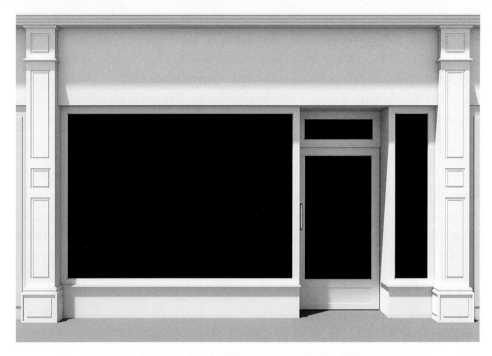

This empty store front could have once been a blossoming fashion retail store. If companies are not profitable, they will not remain viable in the fashion industry. (© concept w/Fotolia)

Step 2: Entering the Fashion Game

Work with others? Work by yourself as an entrepreneur? These are two ways to enter the fashion game. Likely, you will begin by working with others in a corporate or store setting. What makes the most sense for you? If you already have experience and financial wherewithal and have great ideas for new fashion products or services, working as an entrepreneur may be for you. On the other hand, you may need to gain experience. Working with others is a great way to accomplish that. Once you have that basic, all-important decision made, think about what documents and skills you will require.

Step 3: Basic Career Documents and Skills

You are unique. Documents and media you prepare for entering a fashion career should reflect that!

Résumés

Résumés identify you and provide your contact information. More importantly, they describe your education and work experiences. Names and locations of academic institutions, dates of your attendance, and certificates, degrees, and honors earned all constitute information they typically contain. There are several aspects of résumés to consider as you prepare and use them.

First, all information contained should be accurate and honest. Thanks to social media and Internet-related search engines, it has become increasingly easy for potential employers to detect information discrepancies. Second, résumés will likely be electronically scanned by potential employers. This means that they will be subjected to programs set to find key words and phrases

You will need to build a résumé to show any experience that you have in the fashion industry when seeking employment. (© Alexskopje/Shutterstock)

related to the specific job position to be filled. For example, a retail employer seeking an assistant buyer might be especially interested in candidates who note they possess "analytical quantitative skills," "proficiency generating and interpreting spreadsheets," and "use of Excel." What this practice means is that résumés—both hardcopy and electronically stored versions—must be reviewed carefully. As a result, they should both correctly reflect your abilities and mirror language contained in the job posting to which you are responding. How do you look on paper? Your résumé will show!

Cover Letters or Letters of Introduction

Cover letters accompany résumés and reference the position in which you are interested. The main purpose of these is to ask for an interview with potential employer. These are the personal "face" of the résumé, as well. They afford an opportunity for your interest in fashion and of the company to come out. Why are you interested in the job in the first place? Why would you be the best candidate for it? What would you do in the job if you were to obtain it? In other words, cover letters provide you with opportunities to express and detail ways you will add value to the employing organization. In other words, you are providing the potential employer with reasons for wanting to know more about you, information they will find out in the interview process.

Portfolios

Online or in hand, portfolios show technical abilities. These can be those of fashion designers, visual merchandisers, and others seeking employment where their work will be seen by others. Portfolio contents demonstrate both your visual creativity skills and your ability to solve problems. For example, were you assigned a garment to design and make from items on hand, not specially purchased for that task? Were you able to do so in interesting, "hadn't thought of that before" kind of ways? Accomplishments such as that, or for which you won awards or received favorable attention, would be candidates for inclusion in portfolios. Portfolios show off your creative point of view and technical skills.

Like résumés, portfolio contents may have to focus on needs employers express in job postings. Have you, by way of example, developed an entire seasonal collection, one with creative themes and their variations, all focused on a particular, target customer? Can you work creatively with existing brand elements (such as colors and logos) in your design work? Those seeking positions as designers or visual merchandisers may be asked to demonstrate these capabilities. As a result, portfolio contents may have to be oriented around these abilities and not those of less interest to the potential employer. If fashion design is of career interest, you can expect subsequent, specially focused classes to emphasize portfolio planning.

Fashion design course instructors may have more detailed recommendations for portfolio content and form, but in very general terms, they should:

1. Demonstrate superior sketching ability and use of media, such as pencil, pen, watercolor, or computer-assisted design (CAD) programs;
2. Contain outstanding illustrations of individual garments, ones that exemplify knowledge and application of design principles and color usage;
3. Exhibit an understanding of how to put together a thematically consistent collection or series of related garment designs;
4. Present "clean" work, showing no evidence of hurry or carelessness in execution as well as use of clear, precise lettering. Portfolios posted to websites should be easy to access and navigate through.

If you are interested in pattern and sample making, portfolios of completed patterns or lists of the kinds you are able to successfully produce—examples of tailored suits or flowing evening gowns, for instance—will be necessary. Photographic images of completed garments and their details may also be necessary to show your skills. Be sure to take images of successful work, such as styling assignments, you completed.

Other Job Hunting Materials

Many employers, retailers notably, require job seekers to complete preprinted, sometimes highly detailed applications. These are, essentially, résumés, although those, too, may be requested of candidates. Since they are prepared by the hiring company, they usually offer opportunities for candidates to identify and explain their previous employment experiences. Applications also may elicit candidates' comments about how they believe they would be a "good fit" with the company, its business objectives, and its mission or purpose goals. These documents may be completed and left with employers to be referred to when positions become available or in response to posted job openings employers seek to fill. Detailed but necessary, application forms let employers know prospective employees' skills.

To the "traditional" application, résumé, cover letter approach to job searching, it is important to note one updated trend. Now, it is increasingly common for job seekers to prepare folders or binders of materials to give out when prospecting. This means offering them to potential employers, ones applicants are interested in working with but that may not have positions open. These maybe kept on file by the business. As well, such personal brochures may be left with potential employers after interviews. These folders contain easily referenced hard copies of résumés, list of references, and images of work—anything showing applicants' abilities to best advantage and written materials making the case that they are best candidate for positions available.

Today, electronic media abounds with ways of presenting your credentials and highlighting your abilities. As noted, it is now relatively easy to set up personal Internet sites, even more so to begin a blog. One way to show these off either informally to friends or during formal interviews is through the use of iPads or other tablet devices. Obtaining and using these allow you to easily "tote" all the many documents, images, and other media you might need. In addition, it gives you the means during an interview to show your prowess with design and graphic programs. You can, for example, literally render ideas, complete with colors and suggested fabric designs, in front of your interviewers. Keeping up with new technologies and using those advances can further a successful job hunt while adding luster to your own career brand.

Job Skills: Interviewing

Media, no matter printed or electronic, lacks the dimension and depth of personal, face-to-face encounters. The **interview is where both employer and candidate meet to explore whether there is a professional "fit" between the two**. You are aware of the documents such as résumés and other materials required for interviews to come to fruition. What about interviews themselves? What might you expect and recall as important about them?

Whether you are interviewing for a first internship or a management position, perhaps the best thing to remember is to expect anything! Some interviews take place in comfortable conference rooms, others in cramped offices or partitioned off workshop floors with people bustling nearby. No matter what the conditions, suggestions for interview success include:

1. Present yourself authoritatively, as would be expected of a fashion professional. This means appearing appropriately dressed with a nod to trend consciousness. No matter how creative the position or extreme prevailing styles may be, avoid overly revealing, ill-fitting garments.

2. Good grooming and deportment contribute to your authority as well. Exotic makeup or hairstyles (except, perhaps, for jobseekers in those industries) detract from appearing professional. Tattoos and piercings are highly popular and often sources of pride for those who have them. In a job interview context, their display is, for now, considered inappropriate and distracting. Some effort should be made to minimize their appearance. Long-sleeved dresses or shirts and substitution of "mainstream," understated jewelry may be called for. Arriving on time, furthermore, shows consideration for the

Interviews give you the opportunity to expand upon your résumé and market yourself personally. (© wavebreakmedia/Shutterstock)

employer, even if there is a wait for the interview to begin. Often, it takes time for all company participants to assemble. Technology offers many advantages, yet their inappropriate use (such talking or texting during interviews) is decidedly not helpful toward projecting a professional appearance.

3. Your résumé shows your education and previous experiences and your appearance and deportment show your seriousness, but what demonstrates your passion? That includes both your passion for the job to which you are applying and for fashion itself. Using your knowledge (gleaned through personal research) of the industry and company is crucial during the interview. So, too, is showing how you can advance while still remaining open to further learning.

4. The list of interview "dos" and "don'ts" might be endless. The suggestions above are but a few to consider. To them, add eagerness and energy, even excitement for the prospect of working for the company and in the industry itself. Even if you already know a great deal about the company and your chosen career area, research for further information. Doing so will provide you with insights as to further direction of both and thoughts you may use in the interview. Furthermore, demonstrating an ability to think "on your feet" when responding to any variety of questions is another skill of importance. Most employers are interested in knowing how well you work with others, especially in difficult situations. Your résumé should reflect those abilities, and you might want to think how you will emphasize them when asked in an interview. Ultimately, you will be asked why you want the particular job for which you are applying. A clearly expressed, logical answer, one reflecting your past accomplishments and anticipating those you desire to achieve in the future, is the kind of response sought.

To reiterate: expect anything and be ready for it, including your success!

Job Skill: Using Social Media to Start Your Fashion Career

It is estimated that a significant majority of employers now seek new workers through social media outlets. Facebook is one such platform discussed previously. There, as you likely know, individuals are able to post personal profiles and interact with others. Over time, its use has extended to business applications, such as job hunting and career advancement. Its users increasingly are adding pages about their professional lives to personal ones for that reason. Twitter keeps information flowing between diverse individuals and groups as it develops in real time. Everyone stays up-to-the-minute through it, especially when social media platforms are used in conjunction with mobile technologies. Social media brings jobs and people together, especially in fashion and retail industries.

LinkedIn is another social media platform, one that is highly important. Experts estimate that it is the main social media outlet used for making business connections such as hires. It is followed in importance by Facebook, and then Twitter. Like Twitter and Facebook, LinkedIn requires users to register to use its service and interact with others. Unlike them, however, LinkedIn focuses almost exclusively on careers: bringing employers and potential employees, consultants, and other professionals together. LinkedIn does not operate in real time as does Twitter. Thus, it remains important to keep posting on it as up to date as possible. Other platforms exist as well. It seems as if each year there is a "hot" way to get connected! Keeping

BLOG   COMMUNITY   CONTACT

DATA   INFORMATION   MORE INFO

PORTFOLIO   WEB SITE   WWW

All of the items listed in this image are ways that you can market yourself to potential employers. (© Artsous/Shutterstock)

abreast of the newest ways to do so, in fact, finding and using such technologies before others, is one way to use technology to your and your career brand's advantage!

Social Media Can Make You and Your Career Brand Shine!

Remember the fashion game rule "Be a Big Brand"? You have seen how it may be done personally and the importance of finding a platform to launch it. Where do you go from there? Experts in social media suggest the following tactics:

1. Make clear the range of your abilities in the headline or descriptive area near your name. Job titles may not be enough to convey your range of professional abilities. Thus, think of a slogan expressive of you and your career brand. For example, think how much different the impression a phrase such as "visual trend communicator" makes compared with "associate visual merchandiser."

2. Describe yourself in ways that position you as an expert in your profession or as a thought leader. What have you done that few others have been able to accomplish in your current and past jobs? Have you published articles online or established a blog, one others follow and comment on?

3. Use language that will attract potential employers. Read posting for jobs in your career field. Adopt terms and phrases used in them for your purposes. Use words to demonstrate your abilities to solve problems and bring projects to successful conclusions that result in providing tangible benefits to employers. For example, fashion retail managers seeking to advance their careers might note their "collaborative" efforts to "initiate and implement management objectives among sales and other team members." These statements would be followed by explanations of how those objectives were accomplished and how the company benefited as a result. Potential employers look at social media postings when they are seeking individuals with sought-after skills and experiences. How you position yourself through skillful use of language will be how they find you!

4. Look for real or virtual groups of professionals in your area who regularly swap information and stories about their jobs, either real or aspired. Establish a presence there and who knows what contacts you might make and where those might lead! In fashion, there is definitely a "social pipeline," a network of contacts that you—anyone—can build over time.

5. Maintain your career and contact information through regular updating. For that matter, seek to prevent differences in information among your social media postings and résumé. You, personally, are not present to explain differences in your information. All potential employers have for reference is what and how you express yourself through your postings. Make sure you are easily accessed. This means setting inbox privacy controls to accommodate e-mails and texts from others besides those on your existing contacts lists. It also entails making sure that you are connected to platforms such as Facebook through mobile devices. Your credibility as a fashion professional, being current with trends, extends now to uses of technology! Social media applications and their use advances daily. Part of researching developments in your career field is keeping abreast of these as well as the innovative ways they may be used. It is possible you might become a thought leader by knowing the latest, newest technical advances, applications, and how they might be integrated into businesses.

Using online tools helps to show more variety of your personality than the traditional résumé. (© intheskies/Fotolia)

Other Important Career Documents

Business plans are required of some kinds of fashion careers. This is especially true for entrepreneurs seeking funding from sources other than their own financial reserves. **Business plans are formal, highly detailed descriptions of individuals and their entrepreneurial ideas.** These documents contain:

1. A defined result for the business, its "goal" and its "mission statement," purpose, and reason for being;
2. The kind of product or service to be made or offered;
3. The kind of consumers to whom these would be attractive, the "target market";
4. A survey of other businesses offering the same or similar goods and services;
5. How the new business will be structured and managed;
6. Descriptions of ways products will be made, where so, and by whom, or how its services will be established and provided;
7. Financial estimates of costs required to begin and run the entity for a set time;
8. Estimated amounts of monies likely to be received from operations;
9. Marketing and advertising initiatives needed to promote the business;
10. Information about other functions needed to support the business such as legal, accounting, and human resource management;
11. Formal SWOT (strengths, weaknesses, opportunities, and threats) analysis with details about each component.

Maybe you are not—just yet—ready to start your career as a fashion entrepreneur. Practically speaking, what thoughts might you take away as you prepare for a career in fashion? Ideas to keep in mind:

1. Attending **job fairs** and networking at them are great ways to make your presence and interests known to others. Fairs and industry "meet and greet" sessions with those already in fashion careers let you see what such professionals are like in person, hear what they say, and, ultimately, determine for yourself if you could see yourself performing the tasks they do.
2. First jobs in fashion may not be glamorous, well paying, or even paying at all! They allow you, however, to see the industry up close and how it operates. **Internships**, jobs in which students and recent graduates work for established fashion companies in a variety of supporting capacities, are often first career steps for many.

Internships often require long, long hours doing such things as monitoring social media postings, answering phones, cleaning up, or maybe running personal errands for "the boss." It is for you to decide whether you have interest in an internship and have other financial resources to support you while you engage in internship work. True, you will gain experience and opportunity from doing so, as many have found. You can begin your own social network as an intern and go from there.

If your school offers formally organized internships as part of receiving a grade or a diploma, be sure that you understand what activities and tasks you will be required to participate in and perform as an intern and how you will need to document any such work with an advisor both at your school and at the place of work. Failure to do so might result in failure to receive credit for your efforts. If you have to find internship work on your own, balance what you have to gain from working as an intern against what you might likely have to spend of your own time, energy, and other resources, just to have enough money to get by on. Would you, for example, be better off financially and career-wise working in retail sales or as a paid administrative assistant in a fashion company to begin with? Only you can know.

Many internship positions hold out promises of future, full-time, paid employment "if things work out." Ask yourself how realistic such promises are and the extent to which you are willing to see them through before you know if you will be hired for a "real job." Ask how many interns are ultimately hired by the company. Fashion careers are about options. Your knowledge of fashion and the fashion game strategic approach learned here may well help you parlay "unpaid" into "professional." Are you ready for that challenge?

summary
Section Finale

In one place, you have encountered ideas of what may lie ahead for you in a fashion-focused career. You have also gotten some ideas about how to pursue those goals. All of this information will be important to consider, to know, to recall, and to apply once you begin work. But what might that work be? That's a question you will have to answer. What really interests you?

Ask yourself whether that interest is strong enough, lasting enough, and, let's be honest, tough enough for a fashion career. Do you have the kind of motivation to go through with the kinds of activities and actual work the fashion game has described and the challenges that come with them?

The game paradigm, at its core, is about providing a straight-forward way to think about, build on, and benefit from a fashion career. Make a bold first move, one right for you, your interests, and your personal goals, knowing that the fashion game strategy can help you. Whatever you do, however you contribute to fashion, just know that you've made the right choice: your choice!

Good Luck!

questions
Review Questions: What Did You Discover?

1. Describe how the four rules of the fashion game are applicable to those seeking careers in fashion.

2. What basic career paths are there in fashion? What are their characteristics, their benefits, and their challenges?

3. Describe the purpose and content of résumés and portfolios.

4. What kinds of documents might an entrepreneur use and what are their characteristics?

5. Describe the importance of "people skills" when seeking fashion-industry jobs. What are two instances where such abilities would be of importance to job prospects?

terms
Terms to Know

Résumé	Cover letter	Stakeholders
Interview	Personal Internet sites	Profit centers
Portfolio	Social media	Cost centers
Business plans	Blogosphere	
Job fair	Personal networking	

What Happened at Market Day?

Project Purpose: After all your preparations . . . and excitement . . . how did your market day presentation turn out? What occurred during the event? In this project you will describe your efforts.

Step One: How many visitors did your presentation have?

Step Two: What did they say? Record some of their comments. . . .

Step Three: Rate the competition! Describe other participant's contributions to Market Day. Were there any standouts? Why were these so interesting?

Step Four: What might you have done better? Were there any "surprises" you might have avoided?

Section 12: How Will You Play The Fashion Game (Optional Project)

Where Do You See Yourself?

Project Focus: By envisioning the future of fashion . . . and of your career . . . you can gain insight about what and how your contributions can be to make both successful.

Step One: Describe what you would like to accomplish in your fashion career **5 years after your graduation.**

What do you foresee happening in the fashion industry in that time? How will you benefit from those changes?

Step Two: Describe what you would like to accomplish in your fashion career **10 years after your graduation.**

What do you foresee happening in the fashion industry in that time? How will you benefit from those changes?

Step Three: What are your greatest strengths . . . and weaknesses . . . when it comes to having a career in fashion? How might you play up the first and develop the second?

additional worksheets

Market Day Simulation Project Worksheet
Tracking Market Day Preparations
Work Day # 2:   **Completing Tasks Checklist**

Purpose: Do you need additional help with your project? Use this worksheet to help.
Make copies, if you need additional worksheet to track progress, or help other team members accomplish their tasks.

What have you accomplished so far?

_____

_____

_____

_____

_____

_____

_____

What remains to be done? Make a list for your and/or your team's reference:

_____

_____

_____

_____

_____

_____

_____

_____

_____

_____

_____

_____

_____

_____

_____

Profile a Fashion Retail Store

Purpose:	Retail stores have personalities of their own! In this project, you will investigate a particular store of any format which you find interesting. Then you will gather information and write what you find out in a short memo you will share with others.
Step One:	Identify your selected store: _____
Step Two:	How would you classify the store (luxury, mass-merchant, etc.) _____
Step Three:	Describe the type of fashion consumer you believe would be attracted to the store and its merchandise: _____ _____
Step Four:	What services does the store offer that supports its image? _____ _____ _____
Step Five:	What does the store do particularly well in your estimation in its efforts to attract and keep its target consumers? _____ _____ _____
Step Six:	What might your selected store do better in those same efforts? _____ _____ _____
Step Seven:	Select images representing your chosen store and explain how they represent its image.

You may skip bibliography sections in other texts, but take a look at this feature of *The Fashion Game*. There's something here if you wish to know more about just a few of the sources used to compile this text. The following references are highlighted because they are both interesting and readable. As such, they may be helpful, easy starting points for research in other classes. The sources here may be inspirational, too—places where you will find information that will further your personal interest in and knowledge about fashion. Also, most of these resources contain engaging images that will expand your visual "vocabulary."

These sources should be available in your school's library and through Internet resources such as *WWD* online. More esoteric ones may require further research, but all are available as of this text's publication date. Fashion, like any other profession, owes much to its past and commentary on its current meaning. With your interpretations, these sources can become foundations of fashion's future.

I. General Interest and Current Events Related to Fashion and Retail

Boucher, Francois. 1987. *20,000 Years of Fashion: The History of Costume and Personal Adornment, Expanded Edition.* New York: Harry N. Abrams, Inc.

Detailed recounting of costume history, encyclopedic in scope and detail for research purposes, yet fascinating on its own to read.

Drake, Alicia. 2006. *The Beautiful Fall: Lagerfeld, Saint Laurent, and Glorious Excess in 1970s Paris.* New York: Little, Brown & Co.

The stories behind fashion juggernauts Yves Saint Laurent and Karl Lagerfeld are joined in this exciting work, much of which was derived and written from the author's own original research. Fascinating firsthand recounts and interviews.

Hethorn, Janet, and Connie Ulasewicz. 2008. *Sustainable Fashion: Why Now?* New York: Fairchild Books.

This is a new era, and a new consumer has emerged: one who is concerned with making as small an impact on the environment as possible. A good "first read" for those interested in this growing area of the fashion business.

Hsiung, Ping-Chun. 1996. *Living Rooms as Factories: Class, Gender, and the Satellite Factory System in Taiwan.* Philadelphia, PA: Temple University Press.

The darker side of garment manufacture is described in this work. Some fashion companies now expressly forbid "take home" piecework in an effort to prevent entire families, including children, from becoming de facto laborers.

Landis, Deborah Nadoolman, and Anjelica Huston (Foreword). 2007. *Dressed: A Century of Hollywood Costume Design.* New York: HarperCollins Publishers.

Hollywood has had an undeniable influence on fashion. This work explores that concept in thrilling detail. As well, costume design for film and theater could be a practical career for those interested in fashion history; a work such as this is a good starting point to learn more about what is involved.

Marcus, Stanley. 1975. *Minding the Store.* New York: Signet Press Paperback.

Legendary Dallas, Texas, retailer Stanley Marcus lived much of retail history in the twentieth century. From taking over management of the Neiman Marcus stores to establishing World War II–era fabric and clothing construction standards to working with every major (and minor) fashion designer, his influence is still felt.

---. 1979. *Quest for the Best.* New York: Viking Press.

Fashion brands and their development and management explained from the viewpoint of a luxury retailer; Marcus was among the earliest to attempt to define brand image, or in his term, "mystique," a concept he explores in great detail in this work. Marcus is one of the few retailers to write about his experiences and observations as early as the 1970s.

Milbank, Caroline Rennolds. 1997. *Couture: The Great Designers.* New York: Harry Abrams, Inc.

One of the most beautiful pictorial references of fashion history available, it contains images of both well-known and lesser-known, but otherwise highly influential, fashion designers. Detailed and erudite in tone, but a fascinating read.

Neimark, Ira. 2006–2007. *Crossing Fifth Avenue to Bergdorf Goodman: An Insider's Account on the Rise of Luxury Retailing.* New York: Specialist Press International.

As brands become ever more specific as to their intended customers, the "luxury" category has emerged as an important niche. This text explores how one retailer identified and developed a preeminent luxury retail business.

Schnurnberger, Lynn. 1991. *Let There Be Clothes: 40,000 Years of Fashion.* New York: Workman Publishing.

This general-interest book is a humorous, colorful look at fashion history throughout the ages. Presented in "scrapbook" format, it is a fun read.

Strasser, Susan. 1989. *Satisfaction Guaranteed: The Making of the American Mass Market.* New York: Pantheon Books.

Ostensibly about packaged consumer goods, this consumer-interest work details the ways in which such items became as accepted and as commonplace as they are in modern American society; there is much information on how early department stores and visual merchandising efforts were effective to those ends.

---. 1999. *Waste and Want: A Social History of Trash*. New York: Henry Holt, LLC.

---. 2000. (Reprint). *Never Done: A History of American Housework*. New York: Owl Books.

> Both works recount in painstaking detail what life was like before shopping malls and the ready availability of apparel items.

Weber, Caroline. 2007. *Queen of Fashion: What Marie-Antoinette Wore to the Revolution*. Picador, USA.

> And you worry about what to wear? The fascinating political, and sometimes bloody, implications surrounding fashion and the symbolism of dress in eighteenth-century France is explored in this amazing recounting of French fashion's earliest beginnings.

Underhill, Paco. 1999. *Why We Buy: The Science of Shopping*. New York: Simon & Schuster.

---. 2004. *Call of the Mall: The Geography of Shopping*. New York: Simon & Schuster.

> Both should be required reading for those interested in management of fashion brands, visual merchandising, fashion marketing, retailing—in short, for just about anyone interested in careers that rely on enticing consumers to purchase goods offered for sale in physical, brick-and-mortar venues such as malls and stores.

II. Selected Articles and Periodical Publications

Part One: What Is the Fashion Game About?

Newsmakers of the Year: The Twenty Nominees. WWD.com. November 28, 2012. Retrieved November 28, 2012.

Grinberg, Emanuella. Cash-Strapped Millennials Curate Style via Social Media. CNN.com. October 16, 2012. Retrieved November 28, 2012.

Lockwood, Lisa. Hispanics Tip the Fashion Vote. WWD.com. December 3, 2012. Retrieved December 5, 2012.

Conti, Samantha and Evan Clark. Retail Stocks Outpace Market. WWD.com. November 28, 2012. Retrieved November 28, 2012.

Clark, Evan. Women at Work: Fashion's Glass Ceiling Prevails. WWD.com. October 29, 2012. Retrieved November 28, 2012.

Part Two: Fashion Game Players in Action

Friedman, Arthur. Fiber Innovations Answer the Call. WWD.com. November 19, 2012. Retrieved November 28, 2012.

Wilson, Eric. Why Does This Pair of Pants Cost $550? WWD.com. April 28, 2010. Retrieved April 16, 2013.

Clifford, Stephanie. One Size Fits Nobody: Seeking a Steady 4 or 10. WWD.com. April 24, 2011. Retrieved April 16, 2013.

Karr, Arnold J. USA: Consumers Say They Will Pay. WWD.com. September 5, 2012. Retrieved November 28, 2012.

Lewis, Jacquelyn. Spring Breaks: The Launch Craze. WWD.com. September 17, 2012. Retrieved November 28, 2012.

Lockwood, Lisa. Special Report: Catering to the Ever-Demanding Customer. WWD.com. October 24, 2012. Retrieved November 28, 2012.

Getting Personal: Retailers Mine Data to Offer Consumers Tailored Experiences. WWD.com in conjunction with Cotton Incorporated. August 2, 2012. Retrieved November 28, 2012.

Screen Time: Mobile Devices Become Increasingly Essential to Retail. WWD.com in conjunction with Cotton Incorporated. November 15, 2012. Retrieved November 28, 2012.

Part Three: Fashion Game Issues

Ellis, Kristi. Design Piracy Bill Reintroduced in Congress. WWD.com. September 10, 2012. Retrieved November 28, 2012.

Friedman, Arthur, with contributions from Mayu Saini, Ellen Sheng. Manufacturing's Lament: Factory Abuses Persist. WWD.com. November 27, 2012. Retrieved November 28, 2012.

Carpenter, Susan. Yes, Even Clothes Can Be Recycled. *Los Angeles Times* (latimes.com). March 21, 2010. Retrieved September 8, 2012.

Part Four: The Fashion Game in Motion

Clark, Evan. Top 10 Emerging Markets. WWD.com. November 19, 2012. Retrieved November 28, 2012.

Farrar, Lisa. Chinese Homegrown Brands to Watch. WWD.com. December 28, 2012. Retrieved December 28, 2012.

Edelson, Sharon. Recruiting in a Digital World. February 7, 2012. WWD.com. February 7, 2012. Retrieved November 28, 2012.

index